LIFE AND CORRESPONDENCE

OF

Mrs. Hester Ann Rogers,

WITH

CORRECTIONS AND ADDITIONS,

COMPRISING

AN INTRODUCTION BY THOS. O. SUMMERS.

Nashville, Tenn.:
PUBLISHED BY E. STEVENSON & F. A. OWEN, AGENTS,
FOR THE METHODIST EPISCOPAL CHURCH, SOUTH.
1855.

STEREOTYPED BY L. JOHNSON AND CO., PHILADELPHIA.
PRINTED BY A. A. STITT,
METHODIST PUBLISHING HOUSE, NASHVILLE.

CONTENTS.

INTRODUCTION.

Few works have acquired a greater popularity among Methodists than the Life of Hester Ann Rogers. In scarcely any other biography can be found so bright a pattern of holiness as this exhibits. In depth of penitence, strength of faith, ardour of hope, fervour of love, intimate communion with God, constancy of joy and peace, and zealous devotion to the cause of Christ, Mrs. Rogers has had few equals in any age of the church. So brilliant a specimen of the old school of Methodism ought not to be lost from the view of succeeding generations. No unprejudiced person can read the details of her experience without *feeling* that, according to the paradox, she had gained "perfection's height, the depth of humble love." It is obvious that for a long series of years she walked with God—maintaining an intimate and constant communion with the adorable Trinity—her person and performances being accepted in the Beloved.

Nevertheless, some persons seem to be stumbled at certain passages which occur in her writings, indicating, as they suppose, a slight dash of enthusiasm in her experience. They do not indeed think that any of these points affect materially her religious character—perhaps not at all, only so far as her example is concerned.

It is not, for instance, insinuated that her regard for dreams operated unfavourably on her own personal piety, as indeed there is positive proof that it did not; nevertheless, it is imagined that persons of weaker minds from her example might be led to pay an undue regard to them, and the result might be very pernicious.

We will not say that there is no force in this suggestion ; yet it must be observed that good and great men of every age have considered dreams not unworthy of their regard. Thousands, like Bishop Ken, have prayed that God would "make their very dreams devout."

Some dreams "come from a multitude of business," being the continuation and the sequence of our waking thoughts. If we admit that suggestions are made to our minds by divine or diabolical agency when we are awake, it requires no great stretch of faith to believe that this may also take place when we are asleep; and this not only as a miraculous phenomenon, like the divine communications of this sort mentioned in Scripture, but as belonging to the ordinary operations of the Spirit of God. So Elihu seems to have thought:—"God speaketh once, yea twice, yet man perceiveth it not. In a dream, in a vision of the night, when deep sleep falleth upon man, in slumberings upon the bed, then he openeth the ears of men, and sealeth their instruction—that he may withdraw man from his purpose and hide pride from man. He keepeth back his soul from the pit, and his life from perishing by the sword." We suppose none are authorized to say that no dreams of this sort take place in the present age; and therefore no one ought to be charged with weakness for paying attention to such dreams as are marked with logical consistency, and seem calculated to answer the purpose of warning, or encouragement, or some other desirable end. In an answer to a question concerning dreams, propounded at Mr. Wesley's second Conference, it was wisely suggested that "they should not be discouraged or encouraged;" or as he elsewhere expresses it, "They are of a doubtful, disputable nature—they might be from God, and they might not; and are therefore not simply to be relied on, any more than simply to be condemned, but to be tried by a further rule, to be brought to the only certain test, the Law and the Testimony." This, which is unquestionably the proper course, Mrs. Rogers never failed to pursue.

No one can suppose that *sortilege* was practised by Mrs. Rogers and her friends, in their method of consulting the Scriptures. It would be dangerous and highly reprehensible to open the Bible at a venture, determined to be controlled in any pending case by the first passage that might strike the eye. It would, moreover, be unwarrantable to conclude that when one is seeking direction in regard to any matter, the occurrence of a particular passage to the mind is to be attributed to special divine inspiration. A principle of this sort may lead to enthusiasm and fanaticism. We have heard of a man who was not allowed by his master to attend a religious meeting at night. Confined to the house, the only way of escape being by a window at a considerable height from the ground, this passage occurred to his mind: "He shall give his angels charge over thee, to keep thee in all thy ways: they shall bear thee up in their hands, lest thou dash thy foot against a stone:" applying the promise to himself, he sprang from the window, but the angels not being there to prevent the fracture of his bones, he was led to conclude that his mode of interpreting Scripture was more simple than safe.

We know that the Lord does guide his people, and that too by his word as well as his Spirit; and he may do this by sudden and strong impressions upon the mind; but we are not authorized to expect such interpositions, and we never should proceed upon the ground of any of these suggestions, without the collateral and more authoritative indications of conscience, reason, and the general tenor of the inspired oracles. We have no ground to suppose that Mrs. Rogers—notwithstanding the peculiar complexion of a few passages in her life taken by themselves—ever deviated from this rule.

It is clear from the Scriptures that Christians should make every thing the subject-matter of prayer—nothing being beneath the notice of our heavenly Father. It is also certain that many temporal blessings may be granted in answer to prayer, which otherwise would not be granted; and that whenever the impartation of temporal things is not incompatible with the divine will, or with the spiritual interests of the party concerned, such things will be granted in answer to prayer. This does not authorize us to pray for the performance of miracles—these displays of divine power were intended to authenticate the successive dispensations of Heaven, and this being done and the record made, there is no necessity for their perpetuation, and we have no reason to suppose that any miracle has been wrought since the apostolic age, and we have no ground to expect that any others will be wrought until the end of time. The prodigies of Papists, Mormons, spirit-rappers, and other charlatans, are impostures so glaring that they are beneath contempt.

But it is not for us to limit the Holy One of Israel. He has, indeed, limited himself; but we cannot always assign the bounds of his wonder-working power. He can restore vision to one whose optic nerves have been destroyed—he can replace a limb that has been amputated—he can raise the dead; but we have no authority to expect that he will do so; and we act absurdly if we pray for the performance of such miracles. This does not, however, argue that it is useless to pray that he will bless the remedial agents employed to restore our sick friends to health, or to bring them out of temporal straits and difficulties, or to prosper them in any of their worldly enterprises: all these things we know are frequently done by him, and no one can prove that they are not sometimes done in answer to prayer, when otherwise they would not take place. This gives us a large margin in the premises, and we ought to avail ourselves of it, according to the counsel of the apostle: "In every thing, by prayer and supplication, with thanksgiving, let your requests be made known unto God." We are very sure that when the blessing for which we pray is bestowed, it is bestowed by our Heavenly Father—although it might be hazardous to affirm, in any particular case, that had we not prayed for it, it would not have been granted. For wise reasons, God has not seen fit to allow us to connect the answer with the petition with mathematical precision—as cause and effect, or means and end—while in numerous instances he imparts some *spiritual* blessing, or some *other temporal* blessing, instead of that for which we prayed. We asked him to remove the "thorn in the flesh," and it was not removed; but the sincerity, faith, and fervour of our prayer could not be disregarded by our heavenly Father, and he consequently gave us "blessings more divine" and more suitable to our circumstances than those for which we prayed. We are always safe in asking for the bestowal of all spiritual blessings in Christ Jesus, with the assurance that they will be granted; and for the bestowal of every temporal good, with the same assurance that it will be granted, if not contrary to the divine plans or prejudicial to our higher interests. Our obligations to render thanksgiving for favours received, will hold in every case.

It is clear from the general tenor of Mrs. Rogers's experience that she acted upon these sound principles, albeit she speaks of certain extraordinary interpositions of Providence almost as if they were of a miraculous cast, and of certain impressions concerning them as if they were infallible presentiments. Moreover, she was not without her disappointments in reference to objects earnestly desired and confidently expected; and these she well knew constituted an important part of her probationary discipline, and a wise and profitable use did she make of them.

Some persons stumble at a passage in her autobiography in which she speaks of being so desirous of dying as to refuse to take medicine when she was sick. This, of course, was highly reprehensible; but it was just after her conversion, when her mind was singularly immature in religious matters. For example, she was so ignorant as to think that if she were sanctified, she would have an infallible judgment, a perfect memory, with freedom from temptation and bodily pain! It is remarkable that the well-bred daughter of a clergyman should entertain notions so erroneous; but as such was the case, we need not wonder that, like some of the primitive martyrs, she would rather kindle than extinguish the flames that were to bear her soul to God. She very soon, however, acquired correct views on these subjects—qualified her "passionate longings for home"—and not unfrequently expressed a willingness to wait the Lord's leisure, patiently and joyfully, though it might require her to "suffer out her threescore years"—knowing, as Dr. Donne quaintly expresses it, that "no man dies innocently that dies by his own hand or by his own haste." Indeed, she manifested commendable prudence in the care of her health, in order that she might be able to serve God and her generation according to his will, so long as he might see fit to continue her on the earth.

In the interesting Appendix to her Funeral Sermon by Dr. Coke, Mr. Rogers says, that besides innumerable Letters written by his wife, she had left some three thousand quarto pages, of valuable matter, written by her own hand. From these manuscripts principally the materials of the present work have been compiled. The present editor has changed the order of the different portions of the volume—corrected a great many errors—and appended the valuable Letters of Mr. Wesley to Mrs. Rogers to those written by her to him and to others. It is hoped that these additions, alterations, and corrections will secure to this interesting and profitable biography a still wider circulation than it has heretofore acquired.

LIFE OF MRS. HESTER ANN ROGERS

I WAS born at Macclesfield, in Cheshire, January 31, 1756, of which place my father was minister for many years; being a clergyman of the Church of England. He was a man of strict morals, and, as far as he was enlightened, of real piety. I was trained up in the observance of all outward duties, and in the fear of sins, which in these modern times are too often deemed accomplishments. I was not suffered to name God but with the deepest reverence; and once for telling a lie, I was corrected in such a manner as I never forgot. We had constantly family prayer: the Sabbath was kept strictly sacred; and as far as outward morality, my parents lived irreproachably, and in all social duties were regular and harmonious.

I was early drawn out to secret prayer: I believed God was the author of all good, of all happiness; and sin the cause of all misery and pain. If therefore I wished for any thing I had not, I asked God in secret to grant it to me. And in any pain of body, or in any of my childish grief, I fled to him for ease and comfort; and it would be incredible to some, how often I have received manifest answers to prayer, when not more than four years old; and how my tender mind has been comforted. I was deeply affected, and had very serious thoughts of death for some time, and after seeing the corpse of a little brother of mine, who died of the small-pox when I was five years old, I took great delight in the Bible, and could at this time read any part either of the Old or New Testament, always asking questions so as to obtain understanding of what I read. My parents required that I should give an account, every Sabbath evening, of the sermons and lessons I heard at church, and say my catechism to them, which they explained to my understanding. They also required that I should get off the collect for the day, and repeat it with my other prayers every night and morning. These collects I also often repeated in secret, and with great sincerity before the Lord. I never remember going to bed without having said my prayers, except once: I was then diverted by a girl who told me many childish stories, and so took up my attention, that I forgot to pray till I was in bed; and then being alone, I recollected what I had done, and conscience greatly accused me; so that I began to tremble lest Satan should be permitted of God to take me away body and soul, which I felt I deserved! I soon after thought I saw him coming to the side of my bed; when I shrieked out in such a manner as brought my parents up stairs to see what was the matter. This made a lasting impression, and I never after dared to neglect commending myself to the protection of God before I slept. I was at this time about six years old.

When about eight years of age, I heard my father say he had a very remarkable dream, in his recovery from a dangerous illness: that he stood before the throne of God, and saw his glory. But not being able to gaze upon it, fell on his face in raptures of joy.

My mother asked if he could describe what he saw, but he answered, No, it was impossible to convey any idea of it, it seemed almost to deprive him of being. She asked if any thing was spoken to him, but he desired her to ask no more respecting it; nor would he ever tell her any more. I have often thought he received some notice in that dream of his approaching dissolution. A material change was evident from that time in all his conduct and tempers. Anger was ever before a besetting sin, but I never remember to have seen him overcome by it after this. He was more vigilant in public and private duties, more humble and patient under little difficulties and trials, more watchful over the morals of all around him, and took more pains than ever to inform my infant mind in all things which led to piety and virtue. He warned me against reading novels and romances, would not suffer me to learn to dance, nor to go on visits to play with those of my own age. He said it was the ruin of youth to suppose they were only to spend their time in diversions. I believe I shall have reason to bless God forever for several lessons he then gave me, and to all of which I listened with great delight.

In February, 1765, when I was a few weeks more than nine years old, he took his last sickness, a malignant fever, in which he lay several weeks, expressing through the whole of it an entire submission to the will of God, and an assurance of a happy eternity. He sung psalms, repeated various scriptures, and praised God aloud; and was continually commending to his care his dear wife and children. A few days before he died, he called aloud for me; and when I came, he took my hand in his very affectionately, and said, "My dear Hetty, you look dejected. You must not let your spirits be cast down, God hath ever cared for me, and he will take care of mine. He will bless you, my dear, when I am gone. I hope you will be a good child, and then you will be happy." Then laying his hand on my head, he lifted his eyes to heaven, and with a solemnity I shall never forget, said—"Unto God's gracious mercy and protection I commit thee: the Lord bless thee, and keep thee: the Lord lift up the light of his countenance upon thee, and give thee peace, and make thee his child and faithful servant to thy life's end!" I cannot find words to express what were the feelings of my heart on this occasion. Love for my valuable and affectionate parent, grief to reflect I was now losing him, and gratitude that his dying lips had pronounced such a blessing on my head, quite overpowered me. I fell on my knees, gave vent to a flood of tears, and continued to weep till my eyes were almost swelled up. He died the tenth of April, 1765.

My grief for some time would not suffer me to take recreations of any kind; but I would sit and read to my mother, or weep with her. But, after a season, I was invited to the houses of relations and friends; and as I soon became a laughing-stock among them for my seriousness and dislike to their manners and their plays, I began to be ashamed of being so particular. My mother was also now prevailed on to let me learn to dance, in order to raise my spirits and improve my carriage, &c This was a fatal stab to my seriousness and divine impressions: it paved the way to lightness, trifling, love of pleasure, and various evils. As I soon made a proficiency, I delighted much in this ensnaring folly. My pride was fed by being admired, and began to make itself manifest with all its fruits. I now aimed to excel my companions, not in piety, but in fashionable dress, and could not rest long together without being engaged in parties of pleasure, and especially in this (what the world calls) innocent amusement. I also obtained all the novels and romances I possibly could, and spent some time every day in reading them; though at first it was unknown to my mother, who would not then suffer it. After this I attended plays also. In short, I fell into all the vain customs and pleasures of a delusive world, as far as my situation in life would admit, and even beyond the proper limits of that station God had placed me in. Thus was my precious time misspent, and my foolish heart wandering far from happiness and God; yea, urging on to endless ruin. Yet in all this I was not left without keen convictions, gentle drawings, and many short-lived good resolutions, especially till fifteen years of age. God often wrought strongly upon my mind, and that in various ways, of which I come now to speak. But oh! how did I grieve and resist the Holy Ghost! How justly might he have given me up; yea, and sealed me over to eternal destruction.

At thirteen years old, namely, in the year 1769, the Bishop of Chester being to hold a confirmation at Macclesfield, I resolved to attend that ordinance, though it was with many tears and much trembling; for I believed till persons were confirmed they were not alike accountable to God for their own conduct. But when this solemn renewal of the baptismal covenant was made in their own persons, then whosoever did not keep that covenant must perish everlastingly. I therefore endeavoured seriously to understand the import of it, and was deeply convinced I was neither inwardly nor outwardly what it required. The knowledge of this wrought much sorrow, and I formed strong resolutions to lead a new life. Yet sin had so blinded my eyes, that I could not at this time believe, or at least I would not, that dancing, cards, or attending plays were sinful. These, therefore, I did not even resolve against. But I resolved against anger, pride, disobedience to my parent; also the neglect of secret prayer and church going; with all wanderings of heart in those duties, and a variety of other evil tempers, &c., which I knew myself guilty of. Having humbled myself before God, fasted and prayed, and (as I vainly thought) fortified myself by these resolutions, of keeping all God's commands in future, I ventured to take upon me the solemn vow. But such was my fear and trembling at the time, that when I approached the altar I was near fainting, and when returned to the pew, burst into a flood of tears. This was on Whitsunday; and I intended to receive the holy sacrament the Sunday following. But before I came, I was conscious I had already broken my solemn vows; and on the reflection, my distress was great, and I had many doubts whether partaking of the Lord's supper would not be sealing my own damnation. However, one day as I was praying, it came into my mind this holy sacrament is called a means of grace; surely, then, it is just what so sinful, so helpless a soul wants. I will go to it, then, as a mean whereby to receive strength and grace to conquer sin in future. In this view of that blessed ordinance I found much comfort; and I am now assured it was from the Lord, whom ignorantly I was feeling after. I approached the Lord's table, therefore, with renewed vows and renewed hopes; but, alas! these also were as the "morning cloud and as the early dew, which passeth away." For several months I thus repented and sinned, resolved, and broke all my resolutions—sinned and repented again. I dared not receive the Lord's supper without resolving on a new life; neither dared I to stay from it; nor did I ever attend without being wrought on by the Spirit of God.

The latter end of this year I had a malignant fever, and believed I should die. I felt myself totally unprepared to appear before a holy God, and was in great distress; I earnestly entreated him to spare me a little longer, and resolved I would then spend a new life indeed. A patient, forbearing God of love listened to my request, and did not cut the fig-tree down. One night during this illness I dreamed my soul was departed out of the body, and I, with three of my cousins,* (with whom I had a close intimacy, and who I thought had left the body also,) were waiting in dreadful expectation of being summoned to the bar of God; and we all believed our doom would be everlasting darkness! My sins all appeared as in array against me, in the court of conscience, and my mouth was stopped: I had no plea whatever, no hope; for it seemed the justice of God must unavoidably sentence me to endless misery, which I felt to be my real desert, and was bewailing my

* N. B. These three cousins were Robert Roe, whose experience and death is related in the Arminian Magazine, and two of his sisters, Mary and Frances. These are all asleep in Jesus, and their happy spirits rejoicing before his throne; though at the time of this dream they were utterly unawakened.

own folly with bitter cries and lamentations. Their employ I thought was the same—each for ourselves, dreading "the worm that dieth not, and the fire which never shall be quenched"—when suddenly there appeared a cloud of uncommon brightness, and soon after a glorious angel descended in the cloud, and stood before us, clothed in white, with a majesty and beauty not to be described. We beheld his approach with trembling awe, and almost an agony of despair, believing he was sent to summon us to appear, and receive the deserved but dreadful sentence, "Depart, ye accursed!" But, to our inconceivable surprise, he smiled on us with heavenly sweetness, and said, "The Lord Jesus Christ has forgiven all your sins, and washed you in his own blood, and I am come to bid you enter into the joy of your Lord, and to conduct you into his blissful presence!" Being now suddenly transported from depths of misery into joy unspeakable, love beyond compare, and extreme delight, I thought I sprung up, clapped my hands, leaped for joy, and praised my God in ecstasies unknown before, so that it awoke me! Never did I feel any thing like what I felt in this dream, sleeping or waking, before or after, till the Lord did truly speak my sins forgiven. This made a deep impression on my mind for some time. For a month or two I was very serious and circumspect, and read all the religious books I could meet with. One of these I remember asserted, that we are all to be judged according to our works: therefore, if our good works are more than our evil ones, we are in a fair and sure way for heaven when we die; but if our evil works exceed our good, we may expect condemnation. I thought I would impartially examine myself by this rule, and see what hope I should have for my own soul on these terms. I therefore made a little day-book, in which I put down every good and bad action with great sincerity, at the same time praying to God to show me if I was in the way to heaven or not. But then there were many things (as before observed) which I did not account sinful; and again, many things I accounted good actions, because entirely ignorant that an impure motive, in the sight of that God who searcheth the heart, renders our actions, however splendid in the sight of men, abominable before him. Every act of obedience to my elders or superiors, I accounted a good action; as also every prayer I offered, every ordinance I attended, every time I spoke the truth, instead of denying a fault; and in order to swell the number of my good actions, I would sometimes refuse going to a play, or to an entertainment, and read to my mother at home. Nay, with this view I have fasted whole days from morning till evening; but after all I found my bad actions more than my good ones. Yet I went on resolving to be better, and still keeping the account, till being at a dance, I pulled out my day-book with my pocket handkerchief, and it was found, and made the jest of the company. I was then so ashamed, that I resolved to follow this method no more.

I met with another book, which affirmed it was impossible to conquer all sins at once; and if ever we would obtain victory, it must be by overcoming first one and then another. Pride and anger I felt to be my most besetting sins, and therefore set myself against these in particular. But I was foiled in every attempt, and it seemed, as the poet says,

> "The more I strove against its power,
> I sinned and stumbled but the more."

So that this trial only made a more clear discovery that pride was interwoven with my every thought, and word, and action. I was now quite discouraged, and thought it was all vain to strive for a victory so impossible to gain! I then looked round, and considered the conduct of others; and when I saw them more trifling, more wicked than myself, and some of them, who passed for amiable characters, guilty of things which my soul shuddered at, I began to conclude I was very good, compared with these; and surely all these would not be doomed to hell and damnation!—that God was merciful, Christ died for sinners, and therefore if I lived a tolerably moral life, he would pardon the rest, and accept me through the merits of Christ in the hour of death; or at least, I had as good a chance as others; and therefore would cast away fear, and live like the rest of my moral neighbours. It was some time, however, before I had so resisted the convictions of the Spirit of God, as to remain at ease: he strove with me various ways, till I was a little more than fifteen. But I so repeatedly grieved and quenched the motions of that Holy Spirit, that I was then in some measure given up to my own foolish rebellious heart. Dress, novels, plays, cards, assemblies, and balls took up the most of my time, so that my mother began to fear the consequences of my living so much above my station in life. But I would not now listen to her admonitions. I loved pleasures, and after them I would go.

What increased my vanity and pride was, that I was much beloved by my godmother, a lady of very considerable fortune, and often spent most of the summer months at Adlington with her; where I was always treated as if she intended to bestow a handsome fortune on me. She introduced me into the company of those in high life, and enabled me, by large presents, to dress in a manner suitable to such company. Oh how fatal in general are such prospects to a young mind! Yet in all this, I still wished to preserve a religious appearance. I still frequented church and sacraments, still prayed night and morning, fasted sometimes, and especially in Lent; and because I did these things, esteemed myself a far better Christian than my neighbours. Yea, so blind was I, that I had a better opinion now of my own goodness than formerly, when I was far more earnest about salvation. What a proof that sin darkens the understanding!

In the summer of 1773, I was at Adlington with my godmother above mentioned, when I heard various accounts of a clergyman whom my uncle Roe had recommended to be curate at Macclesfield, and who was said to be a Methodist. This conveyed to my mind as unpleasing an idea of him, as if he had been called a Romish priest; being fully persuaded that to be a Methodist was to be all that was vile under a mask of piety. These prejudices were owing to the false stories which from time to time I heard repeated to my father, when about seven or eight years old; and also many more which my mother heard after his death, and to the present time: so that I believed their teachers were the false prophets spoken of in the Scripture: that they deceived the illiterate, and were little better than common pickpockets: that they filled some of their hearers with presumption, and drove others to despair: that with respect to their doctrines, they enforced chiefly, that whosoever embraced their tenets, which they called faith, might live as they pleased, in all sin, and be sure of salvation; and that all the world besides must be damned without remedy: that they had dark meetings, and pretended to cast out devils, with many other things equally false and absurd; but all of which I believed. I heard also, that this new clergyman preached against all my favourite diversions, such as going to plays, reading novels, attending balls, assemblies, card-tables, &c. But I resolved he should not make a convert of me; and that if I found him, on my return home, such as was represented, I would not go often to hear him.

When I came back to Macclesfield, the whole town was in alarm. My uncle Roe, and my cousins, seemed very fond of Mr. Simpson, and told me he was a most excellent man; but that all the rest of my relations were exasperated against him. I asked, Is it true, he preaches against dancing? and said I was resolved to take the first opportunity of conversing with him, being certain I could easily prove such amusements were not sinful. Being told what arguments he made use of, I revolved them in my mind, fully determined if I found upon reflection I could answer them, I would. I first considered if any Scripture example could be brought. I remembered to have read of Miriam's dancing; but it was to express her pious joy to the Lord, and as an act of worship, accompanied by a hymn of praise. David danced also, but it was in like manner, and from like motives. Herod's daughter danced, but she was a heathen, and the cause of beheading a servant of God. Nothing therefore which I found in Scripture countenanced dancing in any measure. I then began to consider the objections urged against it. One of these was, that it tends to levity and trifling mirth, so it enervates the mind, dissipates the thoughts, weakens, if not stifles, serious and good impressions, and quite indisposes the mind for prayer. I asked my own heart, Is not this a truth? Conscience answered in the affirmative. Mr. Simpson pleads further, What good is promoted hereby? I would gladly have had it to urge, it promotes health; but many instances of those who had lost health, and even life, within my own knowledge, through attending this very diversion, would not permit this. Among others, I had a recent proof in Miss H——, who by a violent cold and surfeit got at an assembly, was thrown into a galloping consumption, and in a few months fled to an awful eternity. Again he pleads, are you made better Christians, better husbands, better children hereby? Better Christians I was conscious none could be for having the mind dissipated and unfitted for prayer. Some husbands I knew who were not made better, and some wives, who, to support extravagant dress on such occasions, had greatly injured their families. For my own part, I was conscious it had led me to dress and to expenses not suited to my present situation in life. These thoughts brought powerful convictions to my mind notwithstanding my desire to resist them. I could not deny that truth in particular, that those who habitually attend such pleasure, lose all relish for spiritual things: God is shut out of their thoughts and hearts: prayer, if they use any, is full of wanderings, or, perhaps, wholly neglected; and death put as far as possible out of sight, lest the thought should spoil their pleasures. I was conscious beyond a doubt, these were the fruits this delusive pleasure had wrought in my own soul; and comparing my present state of mind with what it was before I entered upon this diversion, so mistakenly called innocent, I found cause to be deeply ashamed. But then, if this is really true, (said I to myself,) I ought not to follow this amusement any longer. And can I give it up? My vile heart replied, I cannot, I will not. The Spirit of God whispered, Will you then indulge yourself in what you know to be sin? Would you wish to be struck dead in the ball-room? My conflict was great, yet I was resolved to run all hazards rather than give up this pleasure. Therefore I stifled these convictions with all my might; and after this ran more eagerly into all pleasurable follies. O my patient, long-suffering God, tears of grateful love and praise overflow mine eyes, when I consider my deep rebellion, and thy sparing mercy.

About this time I grew tired of novels, and took great delight in reading history. I went through several English and Roman histories, Rollin's Ancient History, and Stackhouse's History of the Bible, intending to go through the Universal History also. And now I believed myself far wiser than any person of my age. Upon the whole, I believe I was at this time on the pinnacle of destruction. And had a just and noly

God then cut the brittle thread of life, I know I should have sunk into hell. But love had swifter wings than death, and mercy to my rescue flew.

In October, 1773, a neighbour of my mother's being very ill, and very poor, I went to visit her, and found her, to my great surprise, joyfully triumphing over death, yea, longing to be gone. This affected me much; for I felt I was in a quite different state—that if death should approach me, he would be a king of terrors. And I had no hopes of happiness beyond the grave. About this time, also, Mr. Simpson's sermons began to sink more deeply into my heart. So great were my obstinacy and folly, that I would come out of the church weeping, and, with the next person I met, would ridicule the sermon that affected me, lest I should be thought or called a Methodist. I began, however, in my serious moments, to resolve again and again I would break off my sins by true repentance, and especially that I would dance no more. Yet time after time I was prevailed on by my carnal friends, and broke the promises I had made to my God

January the first, 1774, I was deeply wrought upon by a sermon preached on, "What shall it profit a man if he gain the whole world, and lose his own soul?" And soon after, under another, on the epistle to the church of Laodicea. Again, while Mr. Simpson preached on the new birth, from John iii. 3, I saw, and felt as I had never done before, that I must experience that divine change, or perish. But I had still one great hinderance which I have not yet mentioned, namely, a young person, for whom I had a sincere affection: he and two of his sisters, with whom I had also formed a strict intimacy from the death of my father, were my constant companions, and were more seriously disposed than any of the rest. However, I was sensible, if I renounced my pleasures, and became what God and my own conscience now required, I must, in the first place, give him up, and that fully, or he would be the means of drawing me back; for he was yet unawakened, though outwardly moral.

But I could not yet make this sacrifice. Therefore I continued to go to assemblies, though conscience bled; and often in the midst of the dance, I felt as miserable as a creature could be, with a sense of guilt, and fears of death and hell. Sometimes those words were applied, "It is hard for thee to kick against the pricks." And, indeed, so I felt it. Yet I would not acknowledge my unhappiness to any, but carried it off with the appearance of gayety; and at the last assembly I ever attended, never sat down the whole night, but danced till four o'clock in the morning. Soon after this, however, the Lord wrought a much deeper work upon my soul.

In April, 1774, on the Sunday before Easter, Mr. Simpson preached from John vi. 44, "No man can come unto me, except the Father which hath sent me draw him." Explaining the drawings of the Father, he related his own experience, under the name of Eusebius, brought up in all moral duties, an attendant on church and sacrament, and one who said many prayers, yet, when twenty-two years old, was deeply convinced he had never been a Christian—could then say feelingly, what he had often before repeated in words only, "The remembrance of my sins is grievous unto me: the burden of them is intolerable." [All this sunk into my very soul: this was just my case.] He mourned, and wept, and prayed! And one day as he was in prayer, and had such a view of his past sinfulness, and present guilt and pollution, as almost deprived him of all hope, the Lord suddenly removed his burden, and spoke pardon and peace to his soul, so that he felt his sins were all forgiven. Lord, said I, if this is truth, (and I cannot disbelieve it,) never let me rest till I obtain a like blessing. He went on to observe the nature of this change, and the objections made in our day to this doctrine of the new birth. One of these objections he dwelt upon, viz. "We are born again when baptized;" but proved, if it were even so, we must still repent anew, and be forgiven, since all have broken the baptismal vow. Then he appealed to each: "Have you renounced the devil and all his works, the pomps and vanities of this wicked world, with every sinful desire?" while I could only plead guilty, guilty. "Have you never taken the name of God in vain? never profaned his Sabbaths? never set up idols in your heart? If you have done these things, you have broken the first four commandments of God." I pleaded guilty here also; for though with respect to the third, I could not accuse myself of profanely swearing, or even naming my Maker in conversation, as many do, yet this prohibition also condemned me, in having taken the name of God in vain into my polluted lips in his house of worship, and appearing before men engaged in devotion, while my heart was wandering to the ends of the earth. As he passed through the rest of the commandments, I could still plead nothing but guilty. And when in the application of his sermon he asked, "Now what think you of the state of your souls before God?" I felt myself indeed a lost, perishing, undone sinner: a rebel against repeated convictions and drawings: a rebel against light and knowledge: a condemned criminal by the law of God, who deserved to be sentenced to eternal pain! I felt I had broken my baptismal vow, my confirmation vow, my sacramental vows, and had no title to claim any mercy, any hope, any plea! I wept aloud, so that all around me were amazed; nor was I any longer ashamed to own the cause. I went home, ran up stairs, and fell on my knees, and made a solemn vow to renounce and forsake all my sinful pleasures and trifling companions.

I slept not that night, but arose early next morning, and without telling my mother, took all my finery, high-dressed caps, &c. &c., and ripped them all up, so that I could wear them no more; then cut my hair short, that it might not be in my own power to have it dressed, and in the most solemn manner vowed never to dance again! I could do nothing now but bewail my own sinfulness, and cry for mercy. I could not eat, or sleep, or take any comfort. The curses throughout the whole Bible seem pointed all at me, and I could not claim a single promise. I saw my whole life had been nothing but sin and rebellion against my Creator, Redeemer, and Sanctifier; and I feared it was now too late to seek mercy.

Thus I continued till Good Friday. My mother thought I was losing my senses, and all my friends endeavoured to comfort me in vain. After many conflicts and strong fears, I ventured, however, once more to approach the Lord's table, encouraged by these words, "A broken and a contrite heart, O God, thou wilt not despise."

As Mr. Simpson was reading that sentence in the communion service, "If any man sin, we have an advocate with the Father, Jesus Christ the righteous; and he is the propitiation for our sins," a ray of divine light and comfort was darted on my soul, and I cried, Lord Jesus, let me feel thou art the propitiation for my sins. I was enabled to believe there was mercy for me, and I, even I, should be saved! I felt love to God spring up in my heart, and in a measure could rejoice in him, so that I would have given all the world to have died that moment. But, alas, this was only for a short season! In the evening one of my cousins calling on me, who had been a witness to my late distress, I told her of the comfort I had received, and added, I am now not afraid to die. She immediately exclaimed, it would be great presumption to say so, for even Mr. Simpson, whom she believed the best man on earth, said he deserved to go to hell. My joy was damped immediately; and Satan telling me I had deceived myself, I gave up my confidence, lost my peace, and became again very unhappy.

It had been well for me if I had then known the Methodists; but I had none to instruct me.

Yet my distress was not the same as before. I had now a ray of hope in God, that he would make me a new creature by grace; and those horrible and slavish fears of hell were removed. I felt my nature all depraved, and my soul full of wounds, and bruised by sin. Yea, and I abhorred myself, truly repenting before my God, and seeking him with my whole heart, in every means of grace. I had never yet heard the Methodists; nor had I lost all my prejudices against them; but a neighbour, who had lately found peace with God, advised me strongly to go, and assured me they had been the means of great blessings to his soul. I would not promise, but resolved to go privately, so that neither the preacher nor any other person should know of it till afterward. I soon after went at five o'clock one morning, and got into a private seat. Mr. Samuel Bardsley preached from "Comfort ye, comfort ye, my people, saith your God." I thought every word was for me! He spoke to my heart as if he had known all the secret workings there; and pointed all such sinners as I felt myself to be, to Jesus crucified. I was much comforted: my prejudices were now fully removed, and I received a full and clear conviction, "These are the people of God, and show," in truth, "the way of salvation."

But now I had new difficulties to encounter: I

4*

knew if I persisted in hearing the Methodists, I must literally give up all. My mother had already threatened, if ever she knew me to hear them, she would disown me. Every friend and relation I had in the world, I had reason to believe, would do the same. I had no acquaintance then among the Methodists to take me in, nor knew any refuge to fly to but my God. I used much prayer, and entreated him to show me his will; when those words were powerfully applied, "Did ever any trust in the Lord and was confounded?" I answered, No, Lord, and I will trust thee! But Satan suggested, "Thou hast no right to trust God: thou art not his child, but a sinner, a rebel!" I fell on my knees, and cried, "Lord, I am a repenting sinner, and thou knowest I have laid down my weapons of rebellion! If I perish, I will perish at thy feet! Only show me thy will, and here I am." It was then applied, "If any man will come after me, let him deny himself, and take up his cross and follow me." I cried, "Lord, I will forsake all, and follow thee: I will joyfully bear thy cross; only give me thyself!" From that time I resolved I would at all hazards attend the preaching. I did so at all opportunities, and it was a great comfort to me.

But when my mother heard of it, a floodgate of persecution opened upon me! In this time of need God raised me up a friend in my uncle Roe, who prevented my mother turning me out of doors. Yet what I suffered, sometimes through her tears and entreaties, and at other times her severity, is known only to God. But he strengthened a feeble worm, and enabled me to endure all with meekness, as seeing him who is invisible. For eight weeks, however, I was closely confined. My godmother came to talk with me, so did my mother's brother, and my father's sister; also a clergyman, and several others; but the Lord gave me a mouth and wisdom to plead my own cause, with arguments from his word, so that they were in some measure all put to silence. In August my mother took me with her to Adlington, on our usual summer's visit, though now quite contrary to my inclination; for I found it a great grief to be separated from the means of grace, and from the dear people of God. Yet I dared not refuse her all obedience which I could render with a safe conscience. And though I believe she hoped to wean me from (what she called) my melancholy and enthusiasm hereby, yet the Lord kept me steadfast and immovable. The deep sense I had of my own weakness and inability to resist evil, or follow that which is good, and the great fears I had of ever again grieving the Holy Spirit, lest he should strive with me no more forever, convinced me of the absolute need of using much and constant prayer. I therefore left all company many times in a day, to retire in secret. I refused to conform in dress, or in any thing my conscience disapproved; and when called upon, gave reasons for my conduct as the Lord enabled me, but always with meekness, and often with tears of self-abasement; so that in a little time, finding all their efforts vain, they began to let me alone; only I was made to understand I had now nothing to expect from my godmother, as to temporal things. This, however, weighed nothing with me, as all my language was,

> "None but Christ to me be given,
> None but Christ in earth or heaven."

In October we returned home, and I now reasoned with my mother, and entreated her not to confine me any more, telling her in humility, and yet plainness, I must seek salvation to my soul, whatever is the consequence. And in order to obtain the end, I must use the means. I am therefore determined to leave you, and go to be a servant, rather than be kept from the Methodists. Yet if you will consent to it, I should greatly prefer continuing in your house, though it should be as your servant; and I am willing to undertake all the work of the house, if you will only suffer me to attend preaching. She listened to my proposals;

and, after consulting with her friends, consented to comply on this last condition; for she and they were agreed that I, who had never been accustomed to hard labour, would soon be weary, and give it up. But they knew not the power and goodness of that God who had strengthened me in all my tribulation.

November the first, I entered upon my new employments joyfully, undertaking my every labour for His sake who bled for me on Calvary! and began to feel at times much comfort, and reviving hopes, that my redemption drew near, and the happy hour when I should praise a pardoning God. Mr. Wesley's Sermon on Justification was a great encouragement to me, on those words, "To him that worketh not, but believeth on him that justifieth the ungodly, his faith is imputed to him for righteousness." This sermon I read many times over with prayer, and could sometimes almost embrace the promises.

On Monday, November 10th, I had strong conflicts with Satan, who told me I had as good give up all, for I should never obtain a pardon! I had sinned beyond hope! I felt my heart very hard, and he suggested, "This is a proof that God has given thee up to hardness and impenitence. Where is thy repentance and tears, and brokenness of heart? If thou couldst repent, and weep, and mourn, like others, there would be hope. But where is thy sorrow for sin? Thou canst not shed a tear." I was so burdened and distressed that day, that I could not go forward with my work, and my mother reproached me. But I besieged the throne of grace with strong crying and supplications to Him that was able to save, and who well knew the Spirit's groaning in my heart.

My cousin Charles Roe, then much devoted to God, put into my hands a little pamphlet, entitled, The Great Duty of believing on the Son of God. Jesus was here set forth in all his loveliness of free grace, toward a poor returning prodigal, as every way suited to the sinner's wants, and all-sufficient to save the vilest of the vile—as willing now, even as willing as when he hung on Calvary, bleeding and dying to save sinners, yea, his very murderers! I was much encouraged in reading this, and would gladly have spent the night in prayer; but my mother (with whom I slept) would not suffer it. I therefore went to bed, but could not sleep, and at four in the morning rose again, that I might wrestle with the Lord. I prayed, but it seemed in vain. I walked to and fro, groaning for mercy, then fell again on my knees; but the heavens appeared as brass, and hope seemed almost sunk into despair: when suddenly the Lord spake that promise to my heart, "Believe on the Lord

Jesus Christ, and thou shalt be saved." I revived, and cried, "Lord, I know this is thy word, and I can depend on it. But what is faith? O show me how to believe: show me what is the gospel faith, or I am yet undone. I desire not deliverance except in thy own way: I desire no happiness, but thy favour. What shall I do? O teach me, O help me, or I am lost!" That word came with divine evidence and sweetness to my heart, "Cast all thy care upon him, for he careth for thee." I said, "Lord, dost thou care for me? and is this faith, to cast all my care, even all my sins, (for I have no other care,) upon thee? May I? Dost thou bid me? a poor hell-deserving sinner—against light, and conviction, and repeated vows—can such love dwell in thee? Is it not too easy a way? May I, even I, be saved, if I only cast my soul on Jesus? my burden of sin, my load of guilt, my every crime? What, saved from all this guilt—saved into the favour of God! the holy God! and become his child, and that now, this moment! Oh it is too great,—it cannot, surely it cannot be!" (Oh what a struggle had Satan and unbelief with my helpless, sinful soul!) But the Lord applied, "Fear not, only believe!" Satan suggested, Take care! Suppose Jesus Christ should fail thee: suppose he is not God! What if he was an impostor, as the Jews believe! Oh the agony that my soul felt at that moment! But I cried, "If this be so, I am undone without remedy! None but such a Saviour as Jesus declares himself to be, (God as well as man,) can save my guilty, polluted soul. The blood of *God-man* alone can atone for me! His power alone can change my rebel heart: my disease is too deep for any other: I can only perish, nothing can be worse; so there is no hazard. If he is God, he is able, and he will save me according to his promise, 'Come unto me, all ye that labour and are heavy laden, and I will give you rest.' If he is God, he must be truth, and cannot deceive me And if not, a holy God will be a consuming fire to the sinner! And there is no Saviour, no way of salvation: I must endure the desert of my sins: I must endure everlasting burnings; and therefore here I will lie and perish at his feet!" Again it came, "Only believe." "Lord Jesus," said I, "I will, I do believe: I now venture my whole salvation upon thee as God! I put my guilty soul into thy hands, thy blood is sufficient! I cast my soul upon thee, for time and eternity." Then did he appear to my salvation. In that moment my fetters were broken, my bands were loosed, and my soul set at liberty. The love of God was shed abroad in my heart; and I rejoiced with joy unspeakable. Now, if I had possessed ten thousand souls, I could have ventured them all with my Jesus. I would have given them all to him! I felt a thousand promises all my own—more than a thousand scriptures to confirm my evidence—such as, "He that believeth shall be saved:—Shall not perish:—Is not condemned:—Hath everlasting life:—Is passed from death unto life:—Shall never die:—There is no condemnation to them that are in Christ Jesus:" &c. &c.—I could now call Jesus Lord, by the Holy Ghost, and the Father, my Father. My sins were gone, my soul was happy; and I longed to depart and be with Jesus. I was truly a new creature, and seemed to be in a new world! I could do nothing but love and praise my God; and could not refrain continually repeating, Thou art my Father! O God, thou art my God! while tears of joy ran down my cheeks.

My mother was astonished at the change which appeared in my countenance and whole deportment; and I soon told her the happy cause:—that I, a poor sinner, had received forgiveness, and could call God my Father and my Friend. Now, said I, I am repaid a thousand times for all I have suffered. One hour's experience of what I now feel, is, itself rich amends for all! But I see an eternity of bliss before! and added, O that you knew what I feel. My words and flowing tears made her weep; but she said little, being all wonder. With what joy and gratitude did I now undergo the most servile of all my employments; yea, and it seemed with double strength of body, though I could neither eat nor sleep much for many days and nights. The love of God shed abroad in my heart was now my meat and drink; and the thoughts of the amazing depths of grace which had plucked me as a brand from the burning, quite overcame me!—me, the most obstinate offender, who had so long and so repeatedly resisted, and grieved his Holy Spirit! This love of my God and Saviour, so unmerited and free, overflowed my soul; nor had I for eight months any interruption to my bliss.

> "Not a cloud did arise, to darken the skies,
> Or hide for a moment my Lord from my eyes."

Yet I had daily crosses to take up and endure; but I rejoiced in being accounted worthy to bear the cross for Him who died to purchase my peace. The word of God was sweeter than honey, or the honey-comb. I generally read it on my knees: ever receiving light, strength, and comfort to my hungry soul hereby.

About six months after this, my cousin Robert Roe came from Manchester, to go to the college in Oxford, being intended for a clergyman. The great change in me was matter of much grief to him. But what most astonished him was to find me, instead of being melancholy and mopish, always happy and rejoicing in God—resigned to sufferings and labours, which he well knew I could not once have submitted to. He saw my pride laid in the dust, and my soul sunk into humility. In short, he saw me the reverse of all I had been before; and comparing my present conduct with the Scriptures, he was constrained to own the power of changing grace—was convinced by the Spirit of God that I was right, and of consequence, that he was not what he ought to be, and what he must be if ever he was saved. He soon became so unhappy that he had no rest, and at last wrote to me, entreating for his soul's sake, I would answer him the following questions: "How did you obtain the happiness you speak of? Are you certain it is real and from God, and not a delusion, or imagination only? Does it arise from an express declaration from God, or a consciousness of having performed your duty? Is it some visible manifestation you enjoy, or some hoped happiness? I know I am a great sinner! I am miserable beyond expression, and can hardly hope for any thing but misery in time, or in eternity? I would give up all the world to obtain the favour of God you speak of, but I know not which way to attain it. If you can lead me in the heavenly path, you will render me happy indeed. Oh! pray for your unhappy friend, &c. R. R."

These lines appearing the genuine language of sincerity, I wrote immediately in answer a brief relation of all the Lord's dealings with my soul, inviting him to the same loving and all-sufficient Saviour. I advised him to hear the Methodists, and go to class meeting: in which he found much comfort, and advanced in grace daily, desiring and seeking nothing but Jesus crucified. And, on October 17th, 1775, a few weeks only before he went to Oxford, the Lord set his soul at liberty, and he rejoiced in a clear sense of his pardoning love. [The reader may find a more particular account of the life, trials, experience, and triumphant death of this Israelite indeed, in whom was no guile, in the Arminian Magazine for the years 1783 and 1784, vols. vi. vii.] But to return.

About seven months after I undertook to be servant to my mother, she was seized with a fever, and when just recovering, had a relapse which threatened to be fatal: so that for near six weeks I had to sit up with her every other night, till at last my body began to fail. Indeed, it was no wonder; for, besides all my labour and fatigue, I used rigorous fasting. The doctor who attended my mother was moved with compassion, and insisted I should no longer go on with what he called sacrificing my life. He spoke to Mrs. Legh, my godmother, who came next day in her chariot to see my mother, and to see that a proper servant, and all needful attendants, should be got immediately. I was now freed from my happy toil, about eight months after I undertook it, namely, in August, 1775. But it was then nearly too late: my health had received such a wound, as it did not recover in many years.

My outward oppositions now began to abate, and many of my enemies were at peace with me. And now also the Lord began to reveal in my heart that sin was not all destroyed; for though I had constant victory over it, yet I felt the remains of anger, pride, self-will, and unbelief often rising, which occasioned a degree of heaviness and sorrow At first I was much amazed to feel such things, and often tempted to think I had lost a measure of grace; yet when I looked to my Lord, or whenever I approached him in secret, he shed his precious love abroad, and bare witness also with my spirit, that I was still his child. Yea, and at this time I received many remarkable answers to prayer, many proofs of his undoubted love and goodness to my soul; and I ever felt I would rather die than offend him, so that I was a mystery to myself! I resolved, however, to use more self-denial of all kinds, and (whatever it cost me with respect to health or life) more fasting and prayer; for I hoped by these means to mortify and starve the evil tempers and propensities of my nature, till they should exist no more; and if my body expired in the combat, I thought I was certain of endless life. I met with some also who told me nothing but death would end this strife!—that this is the Christian's warfare, which cannot end but with the life of the body. After some time I began to believe these miserable comforters, and of consequence, longed for nothing so much as to die: yea, I was impatient to be gone, that I might be freed from sin; for I truly felt, and more so every day,

> "'Twas worse than death my God to love,
> And not my God alone."

My body was reduced now to a very weak state, and I was pronounced far gone in a consumption, which I esteemed blessed tidings. I looked on myself as one that had done with earth, and cried, "O that I had wings like a dove, for then I would flee away and be at rest." Yea, so desirous was I to quit the vale of sin (as I called it) here below, that I could not be prevailed on to take any thing which I believed would tend to restore my health, and therefore continued to decline very swiftly.* In the latter end of December, I was brought so weak that I could not walk about the room with-

* See Introduction.

out help, and soon after took my bed, seeming apparently on the verge of eternity. One day, after sitting up a little, I felt myself so weak that I believed I should rise no more till my soul took its flight to the bosom of Jesus. My joy on this occasion was inexpressible! I begged of the Lord strength to go on my knees once more; and in holy triumph committed body and soul to him for eternity. I believed my work on earth quite finished; and was filled with assurance that the moment of death would be to me the beginning of endless glory—a taste of which I then felt, a drop out of the ocean, a beam darted from the unclouded Sun of righteousness, which quite penetrated and overwhelmed my soul, and left me in speechless rapture at his feet! Yes, I have ever believed that what I then felt was what those feel and experience on leaving the body, who are really dying in the Lord! But infinite Wisdom saw good to lengthen out the thread of life; and I have often believed it was in answer to the prayers of his dear children.

A few weeks after this I felt a degree of disappointment and sorrow on finding a measure of returning strength: just like a mariner, who, got within sight of a desired port, is beat back again into a tempestuous ocean. One of my cousins, coming to see me, recommended a strengthening medicine, which I was unwilling to use, and told him I would rather die than live. He sharply rebuked me for this, saying, you set up your own will, while you pretend to submit to the will of God, and by not taking proper medicines you are a murderer! I wept and said, I think I am resigned. He asked, are you willing to live forty years, if the Lord please? I found a shrinking at the thought, and felt I could not at that moment say I was willing. He left me, but his words made a deep impression. I fell on my knees as soon as left alone, and cried, Lord, perfectly subdue my will. That promise was applied with much sweetness, "Ask what thou wilt, and it shalt be done unto thee." I felt assuredly my Lord permitted me to ask life or death, and was brought to a stand. I felt a thousand fears suggested, that if I lived, I might lose what I now enjoyed of the love of God, and perhaps be one day a dishonour to his cause. But I said, Lord, thy grace is ever sufficient: thou art as able to keep me a thousand years as one day! Again, it was suggested, if thou livest, it will be to suffer. I cried, Lord, thou canst give me suffering grace, and if by suffering I can in any wise glorify thee, "Not as I will, but as thou wilt." I know to die now would be instant glory! But here I am: do with me whatever thou wilt: thou knowest all things, and seest at one glance, past, present, and future. One request only, therefore, will I make: if thou knowest my life would glorify thee, I submit to thy will—willing to suffer, or to do! But, if thou foreseest I should, in living, lose any measure of what thou hast bestowed, Lord, suffer me not to live any longer. Or, if hereafter, at any time, thou seest a danger of my heart departing from thee, O snatch me to thy bosom, and let me not live a moment longer than I live wholly for thee. And now, O Lord my God, I vow and promise unto thee, I will henceforth entirely renounce my own will respecting life or death! I leave it fully in thy hands and to thy pleasure, to take me now, or to spare me twenty, thirty, yea, forty years, or as long as thou seest my life will bring glory to thee and profit to immortal souls; relying on thy faithful promise given me this day, that what "I ask shall be done," and accounting it a solemn covenant betwixt me and thee! that whensoever thou seest me about to be overcome by trials, by temptations or snares, so that I shall in heart or life depart from thee, or wound thy cause, that then thou wilt put in thy sickle and gather me home; yea, if even at that time I should be so foolish as to desire life!—Amen and amen. What I felt of heaven, of God, of love, at that season, cannot be expressed. I had communion with my Lord, as if face to face, and could henceforth choose nothing but his will.

From this day forth I speedily recovered strength; and in a few weeks was enabled to attend some of the means of grace. The Lord was pleased to make the preaching of Dr. Wright a great blessing to me. He clearly explained the nature of salvation from inbred sin: showed it to be as freely promised in Scripture, and as fully purchased by the blood of Jesus, as pardon. Also, that though sanctification in believers is a gradual work, yet the death of sin is instantaneous, and to be obtained by faith alone—just in like manner as justification. He recommended Mr. Wesley's Plain Account, and Farther Thoughts on Christian Perfection; and Mr. Fletcher's Polemical Essay, especially his Address in the end of it, to imperfect believers. These yet further opened my eyes respecting that great salvation; and for reading them I shall praise God to all eternity. I now was powerfully convinced, that whenever sin is totally destroyed, it is done in a moment. From hence I could not rest, but cried to the Lord night and day, to cast out the strong man, and all his armour of unbelief and sin—assured that the power of the living God, and not death, must be the executioner! the blood of Jesus the procuring cause; and faith the only instrument. I had a deeper sense of my impurity than ever; and though by grace I was restrained from giving way outwardly, yet I felt such inward impatience, pride, fretfulness, and in short, every ill temper, that at times I could truly say, I was weary and heavy laden.

I here transcribe a brief extract from my journal, kept at the time, as it will most clearly describe the language of my heart.

Thursday, January 18th, 1776, I was much comforted by a manifest answer to prayer. Afterward, reading three of Mr. Fletcher's Letters to his Parishioners, was a great blessing. Yet in the evening I found many wanderings, and much deadness: I felt dissatisfied with myself, and all around me, and knew not why. It might in some measure be owing to the indisposition of my body, but I fear it was more owing to the evil of my corrupt heart. Oh when shall I be holy?

Friday, 19.—I have been greatly tried inwardly and outwardly, though I have had some refreshing visits of love; but I feel many evil tempers, much self-will that would not be contradicted, (though none saw it but the Lord;) peevishness, pride, and unbelief greatly distressed me. My cry was this evening, "Create in me a clean heart, O God, and renew a right spirit within me." And in private prayer I was blessed in a wonder ful manner. I lay at the feet of my Lord, as clay in the hands of the potter, only beseeching him to stamp me with his lovely image.

Thursday, 25.—The Lord shows me more than ever, I must be made holy before death; and this day I can say, "As the hart panteth after the water-brooks," so thirsteth my soul for the perfect love of God. O may I never rest till I have received this blessing. Lord, I have in this respect been a trifler: I have been too easy, too lukewarm, while thy enemies have had a lurking place in my heart! O forgive me, and help me to be more in earnest. Those words were applied, while engaged in wrestling prayer, "All I have is thine!" And is not this salvation from sin His gift? It is, and shall be mine.

> "O joyful sound of gospel grace,
> Christ shall in me appear:
> I, even I, shall see his face,
> I shall be holy here."

Saturday, 27.—Mr. Wesley's Plain Account of Christian Perfection was this day a greater blessing than before: Oh how very ignorant, how stupid have I been, respecting this great salvation; and even yet I seem to know nothing. Lord, teach me, and save me fully. I find while pressing after entire purity, my communion with God increases, and I have more power to do his will.

Friday, February 2.—I awoke several times in the night, praying for sanctification. Oh the depth of unbelief and of pride! And these seem only the roots of many other evil branches. O my God, I feel my heart as a den of thieves. I loathe my self, but oh! I fall—a leper at thy feet. I believe "the blood of Jesus Christ cleanseth from all sin." But when I would come to the fountain, I seem all ignorance and helplessness. O Lord, teach and strengthen me, for thy mercies' sake!

Saturday, 3.—I have had deep communion with my God, and much power at a throne of grace. I have a clear evidence of his pardoning love, and want nothing but his whole image stamped on my heart.

Thursday, 8.—I was greatly comforted this morning in spreading open the word of God on my knees, and praying for a conformity to it. I opened on 1 Thess. v. 16–ult. I see what is there required is the very salvation my soul needs. Oh how is it summed up in that prayer of the apostle, "And the very God of peace sanctify you wholly; and I pray God your whole spirit, and soul and body, be preserved blameless unto the coming of our Lord Jesus Christ." And would St. Paul pray for what they could not obtain? Oh no! he believed that they should be both sanctified and preserved blameless; for he says, "Faithful is he who hath called you, who also will do it." Amen, Lord! Let me, thy worthless creature, prove this word for Jesus' sake.

On the morning of February 22, I awoke poorly in body, and felt a strange hardness on my heart, and a great backwardness to private prayer. Satan told me, if I prayed, it would be only solemn mockery; for my body would so weigh down my soul, that while my words flew up, my thoughts would remain below, and I should obtain no blessing. But I cried, "Lord, help me," and fell instantly on my knees: for a few moments my ideas were all distraction; but the mighty God spoke to the troubled ocean, "Peace, be still!" and there followed a great calm throughout my soul. My intercourse was now opened with my Beloved, and various promises presented to my believing view. I thought, shall I now ask small blessings only of my God? Lord, cried I, make this the moment of my full salvation! Baptize me now with the Holy Ghost, and the fire of pure love. Now "make me a clean heart, and renew a right spirit within me." Now, enter thy temple, and cast out sin forever. Now, cleanse the thoughts, desires, and propensities of my heart, and let me perfectly love thee. But here Satan raised all his force of temptations to oppose me, telling me, I had not been long enough justified—I had more to suffer first, &c. And my ideas not being yet clear in the nature of this blessing, gave the enemy an advantage. For I thought when fully saved from sin, I could suffer no more; feel no more pain; make no more mistakes; my judgment and memory would be perfect, and I should feel temptation no more! Therefore, this suggestion, that I had to suffer much first, had the more plausibility. But in that moment, I received light from above, and cried, "Lord, till my heart is renewed, I cannot suffer as I ought: give me perfect love, and I can then bear all things!" But, said Satan, if this blessing were given, thou wouldst soon lose it again, in such and such trials which lie before thee: get those trials past, and then come for this blessing. But I cried, "Lord, I cannot stand those trials without it. O purify my heart, that I may be able to stand in the trying hour! If I face my subtle enemies, while I have a traitor within, ever ready to betray me into their hands, how shall I be able to stand?" But if that "strong man armed, be cast out with all his armour," how much more shall I be able to contend with my outward enemies! Many other temptations were injected; but I cried so much the more, "Lord, save me!" And the Lord gave me that promise, "I will circumcise thy heart, and thou shalt love the Lord thy God with all thy heart," &c. I said, "Lord, thou art faithful, and this is thy word, I cast my whole soul upon thy promise: make known thy faithfulness, by performing it on my heart. Circumcise it now, fill it now with thy pure love: sanctify every faculty of my soul: I offer all to thee, I give thee all my powers; I take thee, Almighty Jesus, for my wisdom, my righteousness, my sanctification." Now "Cleanse me from all my filthiness and from all my idols: take away the heart of stone, and give me a heart of flesh." I come empty to be filled: deny me not. It would be for thy own glory to save me now; for how much better could I serve thee! It is true, I have no plea but thy mercy! the blood of Jesus, thy promise, and my own great need. O save me fully, by an act of free grace. Thou hast said, "He that believeth shall be saved:" I now take thee at thy word: I do by faith cast myself on thy promise. I venture my soul on thy veracity: thou *canst not deny!* Being purchased by thy blood, thy justice is engaged: being promised without money and without price, thy truth is bound: thus every attribute of my God secures it to me.

Ah! why did I ever doubt his willingness, when he gave Jesus! gave him to "destroy the works of the devil—to make an end of sin!" The hinderance lay in me, not him. He desired to make me holy, but unbelief hid it from my eyes—accursed sin! But, now, Lord, I do believe: this moment thou dost save. Yea, Lord, my soul is delivered of her burden. I am emptied of all: I am at thy feet, a helpless, worthless worm; but I take hold of thee as my fulness! Every thing that I want, thou art. Thou art wisdom, strength, love, holiness: yes, and thou art mine! I am conquered and subdued by love. Thy love sinks me into nothing: it overflows my soul. Oh, my Jesus, thou art all in all! In thee I behold and feel all the fulness of the Godhead mine. I am now one with God: the intercourse is open: sin, inbred sin, no longer hinders the close communion, and God is all my own!

Oh the depth of solid peace my soul now felt! but not so much rapturous joy as at justification. It was

> "The sacred awe, which dares not move,
> And all the silent heaven of love!"

Yet when I rose from my knees, Satan once more assaulted me with, "Thou art going to face various trials, and a cooling world: thou wilt soon lose this blessing." But instantly that scripture was given me, "He that keepeth Israel, neither slumbereth nor sleepeth: the Lord himself is thy keeper! It is even he that shall preserve thy soul: the Lord shall preserve thy going out and thy coming in, from this time forth and for evermore."—"Lord," said I, "I feel my own insufficiency: I can do nothing: I can resist nothing; but I commit the powers of my soul, the avenues of my heart, to thy keeping." Again he graciously applied—"Blessed is she that believed; for there shall be a performance of those things which were told her from the Lord." "My God," said I, "it is enough! My soul does trust thee, and I will praise thee."

I now walked in the unclouded light of his countenance, "rejoicing evermore, praying without ceasing, and in every thing giving thanks." I resolved, however, at first, I would not openly declare what the Lord had wrought; but it was seen in my countenance; and when asked respecting it, I durst not deny the wonders of his love! I soon found that repeating his goodness, confirmed my own faith more and more. And so did the Lord bless me in declaring it, (yea, and blessed others also,) that I was constrained to witness to all who feared him:

"His blood can make the foulest clean:
His blood avail'd for me."

I dared not to live above a moment at a time; and that moment by faith in the Son of God. I never felt till now the full meaning of those words: "In him we live, and move, and have our being"—and again, "I will dwell in them, and walk in them, and be their God: I will put my laws into their minds, and write them in their hearts." Glory be to my God, I felt it written there: it was no longer I that lived, but Christ that lived in me!

> "Yea, Christ was all and all to me;
> And all my heart was love."

Friday, 23.—Glory, honour, and eternal praise be to the God of love, for ever and ever! His own arm hath brought salvation to my feeble, helpless soul. I am now wholly his! I do love the Lord my God with all my heart, and soul, and strength. I am nothing, and Jesus is my all. The enemy is often suggesting, "Thou wilt soon lose the blessing: thou canst not stand long." But my heart answers, I will hang upon, and trust my God, as long as I have any being; and I know he will supply a feeble worm with power! I have also opened on many sweet promises to-day. I find momentarily power now to pray, and believe: yea, I believe by faith!

Saturday, 24.—Last night and this morning I had deep communion with my God. I feel I am indeed one with Christ, and Christ is one with me: I dwell in Christ, and Christ in me. Oh blessed union with him my soul loveth! And the more I feel of his great love, the more I sink at his feet in humbling views of my own nothingness; and here it is, I would ever lie: this is my own place: Jesus alone is exalted; and I, a poor sinner, saved from sin!

Sunday, 25.—Glory be to God for the best Sabbath I ever knew! My body was so very weak and poorly, I could not go to preaching; but the Lord was with me, and gave me fresh discoveries of my own emptiness and poverty, and of his abundant fulness. Those words were also powerfully applied, "Now ye are clean through the word which I have spoken unto you: abide in me and I in you: as the branch cannot bear fruit of itself except it abide in the vine, no more can ye, except ye abide in me." I also feel that gracious promise mine: "If ye abide in me, and my words abide in you, ye shall ask what ye will, and it shall be done unto you." Oh the condescension of God to a poor worm! What a grant is this! My soul draws near and humbly asks,

"Enlarge my faith's capacity,
Wider and yet wider still.
Then with all that is in thee,
My soul forever fill."

Thursday, 29.—I was so happy that I could

not sleep in the night. Oh what deep communion did my soul enjoy with God! It was, indeed, a foretaste of heaven itself. This morning I prayed for a portion of Scripture to be impressed on my heart, that should abide with, comfort and direct me all the day, and I opened on, "Know ye not that your body is the temple of the Holy Ghost, which is in you, which ye have of God, and ye are not your own? For ye are bought with a price; therefore glorify God in your body, and in your spirit, which are God's." Sweet portion! O my blessed Lord, I rejoice that I am thy purchased property, and not my own; and to thee I gladly yield, body, soul, and spirit.

March 5.—For some days it has been a season of outward trials; but I have enjoyed fellowship with God, and great inward comforts. I have ever found, when he gives peculiar grace, he permits it to be tried; but I prove "as my day is, so is my strength." Yes, glory to his name alone, I am more than conqueror! and feel it the constant language of my heart,

"No cross, no suffering I decline,
Only let all my heart be thine."

Sunday, 10.—Mr. Simpson preached from "The kingdom of God is not meat and drink, but righteousness, and peace, and joy in the Holy Ghost." Oh the blessedness of this inward kingdom! With streaming eyes, and heart overflowing with love, I could claim this portion mine—mine in possession, and mine forever! O Lord, how shall I praise thee?

> "Nothing else will I know, in my journey below,
> But singing thy grace, to thy paradise go!"

Thursday, 28.—After a blessed season of communion with God, in secret prayer this morning, I went with my mother to spend the day at Adlington. Every thing I saw there, in house or garden, contributed to fill my happy soul with praise. In such and such a spot, I would say to myself, have I poured out my soul in deep distress unto the Lord, and in such a place he darted a ray of comfort, and bid me go forward. O my Lord, what hast thou done for a worthless worm, since these seasons of weeping penitence! Then I sowed in tears, but now I reap in joy. "Oh what shall I render unto the Lord for all his benefits?" I have nothing. My all is thine already. A poor offering. But,

> "Poor as it is, 'tis all my store—
> More thou shouldst have, if I had more."

Some time after this, I called upon Sarah Oldham, and found her just arrived on the borders of Canaan. It was animating to be near her! She requested us to sing,

"Gladly would I flee away—
Loose from earth, no longer stay," &c.

When we ceased, she cried, "Oh sweet! oh comfortable! I thank you." I asked her, "Have you any doubts or fears of landing safe!" She said, "Oh no! not one doubt." I asked her a few other questions, which she answered to my great satisfaction. Two days after this, clapping her hands together in an ecstasy of joy, she took her flight to glory! Her last words were, "My Lord and my God."

On Monday, April the first, Mr. Wesley came to Macclesfield, and I saw and conversed with him for the first time. He behaved to me with parental kindness, and greatly rejoiced in the Lord's goodness to my soul—encouraged me to hold fast, and to declare what the Lord had wrought. On Wednesday morning he set off for Manchester. He thinks me consumptive; but welcome life, or welcome death, for Christ is mine.

Tuesday, June 4.—I find great weakness of body, but much of the Divine presence, and resigned longings for immortality. I was at five o'clock preaching this morning, and there the Lord shed his love abroad, and all day I have had such a solemn nearness to him as I cannot describe. I called on one who, in the arms of death, is rejoicing in redeeming love, her will perfectly resigned, and her evidence clear for a glorious eternity. What a sight! O Jesus, this is THY victory! O Satan, how art thou conquered!

Tuesday, July 6.—My weakness of body seems to increase, and so does my union with Him my soul loveth. I was so happy in the night, that I had little sleep, and awoke several times, with those words deeply impressed, "The temple of an in-dwelling God." His love humbles me in the dust: it seems as a mirror to discover my nothingness. Sometimes my weakness of body seems quite overpowered with the Lord's presence manifest to my soul; and I have thought I could bear no more and live. But then I eagerly cry, "Oh give me more and let me die! I long to be freed from earth; but I am resigned to live and suffer here." I found the following lines, which I received with some others, very reviving:

"MY DEAR SISTER,—I fear I shall hardly see you again till we meet in paradise. But if you should gradually decay, if you be sensible of the hour approaching when your spirit is to return to God, I should be glad to have notice of it. It is a comfort: to die is not to be lost!

'To earth-born pain superior you shall rise
Through the wide waves of unopposing skies:
When summon'd hence, ascend heaven's high abode,
Converse with angels, and rejoice in God.'

"Tell me, how far does the corruptible and decaying body press down the soul? Your disorder naturally sinks the spirits, and occasions heaviness and dejection. Can you, notwithstanding this, rejoice evermore? I shall be glad to know if you experience something similar to what Mr De Renty expresses in those strong words: 'I bear about with me an experimental verity, and a plenitude of the presence of the ever-blessed Trinity!' Do you commune with God in the night season? Does he bid you even in sleep go on? And does he make your very dreams devout? That he may fill you with all his fulness, is the constant wish of," &c.

I praise my God, who enables me, in a degree, to understand the above, and to answer those deep questions in the affirmative.

Wednesday, September 11. This day I have had much pain and weakness of body, but my peace hath been as a river: O that my righteousness may be as the waves of the sea. My uncle hath disowned my three cousins on account of hearing the Methodists. My cousins R. and J. are steadfast, and more happy in God than ever. Poor C. has given up Christ for the world, and is therefore restored to the favour of his earthly parent. But oh, how will he appear when earth and heaven shall flee away! Lord, make it a warning to me, that I may watch and pray, and implore momentary help.

Sunday, 22.—As I returned from preaching, I called on Mary Etchels, who is in the last stage of a dropsy, just ready to wing her way to eternal glory. She has been a backslider in heart for some years, but in her long affliction has returned unto the Lord, with weeping, mourning, and supplication. Nor did she weep in vain: the Lord hearkened, and spoke peace to her soul some weeks since; and this day she told me she has received the witness of being cleansed from all sin, so that now she is full of love and joy. Her cry is, Oh how I long to be with Jesus! Why are his chariot-wheels so long in coming? O for patience till my Jesus comes! She got hold of my hand after I had prayed with her, and said, Oh what precious sights do I see! Such glory, such glory, I cannot utter it! Soon after her happy spirit fled to her eternal rest.

Monday, Oct. 14.—In the night (for I could not sleep) it was a convenient season between God and my happy soul. And I since find the bonds of divine union more strong than ever. This has been a blessed day! His work, his ways, his word, are my delight. I live by faith; and all hard things are become easy. I can praise him in every conflict; but I feel I could bear nothing, could do nothing, without Jesus. All my dependence is on *Him*, who supplies the momentary power I want; and I can truly say,

> "With every coming hour I prove
> His nature, and his name is love."

Tuesday, 15.—I am still kept in various trials. This day, the following letter was as if sent of God to strengthen me:—

"My Dear Sister,—The trials which a gracious Providence sends, or permits, may be so many means of growing in grace; and particularly of increasing in faith, patience, and resignation. And are they not all chosen for us by infinite wisdom and goodness? So that we may well subscribe to those beautiful lines:

> 'With patient mind thy course of duty run:
> God nothing does or suffers to be done
> But thou wouldst do thyself, if thou couldst see
> The end of all events as well as he.'

Every thing we can do for a parent, we ought: that is, every thing we can do, without killing ourselves; but this we have no right to do: our lives are not at our own disposal. Remember this, and do not carry a good principle too far. Do you still find,

> 'Labour is rest, and pain is sweet,
> When thou my God art here?'

I know pain or grief does not interrupt your happiness; but does it not lessen it? You often feel sorrow for your friends: does that sorrow rather quicken than depress your soul? Does it sink you deeper into God? Go on in the strength of the Lord. Be careful for nothing. Live to-day. So will you still be a comfort to yours affectionately."

Friday, Nov. 8.—My body is very weak; but when my strength and my heart fail, I feel God is the strength of my heart and my portion forever. Reading a portion of Scripture with prayer, every day, is, and has been, a great blessing to my soul. Often have I found, through this means, direction in difficulties, comfort in trials, and heavenly teachings in the way to glory. And the Scriptures I so read are impressed with such divine unction on the heart as makes it lasting food and nourishment to my soul.

Feb. 12, 1777.—Every day I experience more fully that God is love, and his service perfect freedom. What solid bliss is it to be delivered from all dependence on creatures, and to hang by faith upon the *immutable* God! To know this God is mine: to feel he dwelleth in my heart, ruleth my will, my affections, my tempers, my desires: to know he loveth me ten thousand times better than I love him. Oh it is unspeakable salvation!

Feb. 22.—One year this day I have been wholly

the Lord's; and he has kept sole possession of my willing heart. Yes, thou hast been my strength, my refuge, my guide, and my merciful God: my portion, my treasure, and my whole delight. One year I have loved thee with all my heart, and thou hast reigned without a rival. And now, O my Father, Saviour, Comforter, I give myself afresh to thee.

"Take my soul and body's powers,
Take my memory, mind, and will,
All my goods, and all my hours,
All I know, and all I feel:
Thine while I live, thrice happy I,
Happier still, if thine I die."

On Sept. 14, 1778, there was a very awful earthquake. The new church in Macclesfield (where I then was) rocked like a cradle, and nearly threw some of the people, then kneeling, on their faces. And the noise, for a few moments, was like thunder. The scene that ensued was truly an emblem of that day "when all faces shall gather paleness; and many shall cry to the rocks and mountains, Fall on us," &c. Some believed that the church was falling at the steeple end; and therefore flew in crowds to the opposite doors, shrieking and crying for mercy. Some fainted, and were trampled nearly to death, others bruised much; and some did not recover the fright. But oh, unspeakable grace! my soul was kept calm, for I feared not to die. That scripture was brought to my mind: "Yet once more and I shake not the earth only, but also heaven." And I was enabled to exhort those around to be still, and look unto the God of grace for salvation, which they had too long neglected. Many were deeply awakened by this awful providence; and never found rest afterward, till they found it in the manifested love of a blessed Redeemer. And some who may date their conversion from that day, will, I believe, be eternal monuments of grace.

Many are my symptoms of mortality; but God is love, and bears my happy soul far above

"All sin, and temptation, and pain."

I long for his leave to depart and be with Christ, but wait in humble resignation at his feet, till all his will be done.

Though much indisposed, I went to church; and there in partaking of the blessed sacrament, I had such union and intercourse with the Holy Trinity, as is unspeakable! blessed foretaste of drinking the new wine in my Father's kingdom. Yes, these are the streams, but that is the fountain.

Friday, June 18, 1780.—I was closely tried for a few days past, by near and dear relatives; but in God I have deep peace and can say, all his will is welcome, all pain before his presence flies! Compared with his love, how trifling is all I suffer! Am I not a brand plucked from eternal burnings! and the few moments of my existence here, are all the moments of suffering I shall ever know! yea, and these light afflictions, even as I pass through them, are working out for me "a far more exceeding and eternal weight of glory."

Monday, December 18.—I had a day of many blessings in visiting the sick. I called at John Barber's, and found his wife's mother dangerously ill. This poor old Pharisee, now upwards of fourscore years old, would never listen to the calls of converting grace, or be persuaded that she needed to be born again. But now the Lord has laid his hand upon her soul as well as her body.

Some time after I called again, and found she had been incessantly crying for mercy. When I now spoke with her, she cried out, The Lord will save me; but oh pray! I did so; and then asking, How do you now feel? she said, with uncommon earnestness, I shall soon rejoice in him: he will forgive my sins! Soon after she cried aloud, Lord, I hope thou wilt soon forgive me! Lord, thou art forgiving me! nay, Lord, thou hast forgiven me! After this, she continued exceeding happy for five days, and then exchanged mortality for life!

Tuesday, 19.—I called upon that old saint, Thomas Barber, who was seized the day before with a malignant fever. I asked him, Is the Lord precious to your soul? He said, He is all love: I shall soon be with him. It seems worth remarking here, that this good old man had prayed and agonized with God for many years, that his aged wife might see his salvation; and also that she might be first taken home. His request was granted in both these respects. A little before her death, the Lord revealed his salvation to her heart; and for some days she bore testimony of his love, often repeating, "Thy rod and thy staff comfort me." Just before she departed, having taken an affectionate leave of her husband and children, she cried aloud, "Now, Lord, thou art mine forever and ever!" When her breath was gone, her husband said, "Lord, now lettest thou thy servant depart in peace, according to thy word, for mine eyes have seen thy salvation." And from that time his body was perceived to fail.

Thursday, 21.—I found him very ill, but very happy. Yet he told me, "I have been tempted to fear patience will not hold out in all this pain, for I feel as if every limb was tearing asunder from my body; but I know God is all-sufficient." I called again: he told me, "My pain has been extreme, but I feel the presence of God continually; and I sensibly know, he is as near to me as

I am to myself. Whether I die at this time or recover, my will is wholly resigned; but I know if he calls me now, I shall go to glory." In the afternoon his every breath was prayer or praise; and all his attention manifestly taken up with heavenly things. To the doctor he said, "It is of more consequence that you should repent, than that I should recover; for if I die I shall go to God; but if you do not repent you will perish: 'You must be born again.'"

Saturday, 23.—His dissolution evidently drew near. He was sometimes a little delirious; yet of God and spiritual things he spoke clearly and scripturally, and prayed without ceasing. In the evening he broke out in the most solemn manner, and repeated several times, "Christ is God! Christ is God! God out of Christ is a consuming fire!" On being asked how he did, he said, "I am going to the heavenly Canaan, that promised land for which I set out long ago." While the doctor spoke to him of his body, he regarded not, but told him, "I am not afraid to die." And then, with lifted hands, prayed that all around him, and especially his children, might follow him to glory. When I asked him a little after this, do you now feel God graciously near? he said, (looking with solemn steadfastness in his countenance, as if he saw something,) "His spiritual presence is here!" and bursting into a flood of tears, cried, "I am full of God! His glory fills my soul!" Another asked him, Have you any doubts? He answered, "I have not the least doubt upon my mind, but I shall reign with him in glory!" Late that night I called again, wishing to see him once more and though delirious just before, when one said, Here is Miss Roe, he hastily put out his hand and said, "May God bless you." This was his last address to me; and he spake little afterward. At nine the next morning, I found him speechless, and in a dying state, but quite composed, and just as if falling into a sweet sleep. Mr. Simpson came in, and went to prayer by him; but he appeared insensible to all below. The power of God, however, rested on all present in an abundant manner; and in about an hour afterward he expired without a sigh or a groan.

Friday, 29.—Late this evening, my cousin Robert Roe arrived with the corpse of his brother Samuel, who died at Leek, on his way home from Bristol. There was great hope in the end of this once gay young man. My cousin William, and Margaret, also arrived from Liverpool: O that this solemn season may be sanctified to all his weeping relatives and friends! and may those who partook of the follies that employed his youthful years take the awful warning, and seek that acquaintance with Jesus in life, which he felt sc much need of in his last hours.

March 27, 1781.—This day at my uncle Roe's, I saw Mr. Rogers for the first time. He and Mr. Bardsley are come over from Sheffield to see cousin Robert, who respects Mr. Rogers much, having received good from his preaching at Leeds. We had a blessed season in prayer together; and cousin Peggy Roe in particular, seemed stirred up and comforted. Afterward we called on that dying saint, David Pickford, who witnessed a good confession of the love of Jesus, which he has felt experimentally for these thirty-six years; and proves him yet faithful. At night, Mr. Rogers preached from "You that are troubled, rest with us." And at five o'clock next morning, Mr. Bardsley enforced that blessed portion, "Fear not, for I am with thee: be not dismayed, for I am thy God," &c. I felt both peculiar seasons of divine blessings; and though afterward tried at home, it was a day of deep consolation.

April 20.—I was much comforted by hearing of the happy death of Anne B., one I formerly loved much, and dealt faithfully with. She lost much of her spirituality, by a connection with a carnal man, whom she married a year ago. But the Lord loved her, and sent a lingering affliction, slew the body, but saved the soul!

Friday, 27.—I have lately proved more kindness and affection from my mother than for some years. Oh, how good is the Lord! Surely with him nothing shall be impossible. My uncle Roe is seized dangerously ill, and two physicians called in.

Wednesday, May 2.—There is no hope of my uncle's recovery. But he is reconciled to all his children, and calls much upon God! and begs of Mr. Simpson, and others, to pray for him. Yea, though scarce able, gets upon his knees in bed, to pray for himself.

Thursday, 3.—As I went to my uncle's this morning, I met one of the maids, who told me he is fled into a world of spirits! he lay all night quite composed; but about ten this morning suddenly opened his eyes and fixed them, with seeming delight, on some object for several minutes: soon after which, he silently breathed away the immortal spirit! and, I have great hope, is escaped to endless life. I spent the day chiefly with my cousins, and found it a solemn profitable season. Poor cousin Joseph came a few hours after his father's decease, having rode on horseback two hundred miles in twenty-four hours.

Tuesday, 8.—In the dusk of the evening my uncle's remains were carried in great pomp, by his own carriage and horses, to the new church, and accompanied by coaches, torches, and a vast concourse of people; but the horses, unaccustomed to be adorned with such trappings as black cloth escutcheons, they would hardly proceed. He was interred by Mr. Simpson, in the vault he had so lately prepared! Yes, this much feared, and much loved man, is now committed to corruption and worms! it reminds me of Dr. Young's beautiful lines:

"An angel's arm can't snatch me from the grave,
Legions of angels can't confine me there!"

Tuesday, July 3.—I called on Ann Shrigley, who, when I last saw her, was crying for mercy in deep distress; but is now filled with praise, and on the verge of a glorious eternity. On Friday last, having spoken sharply to her husband, she was seized with agony of spirit, and cried aloud, Now I am lost forever: I shall go to hell: there is no mercy for me. But she wrestled in prayer till she prevailed, and the Lord shed his forgiving love abroad in an abundant manner, and bore his witness with her heart that she was born of God. She now told me, I long to be gone. O that all the world knew what I feel: they would soon seek God and find him; for he would save them all. O that blessed eternity! I am going to that blessed eternity! I said there we shall meet to part no more. She said no, never, never part more! we shall be forever with our Lord. O that blessed Saviour! what has he done for my soul! If my bodily affliction was a thousand times heavier than it is, his love would be above all. On Monday, 16th, I went with Mr. Simpson, who administered to her the blessed memorials of dying love; and we all found it a time of the presence and power of God. She continued in the same sweet frame of mind till her spirit fled away.

Wednesday.—Cousin F. R. called on me this morning, and related her dream, which has made a deep impression on her mind, and affected me much. She thought her father's spirit appeared to her, and a person who was with her in the room where he died; and that he asked, in a most solemn manner, "Are my family and children seeking salvation? I say, are all my children and family seeking the full assurance of salvation?" He then disappeared; but quickly came again, as if he was in haste to give them warning, lest any of them should defer it till too late, and perish in their sins; and asked, "Have all my family found the full assurance of salvation?" and added, with the utmost earnestness, "Tell them, never, never, never to rest till they find it! Do you hear me? Tell them never, never to rest till they have found it!" I forbear to mention a few more particulars in this awful dream! those whom it chiefly concerns no doubt remember them, as it was kept no secret. O may it make lasting impressions on all! Some did take warning—found that full assurance—witnessed a good confession to all their friends, and are now safely lodged in Abraham's bosom:—

> "Far from the world of grief and sin,
> With God eternally shut in!"

After his father's death, my cousin Robert determined to fix in Macclesfield; and for that purpose built a good house, conveniently near the new church—a lovely situation, and good air. When this house was finished, at his earnest request, and by the desire of his aunt, Miss S., and several more, my mother undertook to keep the house. She rented the whole dwelling, and he boarded with her. I mention this, because it appears a peculiar providence that placed me there, to be with this child and servant of God in his last moments. From the time of his father's death to that of his own, he gave himself up to the work of God, as fully as health would possibly permit. He boldly and publicly preached the Gospel in and near Macclesfield; and the Lord bore witness to his word, by awakening, converting, and saving souls. And I believe I may safely affirm, that during that season, he never preached one sermon in vain. Sometimes two, three, or four, in one night, were deeply awakened; and once seven; and commonly three or four justified. He was also the instrument of many believing to full salvation.

Friday, August 9.—We removed to my cousin's house, where I enjoyed, for the short season of his life, many spiritual privileges. My mother also had many opportunities she never would before partake of, both in prayer and Christian conversation; for my cousin had constant prayer-meetings, bands, &c., under the roof, and endeavoured to devote his whole time, talents, and substance to God. But how mysterious are the ways of Providence! how quickly was he called from all this!

Tuesday, 20th, he caught a severe cold, which terminated in his death. Every help was procured, but to no effect. His soul, which long panted after holiness, was now deeply distressed to feel the power of the all-cleansing blood, and the witness of being saved from all sin. He called on me many times a day to pray with him, and was often greatly comforted; but nothing less than full salvation would satisfy. Satan, at times, took advantage of his distracted nerves, and suggested terrible fears, so that his conflicts at some seasons were great, at other times he was filled with comfort; and during the whole of his affliction he never expressed the least murmuring or impatience.

Tuesday, 27th, in attempting to walk two or three times across the room, he fainted away, and when recovered, said, "I beg as a particular favor, cousin, that you will be with me as much as possible: don't leave me, and God will reward you." I seldom did after this.

September 2.—I rose at five, and going into his room, found him awake: he said, I feel peculiarly calm, composed, and resigned to the will of God, but have had no sleep: tell me if you have not been praying for me? I answered yes: he said, I thought so. Then he desired me to open the New Testament, and read the verse that first appeared. I did so, and it was this: "For ye are dead, and your life is hid with Christ in God: when Christ, who is our life, shall appear, then shall ye also appear with him in glory." He was greatly comforted. From this time he hastened toward his eternal home!

Monday, 9.—He settled all his temporal concerns, and then praised God for having done so, and was very happy. But in the night he had one more conflict with Satan. I prayed with him above an hour: surely it was the most solemn season I ever knew! The Lord heard and delivered. He fell into a sweet sleep, and awoke rejoicing, yea, triumphing in God. After this he enjoyed the witness of entire sanctification, and proclaimed to all who came near him the love of his God and Saviour, saying, Now I know by experience what I have preached to others is no cunningly devised fable. I feel now the blood of Jesus cleanseth from all sin. I am now entirely a new creature! I can love the Lord with all my heart, and soul, and strength. The enemy tells me, if I get better I shall soon lose this; but I believe I shall not, for I know as long as I have this hold of God, nothing will be able to overcome me. In a day or two after he was often delirious, yet still, in all intervals, was full of happiness, love, patience, and resignation, though he suffered much.

Thursday, 12.—He said, What a peace do I now enjoy! I feel now, and for some days past, what I never felt before. When I am at the worst, (and none but God knows what I suffer,) my mind is peaceable and happy, and I have not a murmuring or repining thought. I can cast all my care on God, as I never could before; and even my helplessness does not discourage me, for I find his grace sufficient. But I see a great fulness yet before me.

Friday, 13.—When he was got up to have his bed made easy, he would not return to it (though every breath seemed as if it would be his last,) till he had given a short account of his whole experience from his first setting out. He went through all his trials, persecutions, temptations, &c. But now, said he, I reap the blessed fruit; and I can say, neither my father's tears nor severity, neither hope of preferment nor fear of suffering, ever made me prevaricate or depart from what I believed my duty to God. And now I prove him faithful: he hath said, "Whosoever forsaketh father, or mother, or brothers, or sisters, or houses, or lands, for my sake and the Gospel's, shall receive a hundred fold in this life; even father and mother, houses and lands, &c., and, in the world to come, everlasting life." This is literally fulfilled in me. I forsook all, and I was restored to my father's favour. I have a house, land, &c., in this life, and I am going to everlasting life! whereas, if I had basely complied with my friends' desires, I should have possessed no more in this life than I now do, and should have been lying here with a guilty conscience, a frowning God, and full of horror, in the views of a miserable eternity! O how good it is to give up all for God! Now I feel it, and I shall praise him forever! O how pleasingly awful was this noble testimony from a dying friend, when obliged to gasp for breath between every sentence. He continued for some time after this praising God, and recommending all his relations and friends to his protection, the particulars of which I omit here, having already referred the reader to them in the Magazine.

Saturday, 24.—He was quite deranged, yet composed, and knew me to the last. At three o'clock on Sunday morning death sweats came on, and about half-past five he fled to his eternal paradise! All in the room sensibly felt the powerful presence of God. Yea, it was as the gate of heaven, while on our knees we watched the last parting breath! Mr. Simpson preached a funeral sermon in the new church on Sunday, the 29th, and Mr. Rogers at the Methodist chapel. The former from "These are they who came out of great tribulation, and have washed their robes, and made them white in the blood of the Lamb:" the latter from "Mark the perfect man, and behold the upright, for the end of that man is peace." I believe many will remember the blessed season to their eternal good.

In the year following I had another awful scene to pass through. Dear Mrs. Rogers, after the birth of her little James, never recovered her health fully. Mr. Rogers, being a good deal in the country parts of the circuit, I was very much with her, and our love for each other daily increased. At different times she opened her whole heart to me on very tender points, for we were as one soul. For several weeks before her death, she entreated me not to leave her, when I could possibly help it. But as her experience and triumphant death are already published, I forbear to enlarge respecting either. O, my Lord, let my latter end be like hers!

I come now briefly to observe, that after a wonderful chain of divine leadings and remarkable providences, (too tedious to dwell upon here,) on August 19, 1784, I was married to Mr. Rogers, in whom the Lord gave me a helpmate for glory— just such a partner as my weakness needed to strengthen me. He hath made us one heart and one soul, and for above eight years hath crowned our union with his constant smile.

We spent a week or ten days after our marriage with my mother, and then hastened to Dublin, where Mr. Rogers was appointed to labour. We were gladly received, and the Lord gave us the hearts of the people. Our hands being thus strengthened of the Lord, we agreed solemnly to devote ourselves and our all to him and his work. And glory to his name, we saw a blessed revival: in three years the society increased from about five hundred to eleven hundred and upwards; and we had good cause to believe about four hundred were converted to God.

In August, 1789, we came over from Dublin to see my mother at Macclesfield. Mr. Wesley and several preachers with families also coming at the same time to England, we took the whole ship. In this passage we were in imminent danger by dashing on a rock called the West Mouse. But prayer was made, the Lord heard, and wonderfully delivered! We landed at Park Gate, and travelled with Mr. Wesley to Macclesfield, where my mother received us with great affection. After the Manchester conference, we returned to Ireland, sailed for Dublin, where we had left our little boy. We spent about a week with our very affectionate friends there, and then proceeded to Cork.

Here also the Lord revived a gracious work. His word prospered and prevailed, and we had cause to rejoice, not only over a few individuals, but several families, who were added to the fold of God. We found three hundred and ninety-seven members in society, and left six hundred and fifty. In the last year we had some close trials through a few individuals; but our spiritual mercies outbalanced them all. I do not know that I ever enjoyed more of the Lord's heartfelt presence than at Cork, excepting the time of a severe nervous fever, and then the cloud was only for a few days, and that, I believe, was merely owing to the body; for though in a week afterward all the feelings of nature were touched, I felt nothing contrary to resignation, patience, or love.

At the time I now speak of, my own recovery was doubtful. Mr. Rogers (oppressed with grief through my illness, and by his attention to me night and day) was very ill. James had a worm fever, the maid confined with sickness, and my little John, six weeks old, dying in convulsions for three days!—Surely, in this scene, the Lord magnified his power in supporting my weakness, and enabling me then to say, "Good is the will of the Lord." After this season, my consolations were abundant; and my faith, love, and communion with God, much deepened.

I had here some encouraging letters from Mr. Wesley. In the two last he mentioned his intention of removing us to London at the ensuing conference. I trembled at the thought of so important a charge; but committed it to God in much prayer. And notwithstanding our various exercises of body and mind since we came to this city, I am certain Divine love has mixed every cup, and ordered all things well. To be with that honoured and much loved servant of God, Mr.

Wesley, for five months, and then to be witnesses of his glorious exit, was a favour indeed. But oh! how awful the scene!—how unspeakable the loss! I peculiarly felt it, being then in a weak state, not quite recovered from my lying-in.

The solemnity of the dying hour of that great good man, I believe will be ever written on my heart! Well might Dr. Young say, "The chamber where the good man meets his fate, is privileged beyond the common walk of virtuous life, quite on the verge of heaven!" A cloud of the Divine presence rested on all! and while he could hardly be said to be an inhabitant of earth, being now speechless, and his eyes fixed, victory and glory were written on his countenance, and quivering, as it were, on his dying lips! O could he then have spoken, methinks it would have been nothing but victory! victory!—grace! grace!—glory! glory! No language can paint what appeared in that face! The more we gazed upon it, the more we saw of heaven unspeakable! Not the least sign of pain, but a weight of bliss. Thus he continued, only his breath growing weaker and weaker, till, without a struggle or a groan, he left the cumberous clay behind, and fled to eternal life in the bosom of his faithful Lord.

When I look back on the trying scene we have passed through since this awful event, and consider we are yet monuments of grace and saving power, I am lost in wonder and in love. Mr. Rogers, in particular, has been tried as in the fire, and exposed through his office, as a mark to shoot at; yet, through infinite mercy, I believe he will come out of it all more fully purified. I might here enlarge on particulars, but shall leave the Lord's faithful servants, as well as the instruments of their sufferings, to Him who will plead the cause of the innocent, and make "all things work together for good to them that love God:" praying, with our suffering Lord, for those who now persecute him in his members, "Father, forgive them, for they know not what they do."

I shall now only observe, as it relates to my own experience, that these trying exercises of my dear partner have been keenly felt by me. And my nervous system, weakened by that dangerous fever at Cork, has also greatly suffered by these things, which, like "wave upon wave, have followed each other!" To this I ascribe it chiefly, that a cloud of heaviness has, at some seasons, hung upon my mind; and that Satan has taken occasion to suggest, in those times of animal depression, various accusations of short-comings in zeal, activity, and spiritual joy. I do not mean that I was ever left in darkness—No: since I first consciously received a sense of favour with

God, I never lost it; but within two years last past, I have not always had so clear a witness of perfect love. At other times I have had that witness fully and clear; and at all times could say—

> "None but Jesus will I know,
> None but him do I desire,
> Whom have I in heaven but thee?
> Thou art all in all to me!"

But in nothing else than full salvation, and the witness of it, could my soul ever rest. O no! What is past experience without present enjoyment? I must feel, or I cannot be happy.

Sunday, Nov. 11, 1792.—This day it is eighteen years since I recovered the knowledge of a reconciled God. O that I were in a deeper sense a "mother in Israel." My Lord has ever been faithful to me! In all my persecutions he comforted me! In the alluring snares of youth, he saved, he kept. It was by his grace I forsook all—denied myself ease, pleasure, friends;—and after he had proved me, he gave me easier circumstances, and one of the best of earthly friends. He has led on my ignorance, and strengthened my weakness. Through various scenes, and in outward perplexities, how often have I received immediate teaching from God! In travelling from city to city, how have I been protected by guardian love, and saved from fear and danger on the watery deep. May I never forget the ten thousand proofs of his love in Dublin, in Cork, in London. He hath given me favour in the eyes of his children in every place, and helped me feebly to serve them. He hath given me spiritual children also, some of whom are lodged safe in his bosom, and others in the way to glory. I have had five lovely children in the flesh; and besides these, my dear Joseph and Benjamin, left with me in charge, and to whom I feel united in all the tenderness of parental love; nor have they ever been wanting in a due return. One, (a fine boy,) my Lord hath taken to the abodes of bliss; and for the rest he assures my heart,

"The children of thy faith in prayer,
Shall all to thee be given."

The witness of his perfect love ever shone upon my soul, till for a season, in my nervous fever; but that season past, it shone afresh, and continued so to do; till at intervals in the two years past, I have not so constantly enjoyed this. I have been jealous over myself with a godly jealousy, lest anxiety about a multiplicity of outward things has too much stolen upon me, and lest at other times I have suffered my mind to dwell too much on disagreeables—lest I have been less active, less zealous, less spiritual. Yet I dare not say I have forfeited the blessing. But I cannot rest when the witness is not clear. I know much I have felt has been temptation, and that Satan has accused when my God did not condemn.

Many also have been my seasons of deep consolation—of deep communion with my God—many, and remarkable, my deliverances, and answers to prayer; and great my divine support in every hour of trial. At present I am sinking into the arms of love, and I do feel I am all the Lord's. Many things that have crucified my will of late have been good for me. I desire to be crucified with Christ, and that he should live alone in me! I feel he now does; but I long for a yet larger measure of his mind, more of every grace, and deeper communion with my God. He does meet me at the throne of grace, and all temptations respecting conflicts with Satan in death are vanished. I know my Joshua will be with me in Jordan, and see me safe through. Sometimes I have thought I shall have to pass that river before it be long; but that I leave to him. I feel no desire of life, but when I see my dear husband oppressed with trials, and my living seems as if it would be a help and comfort to him, or, when a silent, resigned wish arises, to see my children grown, and partakers of regenerating grace; but I am kept from anxiety.

I feel grateful to my God, that I am placed here, (at Spitalfields,) though but for a season, where I can enjoy more retirement, and less of busy life. My God is with me, and I trust he will draw and unite more fully to himself, his helpless, worthless creature! I have power with him in prayer, and I know he will answer my enlarged requests, for myself, my other self, and our offspring. We shall be his: I will be his alone. This day I consecrated to him my soul and body's powers, my life, my all. May his blessed Spirit come and seal me his abode, ratify the *covenant*, and with the Father and the Son, dwell forever in my worthless heart. Amen. O my God, I sign myself over to thee. This solemn hour,

"My soul and body I resign,
With joy I render thee
My all, no longer mine, but thine
To all eternity."

HESTER ANN ROGERS.

EXTRACTS FROM THE JOURNALS OF MRS. ROGERS.

Dublin, Nov. 7, 1786.—This day my soul hath felt much of the power of God, and a sweet solemnity, which I can but faintly describe. In calling to visit a friend who is dangerously ill of the pleurisy, I was led to bring her very near the time when I shall bid adieu to all beneath the sun. I saw it an awful thing to die; yet rejoiced to feel the sting of death entirely gone; and a witness, that if I was called like her to gasp for another and another breath, and to offer up my spirit, it would surely be into the arms of Jesus. But how was the importance of improving my present mercies impressed on my mind—the necessity of now employing every talent for God. In a state like hers, I should be very unfit to call upon God even for my own soul: much less would it be in my power to persuade, warn, reprove, or exhort others. My God has at present entrusted me with precious time and opportunities. O let me improve, and not betray my trust—but only for thy glory live, and to thy glory die.

In the evening my dear husband preached with peculiar freedom from "All are yours." In the course of his sermon he went through "Paul, or Apollos, or Cephas, or the world, or life, or death," &c., and in the last instance observed, "We are immortal till our work is done: till then, men and devils combined cannot kill." He likewise mentioned that memorable saying of King William, who, at the battle of the Boyne, when in the most imminent danger, exclaimed, (to encourage his men,) "Every bullet hath its billet!" —showing our life is the hand of God alone—when, on a sudden, the congregation was all alarmed by a man with a large loaded pistol being seized at the door. I was in the gallery, and therefore ignorant of what caused the uproar; and my employment was to quiet the women, who were all for rushing down stairs, many of them ready to fall into fits. I had no fear whatever: the sermon had been a blessing to my soul, and I was kept in perfect peace. When I came into the yard, and heard the particulars, I found this villain came into the preaching house, and sat opposite the pulpit for half an hour, while Mr. R. was preaching: then, on receiving a watchword from his comrades, went out. And our maid, who at the same time came into the yard, unperceived in the dark, heard them plotting together, and resolving to fire the pistol at Mr. Rogers, and make off. Another friend, who was nearer than they imagined, also heard them muttering and cursing, one of them bidding him with the pistol, "aim at the cushion." In that moment the door-keeper, and two other friends, desired them to quit the yard, when this fellow rushed toward the door with violence, and attempted to knock down brother Ransford with the butt end of his large pistol; but he avoided the blow, and only received a slight hurt on the side of his head. The ruffian was then seized by a number of our friends, and taken to the watch-house. When examined, he denied he had any pistol, and cursed Mr. Rogers, and all the Methodists, bitterly. He was ordered to Newgate, and there confined. The constable came next morning, and told us, Sir Roger Smith, justice of the peace, had examined the pistol, and found it loaded with six leaden balls, which he showed me—they were very ragged and sharp—and a large charge of the best gunpowder.

All these things put together, I was now much more affected than before, as it appeared plain that a deep laid plot had been concerted, and every reason to believe the intention was to have shot my dear husband while he was preaching. The wonderful prevention filled me with awful gratitude and humble praise. While Mr. R. and several friends went to Newgate to interrogate the ruffian, I spent a precious hour of intercourse with my God. And in sweetly committing to him the whole affair, I had some liberty to intercede for the poor wretch, but more in praying for my dear partner, when the Lord graciously applied these words—"Not a hair of his head shall perish: wherefore, in patience possess ye your souls." I blessed him for the promise and the precept, and was filled with divine consolation.

The night after this happened, Mr. Peacock preached with great liberty, from, "Fear not them which kill the body, and after that have no more that they can do." His word was a blessing to me and many, especially his quoting that text: "Touch not mine anointed, and do my prophets no harm." Two persons returned thanks this evening: one for pardon, the other for being renewed in love; both of them under the sermon last night. Well may Satan rage at a work like this, now going forward in this city. As several Roman Catholics have been lately awakened, and joined to the society; and a very rich man, of great note among the priests, had become a constant hearer at our chapel, it is conjectured where this horrid plot most likely originated. And the more clearly doth this appear from the number of friends who visited this villain while in prison, and by whose means his escape was effected before he was brought to a trial.

CORK, August 20, 1789.—I found that text much blessed to me this morning, Isa. xl. 8, "Who are those that fly as a cloud, and as doves to their windows?" How heavy is the dense cloud—yet it hangs in air without any visible hand to uphold it! Such am I, loaded with ten thousand infirmities, various temptations from Satan, and calumnies from malicious men, under which I must sink, yea, and that even after my soul has been attracted from the earth by the Son of righteousness, was it not that I am held up like a cloud in the air, by the mighty power of God. I also feel as one of those silly, helpless doves, and as such, I fly to hide in my Saviour's breast!—There, my Lord, I would forever dwell.

"How blest are they who still abide,
Close shelter'd in thy bleeding side."

We had a good season at family prayer, after which we went upon the water with some friends; and sailing down to Cove, we went on board of Mr. Sholdham's new and beautiful yacht. This vessel is built, it seems, for pleasure, and he intends to sail in it round the known world. Every thing in it is elegant, even to extravagance: much plate, superb furniture in the cabin, and a French cook on board. But can this make the owner happy? Alas! no: it cannot be, unless his soul were first adorned with Christ, and made meet for God. In the evening, Mr. Rogers preached in Cove, to a large company of attentive hearers, from "Ye must be born again." The room was also well filled the next evening, and the day after we returned home in an open boat. We had a high wind and heavy showers of rain the whole passage, and the tide meeting the wind when we came to Lough Mahon, (a very dangerous place,) it was rough indeed. But the Lord sweetly prepared me for it. That verse was so powerfully impressed on my mind, that I could not forbear repeating it:

"O'er the raging billows sailing,
With my all-protecting Guide—
By thy mercy never failing,
I shall all the storms outride!
Join'd to thee by closest union,
And to my companion dear:
By this happy, sweet communion,
Thou wilt banish every fear."

Just then came on a squall of wind, and the swell so very high, that all the passengers shrieked aloud, and some now cried to God for mercy! Even the boatmen turned pale, and our friends clasped around us in a most affecting manner. Yet, though I was sensible of our danger, my soul was kept from fear I recollected Peter on the waves, and said, "Lord, what are these when in the hollow of thy hand? I commit my all to thee! Preserve me from fear, and help me to praise thee." My soul was indeed filled with his goodness. The boatmen, sensible of the danger, turned out of the channel into shallow water, and then the swell was not so great. But we were still in jeopardy, expecting every moment to be stranded in the mud; and if so, all must have perished, as we were near a mile from shore. But the Lord preserved us from all evil, and we landed safe in Cork before night came on. O may I never forget his love to me this day! How fatal might have been the consequences in my present situation, had fear been permitted to take place; instead of which I was kept composed and happy, and returned in better health than when I went. "Praise the Lord, O my soul, and all that is within me, bless his holy name."

Extract of a letter, received January 14, 1789: "The Rev. Mr. E.—— calling to visit one of his hearers, saw a young lady in the parlour who had come for the use of the water on account of her health. Observing her unusually pensive, Mr. E. took the liberty to inquire the reason. She answered, 'Sir, I will think no more of it: it was only a dream, and I will not be so childish as to be alarmed at a dream! But, sir, (said she,) I will tell you my dream, and then I will think of it no more.' She then repeated, as follows: 'I dreamed I was at the ball, where I intended to go to-night. Soon after I was in the room I was taken very ill, and they gave me a smelling-bottle, and then I was brought home into this room: I was put into that elbow-chair, (pointing to it,) and fainted and died! I then thought I was carried to a place where there were angels and holy people in abundance, singing hymns and praises to God—that I found myself very unhappy there, and desired to go from thence. My conductor said, if I did, I should never come there again. He then violently whirled me, and I fell down, down—through blackness, and flames, and sulphur, the dread of which awoke me!' "

The minister endeavoured, by every possible argument, to dissuade the young lady from going to the ball that night, but in vain: she answered, "I will go. I will not be so foolish as to mind a dream!" She did go. And soon after she came into the ball-room she was taken ill, and [as she dreamed] a smelling-bottle was given her. She was carried home into the room, and put into that very elbow-chair represented in the dream: she fainted, and died!

Awful warning! an awful event! O that it may deeply penetrate the hearts of all who are "lovers of pleasures more than lovers of God." She was warned by a dream; but such are now warned by a reality, even her fate! She is gone, gone into a world of spirits—into eternity. But was she unhappy? Very unhappy in the presence of a holy God and his holy worshippers! Oh how does this correspond with that solemn declaration from the lips of truth, "Without holiness no man shall see the Lord." Oh how unmeet is one who liveth in these delusive pleasures on earth for the spiritual enjoyment of God in glory! which is the inheritance and the bliss of the saints in light. Reader, ask thy own heart! Couldst thou be more happy than she in the eternal employ of those who surround the throne, and sing the song of Moses and the Lamb? Be assured thou couldst not, except on earth thou hast learnt their song—"Unto him that loved us, and washed us from our sins in his own blood, and hath made us kings and priests unto God and his Father: to him be glory and dominion forever and ever."—*Thou must be born again.*

What a striking contrast between the young person alluded to above, and an intimate friend of mine in the city of Cork, who died near about that time. Her name was Mary Mahony. When very young, her carnal relations forced her to marry a man for whom she had no affection. He proved a very wicked and a bad husband; but the God of wisdom and love, even out of his evil, brought forth good. The trials she daily endured, led her to seek rest and happiness in the Source of bliss! Beginning frequently, though privately, to hear the Methodists, her mind was drawn out in strong desires after God. But her husband often followed her, and dragged her out of the preaching-house by the hair of her head. After some time he left her entirely, and she saw him no more. She joined our society about eight years ago, and soon found peace with God, which she never lost; and, about three years after, obtained also a clear witness that her soul was cleansed from all sin. In this salvation she walked irreprovably to the day of her death. And though at some seasons she was buffeted with various temptations, yet she always emerged out of them more fully purified. She was called outwardly to follow her heavenly Lord in the way of the cross; but she joyfully took it up, and bore it with the meekness of her lamb-like Saviour! Like him, her language was, "Not as I will, but as thou wilt."

Her love to Jesus, and her zeal for the glory of

God, and for promoting the good of precious souls, was very peculiar. This induced Mr. Rogers to request her to take the charge of a class of young women, over whom she watched faithfully and diligently with tears, fastings, and much prayer. In her last sickness, (thought to be a rheumatic fever,) her agony of pain in every limb was extreme; but she told me and others, "When these hands and feet are tortured with pain—yea, such anguish as is almost insupportable—I look to my precious Saviour, and see by faith his dear hands and feet pierced, and bleeding, and nailed to the accursed tree for my sins! and the view of that mangled body and precious head torn with thorns, and that precious blood streaming for my soul, sweetens all my pain, and makes me willing to bear all he pleases to inflict." After she had thus suffered for nine days, and constantly witnessed to all the goodness of God to her soul, she became delirious. But a few hours before her departure, the Lord restored her reason. She was, however, speechless, till at last, after struggling some time as in an agony to say something, she cried aloud, Jesus is precious! Jesus is precious! and sweetly fell asleep on the 10th of February, 1789, and in the 25th year of her age.

October 24, 1790.—I heard Mr. Wesley preach in Spitalfields chapel with great liberty, from Eph.

vi. 11, "Put on the whole armour of God." I never heard the Christian armour so described before. In the course of his sermon he introduced an account of a French marshal, a very wicked man, but a great warrior, who in the blaze of battle lifted up his hand toward heaven, and swore by his Maker he would never quit the field while there was an Englishman alive in it! He was harnessed with steel, but while pronouncing the oath, with his arm extended, a musket ball entering the joints of the harness, shot him in the armpit, and down he fell. Mr. Wesley showed, in the beautiful contrast, that the Christian being armed with the panoply of God, *i. e.*, his whole armour, no such part is left exposed, but the whole soul is covered and defended against every fiery dart of our common enemy, the devil.

I awoke very happy this morning, with these sweet words—

> "God, the Almighty God, is thine:
> See him to thy help come down,
> The excellence divine."

And oh! how was I blest while musing on that precious scripture, "Now we see through a glass darkly." It was, indeed, a blessed season to my soul, especially for a few minutes, when I felt what I cannot explain. Such a manifestation of God as a Spirit, uniting himself to my spirit: such a

10*

real enjoyment of God as love, as holiness, as heaven, that fulness which thought cannot fathom! And all this to me. My All in all! united inexplicably to my spirit, more than filling all my powers with his effulgence, so that I was wrapt in God. O my Lord, and shall I prove forever this vision, this fruition of thy fulness? I know I shall. Thou hast given my soul a taste, and thou wilt give me the abiding reality when time is no more. O thou thrice holy God of love, my soul is lost! Wonder and love overpower me quite! I am abased before thee, while I feel the sacred blessing mine.

Nov. 4, 1792.—My closet was truly a Bethel, while my soul was engaged in prayer and holy meditation on those deep words, Col. iii, 3, 4, "Our life is hid with Christ in God," &c. I was led to inquire as follows: But how is my life hid? My animal life being the breath of God, he continues or withholds it at his pleasure. But who can tell how he animates the clay body? or how we continue in that state of animation? When he takes away our breath, we die, and are turned again to our dust. How is it that we now feel, hear, smell, taste, and see? How is it that we think, judge, fear, love, desire, and enjoy? To say we are made capable of all these, is to say nothing. From what arises that capability? The soul actuates the body;

but how? And who informs and actuates the soul? All is hid with Christ in God. He is the source, but we cannot search out his ways.

Our spiritual life is hid also. By nature we are dead. From him we receive the first seed of spiritual life, "Not of blood, (from our natural parents,) not by the will (or power) of man, but of God." And how hid from the wisdom of a natural man, are all the workings of divine grace? We are told he cannot know them. Nor can a soul possessed of this spiritual life, impart what he feels to another: it is that "new name which none knoweth but he that receiveth it." What a mystery: Christ in us! And what a mystery also is that faith which justifies and saves, to a carnal mind?

How frequently is this life so hid, that our actions, words, and motives, are mistaken by men? And often is the saint condemned through this, when approved of God! But soon will this hidden life be revealed in open day, when all shall see and admire the unaffected integrity of him who was despised and rejected by the wicked—mistaken even by his friends, (and perhaps grieved sore through such mistakes,) when his innocence shall shine forth as the light, and his just dealing as the noon-day, while many shall be amazed at his salvation, so far beyond all they looked for on earth! Perhaps a well painted hypocrite might be thought more holy than the Israelite without guile! But then the mask is no more! God will own his jewels, and they shall shine in his presence forever. And if sorrow or tears could possibly be in heaven, surely those who have been (through mistake) cause of grief to these on earth, will sorrow then, and love them more, perhaps, on that account.

Again: much is hid from even the soul posessing this life. The humility of the true saint, arising from the sense of many infirmities which he feels, hides his grace from his own sight, so that, at certain times, he is even discouraged while Satan, the accuser, fails not to to magnify unto him various short-comings. His extreme weakness, his failures in judgment, memory, or zeal. His ignorance of many things; or some constitutional infirmity, though not yielded to, may often beset, and be a burden to his mind. These, and such like, may, for a time, damp the joy of one whose "life is hid with Christ in God." But when such feel their utter helplessness, the Sun of righteousness shall break forth; and, by a word—a single look of love, dissipate all the gloom, and display his graces and himself, and fill with unknown peace! But when these come to pass through the valley, there they shall find Jesus their life indeed with whom they shall then appear in glory! Yes, yes, he will then be revealed to their ravished views, when they shall fearless

> "Pass the watery flood,
> Hanging on the arm of God."

For he will stand in Jordan to see them safe through, and landed all in Canaan, where he will display before them his bleeding wounds, their only title to eternal bliss! And oh! what then shall be revealed to the disembodied saint! Divine amazement and glory all! But oh! to prove the blissful reality mine! This, this is all; and while my soul exults in the sweet assurance, I deeply feel the importance of that question, "Simon, son of Jonas, lovest thou me?" and can tell my Lord, as Peter did, "Thou knowest all things, thou knowest that I love thee." Yes, with all my heart. I have communion with my God, as a man with his friend. I feel an intimate union with Jesus; and through him with the Father; and such overflowing emanations from the Holy Ghost, as I have rarely felt before. I think a little more would burst the earthen prison, and set my longing spirit free.

I have found it very profitable to read Horæ Solitariæ, on the Name and Titles of Christ: especially that of *Jehovah Adonai.* His remarks are very sweet and spiritual, only his Calvinism I pass over. Yet I can allow and join in all that gives glory to Christ, and tends to humble the sinner, ascribing also, with him, my whole salvation to grace unmerited and free. I believe, he who hath loved me, died for all, that they who are dead might henceforth live, "not unto themselves, but unto him who died for them and rose again."

Feb. 19, 1794.—Having heard much respecting public matters, and about an expected invasion, with all its consequences, I have been led much to secret prayer, and feel I can say to my God, "Naked came I into the world, and thou hast cared for me, nurtured me in infancy, preserved me in youth, provided for the wants, yea, even for the comforts of my riper years, and now I am still thine, and I commit myself, my dear husband and children, my all unto thee." I received for answer, "There shall no evil befall thee, neither shall any plague come near thy dwelling." The day after I had some subtle temptations from the enemy; but the Lord assured my heart, he would not suffer me to be tempted above what I am able to bear. Whenever I approach the Lord in secret, Satan vanishes, and Jesus tells me, "All that I have is thine." Yea, he truly leads me into green pastures, and by the still waters of comfort!

"O to grace how great a debtor
Daily I'm constrain'd to be."

My mind has been led of late to meditate on the latter day glory; and the Lord's presence rested upon me in a peculiar manner, while attending to those beautiful ideas of Mr. Fletcher on the millennium, especially where he observes, "That as now the world is overspread with iniquity, so shall it then be with holiness: insomuch that a wicked man shall then be as great a wonder upon earth as a father in Christ is now! that the curse shall be taken away from universal creation, vegetable, animal, and elementary: the bodies of men no longer subject to pain and weakness: no sorrow in child-bearing, no temptation. The lion will then be as inoffensive as the lamb; and the leopard lie down with the kid: For they shall not hurt nor destroy in all my holy mountain, (saith our God,) for the earth shall be full of the knowledge of the glory of the Lord, as the waters cover the sea."

THE DYING BED OF A SAINT AND SINNER CONTRASTED.

Dust we are, and unto dust we shall return. A few more rolling years: a few more months or weeks: nay, perhaps, a few more setting suns, or fleeting moments, and we are gone. Gone, where?

Oh! that awful, dreadful, blissful thought! Awful to all, dreadful to the unholy, to sinners, and blissful to the saints of God. See a man approaching to the verge of eternity: how are all his views changed!—How trifling to such a one appears all below the sun! How important the things of God, and the salvation of his never-dying soul? Let us consider one ignorant of God through life, immersed in pleasure, lost in pride, careless, secure, surrounded and beloved by his carnal friends, and possessed of a moderate share of wealth—such a one in the bloom of life. Some fatal distemper seizes his brittle frame: he is racked with torturing pain, surrounded by weeping friends, whose help is all in vain: the physician gives no hope of his recovery; and he perceives he is ere long to launch into a boundless eternity! What are his views in such a state? Such a scene have my eyes beheld, and therefore with greater certainty I may describe it.—"Wretched man that I am, (methinks I still hear him cry,) where are my pleasures now? What hath pride profited me, or what good hath riches, with all my vaunting, done me?—These are passed away as a cloud, and now, O horror, to think!

'Now leaving all I love below,
To God's tribunal I must go,
Must hear the Judge pronounce my fate,
And fix my everlasting state.'

But can I hope to dwell with God? Ah! no it cannot be. He is holy, I am vile: he is just, and will punish the guilty. He called, and I refused: he stretched forth his hand, and I would not regard; and now he laugheth at my calamity, and shutteth his ear to my cry. Then I would not, now I cannot pray: he often knocked at the door of my heart, saying, by an inward whisper, Thou art wrong: repent, and turn to God. Seek the Lord while he may be found, call upon him while he is near.—Turn ye, turn ye, why will ye die? But I would none of his counsel, and turned away mine ear from his reproof. I refused the yoke of Jesus, despised his ministers, and neglected that salvation which was long offered to me by their means. But now I feel the dire effects! Me miserable: which way shall I flee infinite wrath and infinite despair? Oh eternity! eternity! eternity!—Fall, fall ye rocks, and hide my guilty head: hide me from Him that sitteth upon the throne, and from the wrath of the Lamb!—But oh! even this cannot be: I must endure his indignation: I must suffer the vengeance of eternal fire! My damnation is sealed! Who can dwell with devouring fire? Who can endure everlasting burnings? Take warning, O my careless friends! A gaping hell awaits me! My soul is going! Fiends are waiting to receive it: they encircle me round: Oh horror, and eternity!"

The person described above, was afterward reprieved for a short season from the jaws of death; but he did not manifest any genuine repentance; and, in about six months after, died in raging despair.

Let us next see the child of God! the heir of glory, (pleasing contrast,) how different his prospect! He longs to reach his Father's house, and kisses the kind rod of his afflicting hand. The welcome news that he shall soon be there, elevates his soul with rapturous joy: he has a foretaste of those pleasures which are at God's right hand for evermore, and the language of his heart is,

"Haste, my Beloved, fetch my soul
Up to thy blest abode:
Fly, for my spirit longs to see
My Saviour and my God."

Yes, blessed Saviour, and this thou knowest, is also the language of my heart, while I now bid adieu to earth and all terrestial scenes.

Farewell, my dear beloved children, I leave you, but your parents' God hath promised to care for you. Choose him for your portion, and then if we both leave you exposed to the waves of a dangerous world, the faithfulness of an unchanging Jehovah is engaged to pilot you safe into that haven where we shall meet you all again, being bound up together in the bundle of life, with the Lord our God.

Farewell, in particular, my ever dear husband. How was our friendship ripened almost to the maturity of heaven. How tenderly and closely are our hearts still knit together! Nor shall the sweet union be dissolved by death; but being one in Christ, we shall be one forever. Mourn not that I go to him first. He saw it best for my weakness: my feeble frame might not have supported your absence! A very little while, and you will follow me; and oh, with what joy shall I welcome your arrival on the eternal shore, and conduct you to Him whom our souls love! Till then adieu, my dearest companion in heaven's road, whom God in the greatest mercy gave to me. I leave with thee most grateful sensations for all the kind tokens of affection which I have ever had from thee. For all thy care, thy love, thy prayers, I bless my God and thank thee. But I now go to Jesus, who is yet infinitely dearer to me. With him I leave thee, nor doubt his care, who hath loved and given himself for thee. It is but a short separation: our spirits shall soon reunite, and then never, never know separation more!

Farewell to all my dear friends: weep not for me, but love my God. O make your peace with him, and you shall follow me to glory. He is worthy of your hearts, and only he! O give them wholly to him. I have not served my God for nought: I have lived a heaven below in Jesus' love, and now eternally shall praise the glories of his grace! And you who know my God, O love him more, and never leave him; so will he be to you what he is now to me. Continue "steadfast and unmovable, always abounding in the work of the Lord;" for, I can testify to his glory, "your labour shall not be in vain." Be faithful unto death, and he will give you a crown of life; which I am now hastening to receive. "The chariots of Israel, and the horsemen thereof," 2 Kings, ii. 12, are all in waiting to carry me home!

"See the guardian angels nigh,
Wait to waft my soul on high!
See the golden gates display'd,
See the crown to grace my head!
See a flood of sacred light
Which shall yield no more to night:
Transitory world, farewell,
Jesus calls with him to dwell!'"

He cries, "Arise, my love, my fair one, and come away." *Amen*, saith my willing, joyful soul, "Even so, come, Lord Jesus." My soul is on the wing. Burst asunder ye bonds of clay which hold me from my love: how welcome the stroke that shall break down these separating walls, knock off my fetters, throw open my prison doors, and set me at liberty. This corruptible body, this tottering house of clay, which now cannot sustain his weight of love, shall soon be made a glorious body incorruptible—

"Shall the stars and sun outshine,
Shout among the sons of glory,
All immortal, all divine!"—

and able then to enjoy the full fruition of my God. Yes, I shall soon see him as he is, not through a glass darkly, but face to face. The beatific sight

"Shall fill the heavenly courts with praise,
And wide diffuse the golden blaze
Of everlasting light."

"Waiting to receive my spirit,
Lo, my Saviour stands above,
Shows the purchase of his merit—
Reaches out the crown of love."

Angels surround my bed to carry me away. I come, I come, blest messengers of my God! Haste and convey me to his loved embrace! My faith already beholds the crucified Redeemer: methinks I see him smile, while around him stand the heavenly host exulting! Oh glorious train of blood-bought souls! What an innumerable company! And I shall join the choir—

"Shall shout by turns the bursting joy—
And all eternity employ,
In songs around the throne."

How delightful the theme! It hath set my soul on fire; yet I cannot express a thousandth part of my ideas, or the prospect that lies before me. But I shall prove the unutterable bliss! The inheritance is mine! A foretaste now I feel. Nay, so am I filled with glory and with God, that more I could not bear and live! O may I ever feel the sacred flame, and through eternity proclaim the depth of Jesus' love! Amen and Amen

HESTER ANN ROGERS.

SELECTIONS FROM THE CORRESPONDENCE OF MRS. ROGERS.

LETTER I.

(Written in the nineteenth year of her age, to a lady of considerable rank and fortune, who, being offended at her *turning Methodist*, required an account of her conduct for so doing.)

MACCLESFIELD, Nov. 12, 1775.

DEAR AND HONOURED MADAM:—I beg leave to return you my most sincere and humble thanks for your kind letter and advice; and as you are so kind to express a concern on my account, I hope you will pardon the liberty, and allow me to say what is my opinion and belief, and on what *alone* I can build any hopes of heaven and happiness.

Man, as he came out of the hands of the Creator, was perfectly holy and happy. In him shone all those amiable and lovely attributes of the Deity: goodness, truth, justice, mercy, and love. But, by disobeying the Divine command, he entailed upon himself and his whole posterity (for he acted as the parent or head of all mankind) the sure wages of sin, which is death—death temporal, spiritual, and eternal. The body of man became that day mortal: his soul spiritually dead, and he was every moment liable to death eternal. The guilt of Adam, and the depravity of soul which he contracted by the fall, immediately devolved upon his unhappy offspring. And, we are told, when he begat a son, it was *in his* OWN *likeness, after* HIS *image:* so that now man is born in sin, and under the wrath of God, and if he die in that state, will stand exposed to the sentence of eternal death.* And what can a lost man do in this case! Atonement for himself or offering meet, he hath none to bring; and to pardon sinners *without* a satisfaction, would not be what is commonly called mercy, but it would be giving up the essential glories of the Godhead. What must be done then? Why, God of his *free grace,* and unlimited bounty, has provided a ransom, an all-sufficient ransom, even his well beloved Son! He who is the brightness of his Father's glory, and the express image of his person, became man to die, that man might live.

* It is hardly necessary to say that this is an unguarded way of stating the doctrine of original sin. [EDITOR.

All that was necessary to be done to complete our salvation, consisted chiefly in these three things :—First, a perfect obedience to the *Divine law* :—Secondly, an infinitely meritorious satisfaction to the law and government of God, for the dishonour brought upon them by the sin of man :—Thirdly, a restoration of the moral image of God to the soul, which image was lost by the fall of man. The first of these was completed by the life of our Redeemer, the second by his death, and the third is effected by the Holy Ghost. This provision (ample provision) is made for the salvation of man, so that God can preserve untainted his adorable perfections; or, as St. Paul declares, he can now be just, and yet justify and save penitent, believing man.

That Christ suffered in the place of sinners, is expressed by St. Peter in these words, "Who, his own self, bare our sins in his own body on the tree." Also, Isaiah saith, "Surely he hath borne our griefs, and carried our sorrows. He was wounded for our transgressions, he was bruised for our iniquities. All we like sheep have gone astray: we have turned every one to his own way; and the Lord hath laid on him the iniquity of us all." St. Paul saith, "He hath made him to be sin for us, who knew no sin, that we might be made the righteousness of God in him." And again, in the third chapter of the Romans, he saith, "There is none righteous, no, not one: there is none that understandeth: there is none that seeketh after God: they are all gone out of the way: they are together become unprofitable: there is none that doeth good, no, not one." Therefore, he adds, "By the deeds of the law there shall no flesh be justified in his sight. But now the righteousness which is without the law is manifest, being witnessed by the law and the prophets, even the righteousness of God, which is by faith in Jesus Christ, unto all, and upon all them that believe; for there is no difference, for all have sinned and come short of the glory of God: being justified *freely* by his grace, through the redemption that is in Christ Jesus: whom God hath set forth to be a propitiation through faith in his blood, to declare his righteousness for the remission of sins that are past, through the forbearance of God: to declare, I say, at this time, his righteousness, that he might be just, and the justifier of him which believeth in Jesus."

With St. Paul, then, I would go on and ask—"Where is boasting then? It is excluded. By what law? Of *works?* Nay; but by the law of faith. Therefore, we conclude, that a man is justified by faith, without the deeds of the law. For, to him that worketh is the reward not reckoned of grace, but of debt; but to him that worketh not, but believeth on him that justifieth the ungodly, his *faith* is counted for righteousness. Even as David also described the blessedness of the man unto whom God imputeth righteousness without works, saying, Blessed are they whose iniquities are forgiven, and whose sins are covered. Blessed is the man unto whom the Lord will not impute sin. Abraham believed God, and it was imputed to him for righteousness: Now it was not written for his sake alone that it was imputed to him; but for us also, to whom it shall be imputed, if we believe on him that raised up Jesus our Lord from the dead: who was delivered for our offences, and was raised again for our justification." Now, from all these, and many more texts of Holy Scripture which might be named, I believe, and am sure, that works are not the meritorious cause of our salvation, yet I believe they are absolutely necessary, and *will* follow as the sure and inseparable fruits of a true faith. If you will be kind enough to read the eleventh, twelfth, and thirteenth articles of the Church of England, they will further explain my meaning.

But there is a third thing also necessary to our salvation, which is, that the image of God be restored to the soul. Now, this is done in regeneration Our Saviour assures us, "Except a man be born again, he cannot see the kingdom of God." And again, "Except ye be converted, and become as little children, ye shall not enter into the kingdom of heaven." Nor, indeed, are we fit for it, till renewed by the Spirit of God. For, *were* it possible to be admitted there, we could not enjoy the pure and spiritual delight of the saints above. Their joy consists in an entire freedom from all sin and corruption; and in serving, adoring, praising the Father of all their mercies, the Son of his love, and Spirit of holiness. And they are so far from being weary of this, that they think eternity too short to utter all his praise! How irksome would be an eternity spent in this manner, to a person who never had his affections spiritualized, and his will brought into a conformity to the will of God! This is a change which must be wrought in this world; for there is no repentance in the grave: as death leaves us, judgment will find us. Then, "He that is unjust shall be unjust still: he which is filthy shall be filthy still: he that is righteous shall be righteous still; and he that is holy shall be holy still!" The Holy Ghost is the author of this conversion or new birth; for no man hath quickened his own soul. It is *He* that must begin, carry on, and complete it.

Now, if any man have not the Spirit of Christ, he is none of his; and the fruits of this Spirit are, "love, joy, peace, long-suffering, gentleness, goodness, faith, meekness, temperance: against such there is no law; and they that are Christ's, have crucified the flesh with its affections and lusts. If any man be in Christ, he is a new creature: old things are passed away; behold, all things are become new." And Jesus Christ is made of God unto us, "wisdom, righteousness, santification, and redemption: that according as it is written, he that glorieth, let him glory in the Lord. God forbid that I should glory, save in the cross of our Lord Jesus Christ, by whom the world is crucified unto me, and I unto the world."

This, dear madam, is what I believe, and this, I think, is agreeable to the word of God, and to the articles and homilies of the Church of England, and no schism of the Church of Christ. Forfeiting your love and friendship is a great trial; but believe me, when I think of seeking salvation in any other way, it seems as a sword piercing my very heart! And seeing my dear mother so very unhappy on my account, gives me more grief than I can express; and the thought of my being detrimental to her in worldly things, and that my conduct should make you less *her* friend, seems strange, and is to me very afflicting. But I think these things ought not to be urged too far, especially when the soul is concerned.

I am afraid I have tired your patience, so will hasten to subscribe myself, honoured madam, your most obliged and dutiful daughter,

H. A. Roe.

LETTER II.

To Mr. Robert Roe, when at College, about six months after his conversion.

Macclesfield, Nov. 13, 1776.

Dear Cousin,—As I find by your brother, you have been reasoning with the enemy of your soul, and thereby, in some measure, have distressed your own mind; and as you request me to write, I dare not refuse, for I know God can use the weakest instruments to comfort his children, and often does, that we may ascribe all glory to Him alone. May He who comforteth those who are cast down be your support.

As to your falling from God, I do not fear it; and I am sure it is your happy privilege constantly to rejoice in his love—that love which so clearly spake your sins forgiven. Oppose that adversary of your soul by faith: this shield (saith an Apostle) "shall quench all the fiery darts of the wicked." Be resolute, and determine to conquer. Jesus in our nature hath bruised the serpent's head; and your union with your living Head will give *you* power to conquer, too. Fear not, saith God, for I will help thee. By a simple, living faith, cleave constantly to Jesus; and though earth and hell combine, they shall not be able to overcome or hurt you. Believe even against hope! and when things seem impossible to *you*, weak and helpless as you are, remember they are possible with God. Lay open to him your every care:

> "His heart is made of tenderness:
> His bowels melt with love."

He delighteth not to see his children mourning, cast down, and oppressed, but kindly saith, "I will not leave you comfortless, I will come unto you;" and again, "I will send you the Spirit of truth, that he may abide with you forever." The privileges of a justified soul are very great; for, "if a child, then an heir, an heir of God,"—of all his promises. Praise God that you feel the necessity of heart holiness, and press after it, even after "all the mind which was in Christ Jesus." He is already your wisdom and righteousness, and he will become your sanctification. O look for it, seek it, expect it—expect it as you are, expect it now. Behold, saith God, I stand at the door and knock: open to your Beloved, and he will come in and fill your happy soul.

Be diligent in your studies. It may be a cross, but take it up for Christ's sake, and it will not hurt your soul. Above all, continue in prayer: often read the word of God upon your knees, and his Spirit will explain it to your heart. With respect to your situation, or any temporal thing, be not careful: live the present moment, and lay no schemes for to-morrow: you may then be in eternity! "Instead of busying our minds," saith Mr. Wesley, "with dwelling on the grievous part of what is past or to come, we should remember that the gospel does not permit us to dwell on any thing but the presence and love of God who fills our souls." However you may be tempted, resolve you will not reason, except with the Lord, at the throne of grace. Seek more union and communion with your God: you may attain much of this, even before you are sanctified. But oh! never rest till all your evil nature be destroyed, and every root of bitterness plucked up—till you have given your God *all* your loving heart. And remember with him, "Now is the accepted time—now is the day of salvation." He cannot be more willing or more powerful than he is to-day.

As to myself, I see no end to my Lord's goodness. I find every day an increase of love, joy, peace, and union, close, intimate union with the Great Three-One.

> "All my treasure is above,
> All my riches is his love."

I feel I am very unworthy, yet offering up myself and my services on that altar which sanctifieth the gift, my God accepts a worthless worm, through his beloved Son. He who is higher than the highest, stoops to dwell in my happy soul; and I have communion with him as a man with his friend. Sometimes in the night he so fills my soul with his glorious presence, that I think it will burst its prison, and wing away; and then, oh then, where should I be? Surrounded with angels, and conveyed by them to my God—my life, my treasure, and my crown! I can even now scarce support the blissful thought. Oh what a present heaven of love I feel!

> "Oh what are all our sufferings here,
> If, Lord, thou count us meet,
> With that enraptured host t' appear,
> And worship at thy feet."

It cannot be long ere we lay these bodies down:

> "Our conflicts here shall soon be past,
> And you and I ascend at last
> Triumphant with our Head!"

"Rejoice in glorious hope: Jesus the Judge shall come,
And take his servants up to their eternal home:
We soon shall hear the archangel's voice
The trump of God shall sound, Rejoice!"

I remain your sincere friend in Jesus,

H. A. Roe.

LETTER III.

To Mr. Robert Roe.

Macclesfield, Dec, 10, 1776.

My Dear Cousin,—I am thankful if my letter was any comfort to your mind: to God be all the glory. I hope you are now enabled to rejoice, and are filled with that peace which from believing flows. I hope your heavenly intercourse is open, and that day by day you open still wider the door of your heart, that you may more and more be filled with God.

"Ready are you to receive,
Readier is your God to give."

I trust your studies are now made a blessing, and that in them you enjoy the presence of Jesus. Let no little difficulties discourage *us* who serve so good a Master—us who have in view a heaven of glory! Jesus left that heaven—to suffer, bleed, and die in our behalf. O, then, let us take up our every cross, and despising the shame, manfully suffer with him! Love makes all things easy:

> "'Tis this that makes our cheerful feet
> In swift obedience move:
> 'Tis this shall tune our joyful song
> In those sweet realms above."

I long to be all dissolved in love; for "God is love; and he that dwelleth in love, dwelleth in God, and God in him."

I have had many trials, and some temptations of late; but I am firmly persuaded, that while I cleave simply to Jesus, nothing shall be able to separate me from his love; no, nor to lessen the divine flame which I feel continually burning in my heart. Those precious words, "My grace is sufficient for thee," shall stand firm as the pillars of heaven; and when the enemy would tell me, in such and such a trial thou wilt be entangled and overcome, I tell him, my Lord hath promised strength equal to my day, and all his darts are instantly repelled. Nor do I only conquer; but after my enemy is put to flight, I have more love, more peace, and nearer union with my God. Oh the blessedness of intimate fellowship with him—of possessing that testimony that we please him! Surely it is a taste of heaven; and yet it is only a drop out of the ocean—as a grain of sand compared with the sands on the sea shore—only the beginning of an eternity of glory. O for an archangel's tongue to magnify our adorable Redeemer's name! We can but lisp his praises here; but we shall join in nobler strains above, to praise for evermore the Three in One:

"The heavenly principle aspires,
And swells my soul with strong desires,
To grasp the starry crown."

The Lord is carrying on a glorious work here. Our love feast last week was a blessed season of the outpouring of his Spirit: every one had reason to say, "This is none other than the house of God, this is the gate of heaven." Several who came there burdened and heavy laden, went away rejoicing: three found a clear sense of pardon, and two others were set at perfect liberty from the remains of sin. The preachers all wept abundantly tears of joy, so were they filled with God; and, indeed, I believe there were few dry eyes. Mr. Percival says, there is just such another pouring out of the Spirit in Bolton: above thirty joined the society there in ten days. I know this will rejoice your heart. O let us pray much for a guilty world! I believe this will be a glorious year of the power of God. I do not cease to pray for you, and remain your affectionate cousin and friend,

H. A. Roe.

LETTER IV.

To Mrs. Salmon, of Nantwitch.

Macclesfield, Nov. 15, 1777

My Dear Sister,—I received your kind letter, which filled my soul with praise on your account. I rejoice to hear your name is enrolled with the despised followers of a crucified Saviour. I believe I shall have reason to bless God to all eternity that I ever joined the Methodists. O may my worthless name never be a dishonour to his glorious cause and people! May you and I, dear sister, never be separated from them but by death, and all of us be united to the living Vine, and bring forth plenteously the fruits of righteousness to his glory and praise, "who hath called us out of darkness into his marvellous light."

With divine assistance, I shall not cease to cry unto God for Mr. Salmon and the little flock committed to his care. May they be such as shall be eternally saved, and their number be increased daily. May holiness unto the Lord be the motto of every heart, and his praise dwell on every tongue. It becometh well the just to be thankful; for who is a God like unto our God? Oh how great are his mercies! how innumerable his benefits! We may exclaim with David, "They are more in number than the hairs of our head;" or with a later poet,

"His nature and his name is love."

O let our souls praise the Lord, and all that is within us magnify his glorious name! Once we were darkness, but now we are light: once we were the slaves of sin and Satan, but now we are set free, in the glorious liberty of the children of God, and our lot is among the saints. Once we were in our sins, and under condemnation, now we are the children of God, and heirs of everlasting life. Once we were enemies to the eternal God, by wicked works and tempers: now we are reconciled through the blood of his Son, and he is become our Father and our Friend. Such grace, such love as this, demands our praises. Others may boast of riches and estates, their high birth and parentage; but we will joy in the Lord, and glory in the Rock of our salvation! We are plucked as brands from the burning, and we will praise our great Deliverer. Jesus is our Redeemer and our Saviour, our Beloved and our Friend; and we will give him our hearts, our lives, our all.

The poor unthinking multitude "see no form nor comeliness in him, neither any beauty that they should desire him," but we know and prove, that "he is the chief among ten thousand, and altogether lovely." He is the Friend that sticketh closer than a brother—that sympathizes in our infirmities, and beareth our sorrows. He careth for our necessities, and supplieth our wants. He strengtheneth our feeble hands, and feedeth our hungry fainting souls with the manna of his love: in him is all we want, and he is all our own: yea, and he will be our satisfying portion forever. "Happy are the people that are in such a case: yea, blessed are the people that have the Lord for their God."

My health has been very indifferent for some time; but, blessed be God, pain is sweet, and life or death is gain: I desire nothing but to do and suffer the will of my heavenly Father, and to increase in all the height of holiness, in all the depth of humble love. I do lie at the feet of Jesus, and find his love forever new. Lord, what am I, that thou shouldest thus regard me!

"He calls a worm his friend!
He calls himself my God!
And he shall save me to the end
Through Jesus' blood."

I hope my dear sister proves, as sweetly as I

do, the great privilege of approaching a God of love in secret prayer. These are precious seasons to me: here we may disburden all our cares and fears to him, who can and will save to the uttermost: by this we may renew our covenant with the Great Three-One, day by day, and receive from him fresh strength; and in this means may delightfully converse with our Beloved—lay open to him our hearts, and praise him who knows every secret there. And how does he melt the soul with his overwhelming grace, that thus seeketh him! They are such ravishing moments with me, that often I know not whether I am on earth or in heaven:—Surely it is a taste of heavenly bliss! I do not forget my dear sister and friend, when I thus approach the gracious throne. O pray for me! Dear Mrs. Salmon, yours in divine bonds,

H. A. Roe.

LETTER V.

Written at a time when she was supposed to be near death, and addressed to a lady of her acquaintance.

Macclesfield, Jan. 9, 1778.

Farewell, my friend! To the care of that

God of truth and love, who hath been so gracious unto me, I commend you. May you prove all the riches of his grace in life, and lay down this earthly tabernacle with the same joy and assurance of hope as I now do. "I have fought the good fight, I have finished my course, I have kept the faith; and henceforth there is laid up for me a crown, a never-fading crown of righteousness, which the Lord, the righteous Judge, shall give me at that day." I joyfully declare, it is by grace *alone* I am saved:—Jesus is all in all, and I am nothing without him.

I believe you will bear with a friend if she leave the following dying cautions; and O may the Spirit of holiness write them on your heart:—Deny yourself wholly, take up your cross daily, and follow Christ fully. Watch, fast, pray. Avoid all occasions of temptation *resolutely;* but, if at any time you are overcome, delay not to fall at the feet of Christ that moment for pardon and strength. The eyes of earth and heaven are upon you: many wait for your halting: more, I trust, wish you success in the name of the Lord: I am sure I do, and therefore write without reserve. Take care of your own understanding: do not suffer yourself to think of it, but with deep abasement that you have made no better use of it. Do not adorn your body now, if you wish to be found adorned with Christ in the day of eternity. I sit under the shadow of my Beloved. While I write, I feel him sustaining my soul. O Jesus, great is thy goodness, great is thy mercy! I feel my insufficiency to speak of the goodness of my God: it is more than I am able to express: I enjoy in him all I want; but am daily more sensible how little I am. O how his grace is magnified in a poor worm! You also have tasted of his love: may you follow him fully and steadfastly. While you do this, though storms should arise, and winds blow, they will only settle and fix you more fully on the Rock which cannot be moved. Believe simply and constantly, so shall you love steadfastly and entirely: then shall the Lord guide you continually, and satisfy your soul in drought, and your soul shall be as a watered garden, and as springs of water which fail not.

Farewell—I was going to say forever; but ah! no. I shall see you again: may it be where we shall rejoice together, in that joy which cannot be taken away from us: then shall we part no more, but live forever in the presence of our Jesus.

There, only there, we shall fulfil his great design,
And in his praise with all our elder brethren join,
In hymns and songs which never end,
Our heavenly, everlasting Friend!

H. A. Roe.

LETTER VI.

To Mr. Robert Roe.

MACCLESFIELD, Feb. 12, 1778.

DEAR COUSIN,—Since I wrote you before, I have been, to appearance, on the borders of eternity. My body was, indeed, brought very low; but my soul was full of heavenly vigour, and longing for immortality. O what heavenly transport filled my ravished breast, when I thought I had done, forever done, with all below; and, as I then thought, in a few days, or weeks at most, I should leave my cumbrous clay, to bask in the beams of uncreated beauty—should stand before the slaughtered Lamb, and see the wonders reserved for me—

"Should fall at his feet,
The story repeat,
And the Lover of sinners adore,"—

when I should be lost in Father, Son, and Spirit—overwhelmed and implunged in the fathomless abyss to all eternity. What I felt cannot be described: it was a real taste of joys immortal: it was a drop of heaven let down. But, behold! I am yet spared. Infinite Wisdom protracts my stay a little longer, and I bow my soul in resignation at his feet. I am not my own, but his; and O! may my language ever be, "Not as I will, but as thou wilt." I find I need not drop the body to enjoy the presence of my God: he dwells in my heart:—in him I live:—he surrounds, supports, sustains, me:—wrapped in his being, I resound his praise! O the heartfelt communion my soul enjoys with him—the intimate converse, the sweet fellowship! My spirit is filled and yet enlarged. It often seems as if mortality could bear no more; and yet my desires are insatiable. I long to plunge deeper into God.

I rejoice to find, by your last letter, that you are cleaving to your Lord, and happy in his precious love. O that every day and hour you breathe, you may sink deeper into him: All, all you want is there. Let not your trials be any discouragement: nay, "Rejoice and be exceeding glad, for great is your reward in heaven." Remember, every cross is a pledge of your crown, and all your sufferings will add to your eternal weight of glory. I hope you are all in earnest for the precious pearl of perfect love: O look up to a present and a faithful God! Ask, and you shall receive: all things in him are now ready: be not faithless, but believing. Hath he said, "I will circumcise thy heart," and will he not do it? Sooner shall heaven and earth pass away than his promise fail, if you only embrace it by believing O claim your privilege—the inheritance of the land of promise, the rest of holiness purchased for you by blood! Go up and possess it—fear not—come now, just as you are—empty, to be filled—filthy, to be cleansed.

> "Sink into the purple flood,
> Rise to all the life of God."

Be assured I ever remember you at the throne of grace, and remain your friend and sister in Jesus,

H. A. Roe.

LETTER VII.

To Mr. Robert Roe.

Macclesfield, March 10, 1778.

Dear Cousin,—I bless God that you learn wisdom by the things that you have suffered; and that you feel every temptation from Satan, as well as your outward trials, does work together for your good. So it shall ever be to *all* who love God, as I am fully persuaded you do.

I have of late been exercised with various and close trials, but not one too many; for all are permitted by my God! He is my portion, and reigneth in my heart alone. I have a happiness, therefore, independent on any creature, or any thing below the sun: God is all, and he is mine!

"All my treasure is above,
All my riches is his love."

O precious portion, invaluable treasure!

"Joys that, never, never past,
Through eternity shall last."

I think believers, in general, do not meditate enough on their privileges, and the great things God hath done for them, and promised to them—from what they are redeemed, and the fulness they are called to possess. Let you and me now dwell a little on the blessed theme: let us look to the rock from whence we were hewn, that we may rejoice the more in what we now are. Were we not once going on in the way to eternal ruin? dead in trespasses and sins, yea, slaves to Satan, and led by that grand adversary withersoever he would; yea, sleeping secure on the very verge of destruction? O my friend, if God had *then* cut the thread of life, and sent us to reap what our sins deserved, we had now been lifting up our eyes in torments! But, stupendous love,—

"When justice bared the sword,
To cut the fig tree down,
The mercy of our Lord
Cried, Let it still alone."

Yes, he spared our rebel souls—he shed his blood to ransom us from death—pleads our helpless cause before the throne, and mercy to our rescue flew. We were awakened by his Spirit to a sense of our danger; and no sooner did we truly seek, but he was found. Yes, *we* found redemption in his blood, the forgiveness of our sins; and, from being the bond slaves of hell, are become the children of God; and now all the Father hath to give is ours—ours by covenant through Jesus. He hath the Holy Ghost to give as an abiding, indwelling Comforter: this blessing then is ours. All the promises are our own:—"They are all yea and amen in Christ Jesus." Jesus hath given himself to us, and the Father is our God. Was it not the word of our redeeming Lord, "I and my Father will come and make our abode with you." And again, "I will send you another Comforter, even the Holy Ghost, who shall abide with you forever: he dwelleth with you, and shall be in you." Here, then, are promises of the whole divine Trinity dwelling in our hearts; and are not these promises sealed with the blood of the covenant! But will God, the eternal Trinity, dwell in an *impure* heart?—O no! but, by entering, he will cleanse it. Every root of bitterness, every remaining sin, and all the strong armour of unbelief, will flee before him. Can they stand his presence? No, no: God is love, and where he dwelleth, nothing but pure love can dwell.

"Thy presence, Lord, I cannot doubt,
Extirpates inbred sin."

O glory be to God, what a precious salvation is here. And this is the privilege, the happy privilege of all who have embraced the Saviour. All he hath promised, all he hath to give, is the believer's portion. Faith believes the record true, without staggering at the promise. The promise, my dear friend, is for you. Receive it, then, and let the humble language of your soul be—"Be it unto me, according to thy word." O rely on the word of a God that cannot lie, and receive him as your sanctification, and as your indwelling, abiding Comforter, your King, and your God. If you feel the flame that is now kindled in my breast, you will:—this will be the happy moment. Speak, thou eternal God, and let thy servant now be clean.

I had been led unawares thus to speak, but I believe it is by the Spirit of God; for, while I write, I am indeed filled with divine and ravishing consolations! My soul feels all I have spoken. Glory be to God, for I am most unworthy. I have much greater depths of humble love to prove, and my soul thirsts after them. O pray for me! Praise, for me, the God I truly love, and believe me ever your affectionate sister and friend,

H. A. Roe.

LETTER VIII.

To Mr. Robert Roe.

MACCLESFIELD, May 15, 1778.

DEAR COUSIN,—I am not much surprised that you are assaulted with the temptations you mention in your last; and though I feel for you, I have no fears on your account. I know the Lord will make your darkness light, your crooked paths straight, and your soul shall see the salvation of God.

It is no marvel that the enemy of souls employs his every artifice to destroy your peace. And will he not the rather do this just at a critical season, when your outward trials are great? He sees you pursuing the things, and espousing the glorious cause which shall overturn his kingdom. Marvel not then at his rage against you. It proves to me that you will be an instrument in the hands of God, of much good to precious souls; and that this dire enemy foresees it likely to be so; and therefore would retard, though he cannot hinder or stop your progress. You say, "you cannot believe till these doubts are cleared up." Here is another device of Satan. Your doubts cannot be removed till you do believe. Faith only is able to quench all the fiery darts of the wicked one—only believe, and you shall be saved from all your doubts: meridian evidence shall put them all to flight. Cast your soul, your fears, your unbelief, your inbred sin, your all, at the feet of Christ; and into the fountain of his blood, the depths of his love. Be determined: Lord, thou shalt be my teacher, wisdom, guide, counsellor—my atonement, my king, my portion,

"Helpless into thy hands I fall:
Be thou my God, my All in all."

Yes, my dear friend, leave Christ to answer every temptation that besets you. He hath said, "My grace is sufficient for thee." This is enough: be not faithless, but believing.

You ask, if I am not in a delusion respecting my experience of perfect love? Blessed be God, I have not the shadow of doubt. Even Satan himself finds these suggestions vain, and has left them off. He would rather lead me to doubt, or care for to-morrow; saying, such and such a thing is at hand, and will overcome thee. Thou wilt fall in some of thy trials; or when death comes, thou wilt be under a cloud. But, through grace divine, I am enabled to discern from whence these suggestions come, and they never distress me for a moment; for, by constant looking to Jesus, I received fresh strength in every time of need. I know I am *now* right, and I trust him for all that is to come; and, though all weakness, ignorance, helplessness, and unworthiness, yet I have the testimony of my own conscience, and the witness of God's Spirit, that I am wholly and unreservedly his—his in body, spirit, soul; nor does any thing but love remain in my heart. But, were I in a delusion—O happy delusion! it brings salvation—it brings heaven below! Nay, with what I this moment feel, I could be happy in the greatest of outward conflicts and distresses, for Christ is in my heart! I dwell in God, and God in me—I dwell in love, and love dwelleth in me—God is love, and he is all I want. And is it possible we should be ignorant whether we feel tempers contrary to love or no?—whether we rejoice always, or are burdened and bowed down with sorrow?—whether we have a praying, or a dead, lifeless spirit?—whether we can praise God, and be resigned in all trials, or feel murmurings, fretfulness, and impatience under them? Is it not easy to know, if we feel anger at provocations, or whether we feel our tempers mild, gentle, peaceable, and easy to be entreated, or feel stubbornness, self-will, and pride?—whether we have slavish fears, or are possessed of that perfect love which casteth out all fear that hath torment?

You ask how I obtained this great salvation? I answer, just as I obtained the pardon of my sin—*by simple faith.* No sooner did the pride and remaining unbelief of my heart submit to be taught, and to receive his precious, full salvation, as a free gift of his grace, by faith alone, without any fitness or worthiness, but I was instantly filled with such humbling depths of love to God, and union with him, with such discoveries of my own nothingness, as wholly swallowed up my soul in gratitude and praise. I knew the faithfulness of my God, and ventured on the promise, in spite of reasoning and unbelief and all the lying suggestions of the enemy, and believed *against hope*, or whatever opposed, when I felt my soul sinking into nothing, and Jesus became my all. I cried, this is what I wanted: I am emptied of self, and filled with God: I am now where I ought to be, a worm at Jesus' feet, saved by grace. But a thousand suggestions were soon darted, such as, thou wilt soon lose it: thou canst not stand—when thou art tried thou wilt fall. I said, Lord, thou alone canst be my keeper—see *thou* to that—I have given myself into thy hands, and I will hang upon thee. Thou hast promised, "My grace is sufficient for thee." O the preciousness of these words! I shall praise God in eternity that they are written in his book. This and such other promises have been proof for me against every opposition and trial I have met with, (which you know are not few;) and by thus trusting the promise and the Promiser, I have conquered; and, glory be to God, through his strength I shall still prevail. It is by hanging on Jesus, as an infant on its mother's breast, I retain my peace, and love, and joy—by watching, prayer and praise: by pressing after deeper degrees of humble love, communion with God and active holiness. Never were the ways of God so sweet as now to my soul: I love the narrowest path his Spirit and his word point out; and all my delight is to do and suffer his will. O may the same God of love fully reveal his great salvation in your heart, and be himself your rich portion forever, prays your affectionate cousin and friend,

H. A. Roe.

LETTER IX.

To Miss Bourn, of Newcastle, Staffordshire.

Macclesfield, Aug. 20, 1778.

My Dear Sister,—I was glad to receive yours by Mr. Hall. It always gives me pleasure to hear from you. In the bonds of divine love, my soul is united to yours; and, from the contents of your letter, as well as the power I had in your behalf with my God, I am assured that before long you will be a happy witness that Jesus can and will, and does destroy the last remains of sin in his children's hearts in this life: yea, in every such heart who does truly hunger and thirst after righteousness. You do hunger and thirst: O that you could look to him this moment as a precious Saviour! Is he not so? Do you not feel his loving presence? Are you not his, the purchase of his blood, the new made creature of his love, born of God, and become his child? Is not Jesus your Beloved and your Friend? Can he then deny his own Spirit's cry in your heart, and that, too, when all you ask is, that he will destroy his own enemies in your soul, and enable you to love him with all your heart? But, as to that temptation, if you receive it now, you will soon lose it: is he not able and willing, and faithful to keep, as he is to save? Yes, glory to his holy name, I know he is. He is the all-sufficient God, and, saith he, "My strength is made perfect in weakness." Trust him, then, poor, weak, and helpless soul. "But it is not long enough since you were justified." Does God tell you so? Has he set any limited time? None that I know of, except the present. He saith, Now, "to-day if you will hear my voice." And again, "Now is the day of salvation." And again, "Come, for all things are now ready." He has commanded, "Thou shalt love the Lord thy God with all thy heart, with all thy mind, with all thy soul, and with all thy strength;" and he hath promised, "I will circumcise thy heart, that thou mayest do it." But does he ever say, Suffer so much, or stay so long, and I will do it? Nay, but he saith, "If any man thirst, let him come unto me and drink. Ask and ye shall receive, that your joy may be full."

My dear Miss Bourn, there are some in this town who have not been justified so long as you, who have received, and do profess this blessing. O then, come once more, even as you came when first reconciled to God, and cast your soul simply on Jesus! Would he bleed for us when rebels, and will he refuse to avenge us of our inbred foe, when we are his beloved children? Surely no: it cannot be. I hope soon to see my dear friend, and that she will be able to tell me she has obtained this precious salvation.

Did you ever read Mr. Wesley's sermon on the Scripture way of salvation? You would do well to consider the conclusion of it attentively. "Hereby," says he, "you may surely know whether you are seeking to be sanctified by faith, or by works. If by *works*, you want something to be done first, before you are sanctified. You think, I must first *be*, or *do* thus or thus. Then you are seeking it by works unto this day. On the other hand, if you seek it by *faith*, you may expect it *as you are;* and if as you are, then expect it *now.* Do you believe we are sanctified by faith? Be true then to your principle, and look for this blessing just as you are, neither better nor worse: as a poor sinner that has nothing to pay, nothing to plead, but Christ died. And if you look for it as you are, expect it *now:* stay for nothing: why should you? Christ is ready, and he is all you want." Let your inmost soul cry out,

"Come in, come in, thou heavenly Guest,
Nor hence again remove:
Settle and fix my wavering soul,
With all thy weight of love."

Glory be to God, he carries on a glorious work among us here. Sinners are convinced, many are justified; and lately, several backsliders are restored. One poor soul, that has been long wandering from her God, was restored last night, while a few of us were at prayer. I am, my dear friend, yours in Jesus,

H. A. ROE.

LETTER X.

To Miss Brown, of Newcastle, Staffordshire.

MACCLESFIELD, Nov. 15, 1778.

MY DEAR SISTER,—Your letter caused great thanksgiving to God on your account: all glory be to him who hath increased your desires after holiness. Fear not, you will surely attain if you follow on. That lovely Lamb that bled on Calvary, was slain for this—"to redeem us from all iniquity." O look to him: behold the glory of God! See the God of angels: O look at his precious bleeding side: his hands, his head, his feet! Behold him gasping, groaning, dying, that you might be made clean! Hear him cry, "It is finished." How finished, if his blood cleanseth not from all sin?—"Without holiness no man shall see the Lord." But, glory to his name, whoever steps into that fountain, which is expressly said to be for sin and for uncleanness, shall be made perfectly whole. O let your faith venture in! wash and be clean:—

"Sink into the purple flood,
Rise to all the life of God."

Open, my dear sister, open your willing, longing heart, and the King of glory will come in. And then be assured, "all evil before his presence shall fly." Sin cannot remain where Jesus fully dwells; for he is holiness, and when he fills the soul, he leaves no room for any other guest. Whenever you can say, Jesus, thou art my all, and I love my God the present moment, with all my loving heart, you that moment possess the blessing of sanctification, and never need to lose it more. It is retained, as well as received, by simple faith. We can have no stock of grace on hand, but live moment by moment, hanging and depending on the adorable Jesus. In him there is a full supply of all we want, or can want.

This, blessed be God, I prove, and that continually. Every hour, every moment, brings me fresh delight in God. He is an inexhaustible fountain of love:—

> "Insatiate to this spring I fly,
> I drink, and yet am ever dry."

I cannot express the sweet union I feel with my God at this moment.

> "My Jesus to know, and feel his blood flow,
> 'Tis life everlasting, 'tis heaven below."

I am much blest when I remember my dear friend at the throne of grace; and often do I beseech my blessed Lord to

> "Fill her with all the life of love,
> In mystic union join
> Her to thyself, and let her prove
> The fellowship divine."

Jesus is unspeakably precious while I write: may you catch the flame I feel:—

> "And when your cup with love runs o'er,
> O may sin never enter more."

So prays, my dear sister, yours in divine bonds,

H. A. Roe.

LETTER XI.

To Miss R. before she received sanctification.

MACCLESFIELD, Nov. 21, 1778.

LAST Thursday evening I was pleasingly surprised by a letter from my dear Miss R., who, I sometimes feared, had forgot all her purposes and promises; and also all the blessings she so often received when we met in our Lord's name. I was glad to find my fears groundless; but much *more* pleased and thankful was I to find, by the contents of your last, that your precious soul was still labouring up the hill of holiness: go on and prosper. Many are the trials we meet with in the way: yea, our Lord hath foretold us, that in the world we should have tribulation, but in him peace, which is the seal of cancelled sin.

I hope you keep a sense, yea, a clear sense, of pardon at the worst of times. This is your privilege, and I am thankful you discern such beauty in holiness. O how sweet are those words:—"Without holiness no man shall see the Lord." You have cause to praise God for the knowledge he has given you of your nature's depravity. It is very good and profitable to know our sinful tendencies. O! my dear, be very watchful against *little* things, and "keep thy heart with all diligence; for out of it are the issues of life" and death. Let God have your first thoughts: let him be first in your affections, so shall your words and works please him; for,

> "What are all our works to him,
> Unless they spring from love."

Daily entreat him to take away all opposition that remains in your will, to his providential order: so shall you find rest in those circumstances, which otherwise would give you much uneasiness. The meditations of your heart leading to him, the affections of your soul cleaving to Jesus, *your* will sinking into *his* will—here is the rest of the saints! while all that is within you calls your Jesus King.—"Whatever ye ask in my name," saith our adorable Redeemer, "you shall receive." Ask, then, my dear friend, for a greater power of faith; for, as you believe, so will you increase in every grace of his Spirit; and your soul will more and more centre in God, till you become one spirit with him, who is the life of all living; yea, the very essence of heaven itself!

> "To his meritorious passion
> All our happiness we owe:
> Pardon, uttermost salvation,
> Heaven above, and heaven below:
> Grace and glory
> From that open fountain flow."

To the bosom of our Almighty Jesus I commend you: O may his face always shine upon you, and his blessed, loving Spirit fill your soul! Pray much, and you shall attain all the salvation you desire. I am yours in bonds of divine love,

H. A. ROE.

LETTER XII.

To a Preacher of the Gospel, in answer to some inquiries relative to the state of her soul.

MACCLESFIELD, Dec. 6, 1778.

DEAR SIR,—To tell you one thousandth part of the preciousness of Jesus, is a task impossible to men or angels. To *my* soul, he is truly the altogether lovely—the one object in which all my desires, expectations, and affections centre—the Alpha and the Omega. To him my more than all I owe, being snatched by his grace, a brand from everlasting burnings! My surety he is, my life, my peace, my treasure, my husband, brother, friend—my wisdom, my righteousness, my sanctification—my all in all, for time and for eternity. Him, and him alone I desire: him, and him alone I love.

"I have no sharer of my heart,
To rob my Saviour of a part,
And desecrate the whole:
His loveliness my soul has prepossess'd,
And left no room for any other guest."

Yet, O how is my heart expanded when I see I have yet received but, as it were, a drop out of the ocean! but a glimpse of his precious fulness, and an eternity of growing bliss lies yet before me! This glorious prospect truly lays me where I would forever lie, at his dear feet, the monument of his mercy. O that I could praise him as I would! but language fails, and I long for that day when I shall praise him in nobler strains above. Were he to give the summons now, and call from earth away, O how gladly could I wing my flight this hour! Loose from creature and created good, I only wait the joyful word, Come up hither!—Then would I exulting

> "Clap the glad wing, and soar away,
> And mingle with the blaze of day."

In that blessed kingdom, dear sir, I hope to meet you, though, perhaps, on earth we may meet no more. In the mean time may you be filled with all the communicable fulness of Father, Son, and Spirit, rejoicing herein with increasing joy, and made very useful in your Lord's vineyard, prays sincerely your real well-wisher for Christ's sake,

H. A. Roe.

LETTER XIII.

To Mr. Robert Roe.

CHESTER, Dec. 19, 1778.

DEAR COUSIN,—I am glad to hear by your sister, that you are restored to a measure of health; and that the Lord, the faithful God, is still your support: may he be so to the end of your pilgrimage. Lean every moment on your Beloved, and attend continually to the lessons of his love. I trust you have learned many sweet and important truths, in your late affliction, and are coming out of it as gold purified in the fire. You have no cause to fear all the legions of your spiritual enemies: tempt they may, and powerfully assault, but cannot harm. I am led to believe all the depressions of mind you sometimes feel, are in a great measure owing to two things: First, not being deeply and clearly sensible what is temptation, and what is sin: and, Secondly, accounting the inseparable infirmities of the corruptible body to be sin: such as, errors in judgment, failures of memory, bodily weakness, or pain; and, at times, through various causes, a depression of animal spirits. This last mistake may arise from another, viz., looking upon elevating, transporting joy, as inseparable from true grace. Now, I think you must allow, that, as free agents nothing but what our will chooses in opposition to the will of God, or, as Mr. Wesley expresses it, "nothing but a wilful transgression of a known law is sin." Granting this, then, and though ten thousand sinful objects, or desires, in all the pleasing forms that Satan can invent, may be darted into our minds, or displayed before the eyes of our imagination, if our will and affections do not embrace or choose them, but we resist and hate them, in this case we do not sin, but conquer.

Secondly: when through various indispositions of the frail, tottering body, we feel a very small degree of joy; nay, perhaps only a degree of *hope* and confidence, and, at the same time, the enemy endeavouring to lay the axe of his temptations at the root of this, this, I say, is a time to take the advice of God by his prophet, "Who is among you that feareth the Lord, that obeyeth the voice of his servant, that walketh in darkness, and hath no light? Let him trust in the name of the Lord, and stay upon his God." This text proves that joy is not inseparable from grace. It is not according to our joy, (for this is the fruit or effect of faith,) but according to our faith he blesses and saves, accepts and loves us. Our love to God, his cause, his people, his precepts, all springing from the root of faith, are so many acts of the soul, which our blessed Lord and Master approves and accepts through the Beloved; and are inseparable evidences of our sonship. But joys, comforts, and communications of the Holy Ghost, are so many free gifts bestowed upon us; because the Lord delights in blessing, comforting, and dwelling in us, and are so many pledges of his unmerited love.

Now, if the Lord permit bodily affliction, so that the animal spirits cannot receive the communications, (I mean, cannot receive them without an extraordinary exertion of his power and love, which, indeed, we often see manifested in the dying hours of those who love God, and I myself have often felt in sickness and close trials,) ought we not, in such cases, to cast ourselves by faith on him, lean on his bosom, and, without giving way to reasoning, believe he will make every affliction work for good? Surely we ought to trust him at all times—it is our privilege. Do not mistake me: I am not condemning a religion that may be felt: I would only prove to you, that faith is the root of joy, and not joy the root of faith; and that you ought not to cast away your shield of faith, because you have not, for the present moment, much joy. When we are beset with various trials, various temptations, and various suggestions: such as, Thou wilt surely fall—such a temptation will prove too hard for thee, &c., "My grace is sufficient for thee," saith the Lord—he who knows all your trials. Now, when by faith we embrace and rely on this promise, knowing he who is faithful will perform his word, we are strengthened by a sweet peace, and well-grounded confidence and hope, that shall never make us ashamed. And, while we continue to live by this faith, we more than conquer, whether our joy be little or great. This is our shield, and God is pleased by afflictions to try and prove this faith, that it may burn the brighter and be more conspicuous to all. Not that he is displeased with us for any thing, nor as a punishment; but, whom the Lord *loveth* he chasteneth. I believe this is often your case; and he calls upon you by his word, "not to cast away your confidence, which hath great recompense of reward. And yet a little while, and he that shall come will come, and will not tarry."

With respect to sanctification, I mean the instantaneous work, you have the word of a God—"I will sprinkle clean water upon you, and ye shall be clean, from all your filthiness, and from *all* your idols, will I cleanse you." Here is a *full*, *free* promise. Do you seek this salvation by faith, or by works? If by faith, then you have no need to tarry for worthiness or fitness, but come now, just as you are. You must embrace the promise, believe it, hang upon it, rejoice in it as your own, trusting God to perform it. Soon as you cast your soul upon him by faith, he will seal the blessing on your heart. May he reveal these things to you by his Spirit, and fill you with his fulness, prays your affectionate friend and cousin,

H. A. Roe.

LETTER XIV

To Mr. Robert Roe.

Nantwich, April 20, 1779.

Dear Cousin,—You are quite mistaken—you do not try my patience at all; but you are made a means of humbling my soul before God, when you think me capable of answering in a proper manner the questions you ask; and yet, as far as the Lord has taught me, I am willing to communicate. I believe your eye is single: you are a child of God, and an heir of glory—a well-beloved of the eternal Trinity. For you the Father gave his only Son: Jesus the Saviour bled for you; and the blessed Spirit hath applied the blood of sprinkling to the pardon of your sins, and the comfort of your soul in all your various trials. I account it no strange thing that you should be assaulted like your heavenly Master, with that suggestion, "If thou be the Son of God,"—surely you will not give way to reasoning, because Satan accosts you as he did the incarnate God. No: rather take comfort, for he that had *no sin* was tempted in this very point, like as you are. A hypocrite may boast he is never tempted—has no doubts or fears—but a child of God (some rare cases excepted) is seldom long together unassaulted by our vigilant adversary, who takes every possible method and opportunity to attack our confidence in the Lord, and to work upon all that remains of the carnal mind, or of unbelief; but he can *only* tempt—he cannot force us to give way either to sin or unbelief. Neither think it strange that you are not inwardly as holy as you ought to be: every child of God feels the same, till fully renewed in love by the power of the Holy Ghost. Till then he has faith, but it is often mixed with unbelief: he has love; but though he loves God above all things, yet the love of self, and of creature comforts, often steals in. He has a blessed measure of true humanity, and yet he is constrained to acknowledge frequently with tears,

> "Cursed pride, that busy sin,
> Spoils all that I perform."

His patience and resignation are not perfect: his will is not fully subdued to God at all times, nor his affections and desires wholly spiritual. The Spirit of God does visit, but does not *dwell:* does, at times, ravish the soul with delight, thereby wooing it to cast away unbelief, and open the door to receive all the precious mind of Jesus—all the stamp of love divine. Now when a soul is obedient to the voice of God, when it does open the door, and grasp the promises of holiness in the hand of faith, he will come into that soul, and plant his own nature there. Then, when perfected in love, faith becomes constant, and unmixed with unbelief. Love takes full possession of the soul, and humility, unmixed with pride, lays him at the Saviour's feet. His constant faith and perfect love now bring forth perfect patience and resignation. His deep-rooted humility having laid all self at the Saviour's feet, his will is now quite subject, and all his language is,

"All's alike to me, so I
In my Lord may live and die."

But even this state is consistent with many ignorances, weaknesses, and infirmities—with many temptations, trials, crosses, and bodily afflictions; and, on account of these, our joy may at times be small; yet our faith may be perfect, and our peace undisturbed. I believe our faith is often made manifest by following God *blindfold*—if I may be allowed the expression—I mean, when our ignorance and blindness cannot account for his providential dispensations—when we are beset with trials, and see no way to escape. In this case, faith says, "It is the Lord, let him do what seemeth him good." Being confident of this one thing, "What I know not now, I shall know hereafter:" I will trust in my God, and not be afraid, for he is my all.

I have not time, room, or expression, to tell a thousandth part of the goodness of my God to my soul. He is ever with me, and assures my heart, "All that I have is thine." All my desires are satisfied in him—I live in him, and walk in him, and he is my God. He is with me in sickness and in health—at home and abroad—in public and in private. In reading or writing I feel his presence; and, O! when I am bowed before his throne, he lets down a heaven of communicated bliss! Language fails when I speak of his love! O may my every breath speak his praise! I remain your unworthy friend, but happy sister,

H. A. Roe.

LETTER XV.

To Miss Salmon.

Malpas, June 16, 1779.

My Dear Friend,—How shall I praise my God for his goodness, his infinite, his stupendous love! O how he heapeth his benefits upon me, and maketh every other blessing sweet, by the gift of himself. Would any thing the world calls great or good, be any thing to me without my God! Ah! no, no: every thing most desirable is hateful to my soul, wherein I cannot taste, or feel, or see something of my blessed Lord; but, all glory be to him, he is my all in all things. Help me to love this only lovely, dearest object of my wishes. Let him, my dear sister, be our Lord and King forever. Yes, Lord, take our hearts:—

"Manage the wheels by thy command,
And govern every spring."

How sweet is the yoke of Jesus! O how gentle, how tender, how compassionate his care! How hath he borne you and me, as weak and helpless lambs in his arms, carried us in his bosom, and defended us from the fowler's snare! Eternal Lord God, thou indwelling Trinity, whom truly our hearts do love, accept the gratitude words cannot speak: in silent adoration we adore thee, overwhelmed at thy amazing grace! I cannot utter, my dear friend, the sweet feelings of my heart, or tell you how divine a union my spirit feels with yours. O may you now, and henceforth, prove all that Jesus can bestow! How much is that? Words cannot tell you; but yours it is, through the merit of his blood!

I intended to begin my letter with thanks for your love and kindness to me at Chester; but I was led to the precious Fountain of all comfort, and when I had once begun his mercy's theme, I could not break off. I bear, however, a grateful sense of the affectionate regard you manifested; and though to tell you so is all I can do, my Lord will surely reward. My love to dear Miss Bennet, and all that family; and to all where you are. I bear them all on my heart before God. I love them all; and if they knew how Jesus loves them, they would not keep back their hearts from him. I got safe to this place, and am treated very kindly by this loving family; but O how I feel for those who love not God! My dear Miss B. is as open and free as before. My soul cleaves to her, and I have great hopes. Pray for her, and for your ever affectionate,

H. A. Roe.

LETTER XVI.

To Miss Loxdale.

Nantwich, June 30, 1779.

Dear Sister,—My dear friend's letter was indeed a pleasure and a blessing to me; and my Lord's great goodness to you is a fresh motive to love and praise him. But fresh motives of this kind are no new things to me: I am ever discovering instances of his goodness, that fill me with wonder and astonishment, and cause me to exclaim, with holy David, "Lord, what is man, that thou art so mindful of him?" Great things, indeed, my dear sister, hath the Lord done for you, and for your unworthy friend; and yet, O stupendous grace! we have only received a drop out of the ocean of his love: an endless prospect, and a maze of bliss, lie yet before us!—opening beauties, and such lengths, and breadths, and depths, and heights, as thought cannot fathom, or mind of man conceive! It is, my friend, the fulness of the Triune God, in which we may bathe, and plunge, and sink, till lost and swallowed up in the ever growing, overflowing ocean of delights. His fulness—O what is it!—shall we *ever* fathom it? ever know a ten-thousandth part? Ah no! a ten-thousandth part of that effulgence we could not bear to know and live! Nay, and when disembodied through the revolving ages of eternity, I am persuaded we shall only seem beginning to know his fulness of love. What thoughts are these! When I enter into them, as into a labyrinth, they almost overcome my natural powers. O how very little of his revealed glory can this earthen vessel contain! but a time is hastening on, (and I eagerly wait for its approach,) when, no longer imprisoned in clay, our eyes shall be strengthened to see him as he is—see him for ourselves, and bask for ever in his smiles. Yes, we shall be with Jesus and behold his glory. He will reveal to us, also, as much as we can bear of the fulness of the Father's glory; and we shall be with Father, Son, and Spirit, filled to all eternity! But I have been led further than I intended: I must return.

Permit me to ask, my dear friend, what are your ideas, what is your opinion, or what your experience of inward, instantaneous sanctification, whereby the root, the in-being of sin is destroyed? I do not mean or allude to a state of angelic or Adamic, but a Christian perfection—a destruction of every temper contrary to love—a state consistent with many temptations of the devil, if our hearts repel those temptations, and our will do not embrace or yield to them; for that cannot be sin in which our *will* has no part. Thus it was with Jesus: "In him was no sin, yet he was tempted in all points as we are:" before his pure eyes did that enemy display all the kingdoms of the world, and the glory of them:—to his spotless soul he suggested disturbing doubts, and presumptuous expectations; but in the Son of God they found no place. Again : what I mean is a state consistent with a growth in grace ; for Jesus, though always pure, "increased in wisdom and stature, and in favour with God and man." Is not such a state expressed and described in the thirteenth of the first book of Corinthians ? and is it not commanded in these gracious words, "Rejoice evermore, pray without ceasing, and in every thing give thanks?" Does not the apostle add, "This is the will of God concerning you?" And after praying, "Now the God of peace sanctify you wholly," does he not pray, that "your whole spirit, soul, and body, (after they are so sanctified,) may be preserved blameless to the second coming of our Lord Jesus Christ?" Then follows the glorious promise, "Faithful is he that calleth you, who also *will* do it." And is not the same thing promised in the sweet passage you named ? "I will sprinkle clean water upon you, and you shall be clean : from all filthiness, and from all your idols, will I cleanse you," &c. And again, did he not "swear to our father Abraham, that he would grant unto us, that we, being delivered out of the hands of our enemies, might serve him without fear, in holiness and righteousness before him all the days of our life." By the state I weakly attempt to describe, I mean that degree of humble love which excludes every temper contrary thereto; and faith that excludes the remains of unbelief, and every tormenting fear: "for he that feareth is not made perfect in love." It is "fellowship with the Father, and with his Son Jesus Christ," through the Spirit, by whose abiding witness we can say, "Abba, Father—my Lord and my God," with an unwavering tongue.

I know this precious Gospel salvation is even derided by some, and exploded by many. Perhaps you may have conversed with some of these; and not have met with many who have dared to speak for God in this respect. Some of my expressions may therefore appear odd or unusual; but compare them with Scripture, and mention with freedom any of them you wish me to explain. As I know your situation, you will excuse the liberty I take in advising you not to meddle with *opinions:* these insensibly eat out of the soul the precious life of God. Dispute not with any; or, if they seek hurtful disputations, it is a good way to propose prayer. But it may be well, as much as may be, to avoid the company of those who love vain controversy. Endeavour after a calm, recollected spirit—a heartfelt union with a holy God. Sweet truth—God is love, and love is the Christian's all. Love in us is his nature imparted: it is the fulfilling of the law, the perfect law of liberty. Whosoever "loveth his brother," hath fulfilled the law to his neighbour; and he who "loveth the Lord his God with all his heart, and soul, and mind, and strength," hath fulfilled the law to him also. To such "his commandments are not grievous," not a task—a wearisome burden, but a delight: they are ways of pleasantness—they are paths of peace. And as we are under a law of love to God, so God our God in Christ, is under a covenant of love, in which is made over to us all *he is* and all *he has* to give—his every attribute, his wisdom to guide and teach, his power to protect, and help, and strengthen, his faithfulness, his truth, his mercy &c, all sealed over, and secured by covenant promises and covenant blood.

O, my dear sister, what a blessed portion is ours! Let us determine to prove it all. We *may*, I trust we *shall*, and together praise in endless day, the great Three One. I am ever yours in him,

H. A. Roe.

LETTER XVII.

To Miss Loxdale.

Macclesfield, Aug. 4, 1775.

I thank you, my dear sister, for your last, and would have written sooner, but a violent rheumatic pain in my head prevented me. I clearly see in your experience a deepening of the work of God. He is preparing your heart for his perfect love: he is emptying you of self, that you may be swallowed up in him: he is crucifying you to the world, that you may live *to* him, and *for* him alone: he discovers to you the beauties of holiness, that your soul and all its powers may be captivated thereby, and enlarged to ask and receive all his goodness waits to give. It is no marvel that Satan shoots his fiery darts, and employs his strongest batteries to prevent this work of grace: he ever did, and he ever will. This precious salvation entirely overturns his kingdom in the believer's heart: he hath no more place, no more power: he finds no inward evil now (in those thus saved) to close in with his temptations. His every dart is now repelled, quick-sighted love discovers all his snares, and armed with the strength of Omnipotence, we more than conquer!

The temptations you find, are the same I was followed with, when the fountains of the great deep of inbred corruption were discovered to my view: yes, I experienced them all, and ten times more.

Mr. Fletcher's Polemical Essay, especially in his address to imperfect believers, seeking Christian perfection, was made a great blessing to me

This, with Mr. Wesley's Plain Account, answered every objection, every doubt; and I earnestly recommend them to your serious perusal. These will lead you to see we are sanctified, as well as justified, by *faith alone,* and not for our merits fitness, or deservings; but faith lays hold of the blood of Christ, as the procuring cause of our holiness, and which *alone* cleanseth from all sin. This blood is all-sufficient:—as prevailing *now* as ever it will be. What then does the believer (hungering and thirsting after righteousness, or inward purity) wait for? The promise is, They shall be filled. Why delay? We may come just as we are; and if so, we may come this moment. It is said, Acts xxvi, 18, "We are sanctified by faith in Jesus;" and the work in that verse is plainly distinguished from justification, or the forgiveness of sins, both being there clearly promised. If then it be by faith alone, it must be also instantaneous, in the same manner as our pardon was. Did we not receive the one in a moment, by, and in the act of believing? And why should we stumble at coming the same way for the other? "By grace are ye saved through faith," in all the different degrees of that salvation which we can receive in the body. If by grace, then it is no more of works, and if not by works, we need wait for none:—we may come just as we are, yea, just now.

May the Lord, while you read these lines, open the windows of heaven, and fill your spirit with his pure love. Do you thirst? Behold rivers of living waters gushing out of your Redeemer's wounds—water that will wash your inbred sin away. Is not the Holy Ghost waiting to apply the efficacious blood, and make you white as snow?—Hovers he not over you?—knocks he not even *now* at the door of your heart? O let your inmost spirit cry,

> "Come in, come in, thou heavenly Guest,
>   Nor hence again remove;
> But sup with me, and let the feast
>   Be everlasting love."

Amen, Lord Jesus, answer the prayer of thy child. Be it unto her as her soul desireth: fill her heart, and fill it *now*. I feel for the trials of your present situation, but the sweet love of Jesus shall bear you above all. Take no thought for the morrow, but momentarily live *to* God, and *for* God, and nothing will be able to harm you. I am, my dear friend, yours in the best of bonds,

H. A. Roe.

LETTER XVIII.

To Mr. Robert Roe, upon the nature of faith, and in what sense it is the act of man.

MACCLESFIELD, Aug. 12, 1779.

DEAR COUSIN,—I can still see all your doubts and scruples in no other light than as temptations and suggestions from an enemy, who is, and ever will be, watching and endeavouring to break your peace. And though I believe you will be brought through them all to the haven of bliss, yet you permit him to rob you of much comfort, which you might enjoy; and he would rather employ you in answering his lying suggestions, than that you should be momentarily looking up to, and depending on Jesus for all you want. For my own part if it were not to answer your queries, I should never enter into the nice distinctions you do. I have much more to learn myself, and am convinced many would solve your scruples much better than I can. Indeed, to speak properly, no one can do it—it is the work of God. Yet, I am ready to impart what himself hath freely given. But, I beseech you to read my letters with prayer, and beg of God that he will attend every observation with the light and blessing of his Spirit.

You say, "The work of justification is greatly obscured by many, and you do not exclude me—

that I tell you, sometimes it is by faith, sometimes by works." So do St. Paul and St James, yet they are strictly consistent with themselves and each other. But I sometimes think you understand by works a meritorious condition: I never mean any such thing. When I speak of the works God requires in a seeker or believer, I only mean a co-operation with, or using the grace given to us. I believe God the Father loved all mankind in their sins, freely and unconditionally, or he had never given his only begotten Son. And it was an unconditional promise, "The seed of the woman shall bruise the serpent's head." God the Son also loved us freely and unconditionally, when he left his Father's glory, and became man—lived, died, and rose again *for us.* I believe too, God the Holy Ghost, unconditionally (with respect to anything *we* can do) enlightens every man that cometh into the world. But then, these things being done for us, by and through the *free grace* of the Eternal Trinity, we are required to *use* the light given.

If the Spirit of God convinceth of sin, which is *his* work, we are required to forsake it; and there is always power to do it communicated. This forsaking of sin is an act of man, and a *condition;* for "put away the evil of your doings," saith God, "from among you, and cease to do evil;" yet this is not a meritorious work. Again: if the Spirit points the guilty, heavy-laden sinner to the Lamb of God, shows the all-sufficiency of his atonement, and that the promises are made to such lost sinners as he is, who are weary of the burden of sin, that he has a right to come, because all are invited; and that "now is the accepted time" with God, "and now is the day of salvation,"—that no price, no worthiness, is required, but he may come without money, and be forgiven freely—when these things are revealed by God, which is *his* work, then it is that we are commanded to act faith. We are to believe the record true, embrace it, rely upon it, and venture our guilty souls on the promises made through a bleeding Saviour. It is after this act of faith, not before it, God gives the witness of the Spirit. Do you not understand me? The witness, or the seal of the Spirit, is God's gift, not our act, given to all who do act faith on Jesus, and the promise made through him. But it is not given till faith be acted. If we, as penitents, had *no* power thus to act faith, how would God be just in declaring, "He that believeth not shall be damned?"

With respect to works after justification, can any one retain his confidence in God without them?—Has he any foundation in the Scripture to do so? God absolutely requires that we should do, do, do, (as you say,) and be, be, be: not in a meritorious sense, but as fruits of the law of love, written in our hearts, acceptable and well-pleasing through Jesus Christ, and with every injunction he gives power to perform it. The power given is of grace, and the use of that power is the act of man. Again: When the Lord, by his Spirit, reveals our inbred sin, and points us to the all-cleansing blood, and to the promises to circumcise our heart, &c., it is his work wrought in us freely. But, when this light is given, we are to embrace the promises, and act faith upon them. God hath said, "I will do it." Let me ask, Do you believe he will do it *in you?* Hold fast that faith, then, for the promise is sure: it cannot fail; and God's time is now. Only believe. God at this moment requires an act of faith in you. He holds out the promise, and bids you believe. But you will say, I do not feel the blessing. Poor Thomas! Because thou hast not *seen*, thou wilt not believe. "Blessed are they who have not seen, and yet have believed!" But you ask, "What must I believe? I answer, that God is faithful—that he *can* and *will*, in a moment, give you what now you do not feel: nay, you will not feel it till after you have believed. If I had given you an apple, it would not be faith to believe I had given it; but, if I had promised to give you one, and to give it you instantly on your requesting it—if you then believed my promise, and took me at my word, though you did not see or handle the apple, this would be your act of faith *in me.* But how much more immutable the promise of a God! You cannot believe him in vain. Even suppose (which is seldom the case) you thus act faith a day or two, or longer, before you receive the witness, shall you be the worse for it? Nay, but far better for having believed: this faith *will* bring power into your soul, and you will sensibly feel what you never felt before; and soon you will prove the Spirit's inward testimony, that it is done unto you according to your faith. But you will say, "How is the work instantaneous, if I must wait a day or two?" I answer, the work is done the moment you believe, though the witness of the Spirit (which is not your faith, but the gift of God) be not fully given till afterward. "He that believeth" (the promise saith) "shall be saved"—from guilt, from inbred sin, and into glory.

It appears to me you labour under another mistake. You expect in being saved from sin, to be also delivered from temptation, short-comings, weaknesses, and infirmities; but these are inseparable from humanity. We shall never have a perfect body till the resurrection: of consequence, shall be liable to a thousand infirmities. We shall never have perfect knowledge in this life, and shall therefore ever be liable to errors in judgment, &c. The perfect law of Adam would condemn these things; but we are under the covenant of grace; or, in other words, under the law of love to Christ, whose blood every moment pleads for these things. May the God of peace and love teach and guide you into his perfect will, prays your affectionate cousin,

H. A. Roe

LETTER XIX.

To the Rev. J. Wesley.

Macclesfield, Oct. 15, 1779.

Rev. Sir,—Since I received your last, I have had a return of the pain in my side, an oppression of my lungs, and sometimes (which I never had before) such a yellowness of my skin, that I apprehended it would turn to the jaundice. After eating and drinking, I was thrown into violent heats, and afterward into cold fainting sweats. Then I was either in great pain at my stomach, or else so sleepy, that I could not keep my eyes open for a considerable time. But, blessed be God! I found it a sweet affliction; for never did I find Christ so precious, my evidence so clear, my will so unreservedly swallowed up in his, nor the intercourse so truly opened betwixt him and my believing soul. Hence I loved, and praised him for every pain; and, had it been his adorable will to have called me hence, how gladly should I have obeyed the joyful summons, and hasted to the presence of my Beloved, my Friend, my All! But seeing he still spares me a little longer, to embrace his will, and bless the merciful hand which brought me down, and hath raised me up again, I see an open field: a boundless prospect of new delights lies open before me: I see and feel that God hath engaged all his attributes in my behalf; and in his strength I fear no cross, no shame, no enemies; for my Leader, my Captain, my King, is the Lord of hosts. His glory is my only aim, and my only happiness. O precious thought! O bliss, not imaginary, but real! not fading, but everlasting: not decreasing, but ever growing! O vast abyss of unfathomable love! And as this is *my* portion, so, dear sir, it is *yours* also. We experience it now, and shall forever know it. On these accounts, how easy is the sight of faith! how delightful the labours of love!

and how welcome the cross we bear for Him, who is our life, our strength, and our salvation!

Dear Mr. S. is still unable to go into his circuit, and I fear he will never be much better. Cold bathing seems to do him most good; but he is very ill, especially in the mornings. His grief at not being able to travel is, I believe, a great hinderance to his recovery. My soul feels great nearness to him; for I believe he is, in a peculiar sense, beloved of God, and a faithful steward of his grace.

I hope, sir, you will remember him at the throne of grace, and that God may either restore him to his former usefulness, or else help him to be perfectly resigned to his adorable will; for you know, dear sir, that to have a soul all on fire for doing good, kept back and hindered by sickness, weakness, or other bodily infirmity, must be a great temptation to the contrary. But as there are none so weak as myself, and, of consequence, who stand more in need of Divine assistance, I hope you will not cease to mention me in your prayers. In so doing you will greatly oblige, Rev. sir, your very unworthy, but most affectionate friend and servant,

H. A. Roe.

LETTER XX.

To the Rev. J. Wesley.

December 11, 1779.

Rev. and Dear Sir,—I should not have been silent thus long, had not my dearest Lord seen good to afflict my body. I have lately been confined, and am just recovering from a sore throat. It was not ulcerated, but attended with a fever. Numbers in this town, or neighbourhood, have been ill, and several have died, four in one family within a month. I applied hartshorn to my throat, and found benefit from it. I am now, I bless God, much better. I have reason to praise him for every affliction; for all he permits does work together for my good. I do love my Lord with all my heart.

"All my capacious powers can wish,
In him doth richly meet;
Nor to my eyes is light so dear,
Or friendship half so sweet."

No, no, all the creation can boast is poor and mean compared with him I love. In him I feel a constant heaven, and my soul truly sits loose to all besides. I have victory, through his grace, over all things, inward and outward, that are contrary to his will. I have at times various temptations; but they find no place in me, nor at any time distress or bring me into bondage. I have (glory be tc God) the inward testimony of his Spirit, that I please him, and that he dwelleth in me. My body and soul are both the Lord's; and I earnestly desire that his whole will may be done in me and by me. I am a sacrifice offered up through Jesus, my adorable High Priest; and am determined, through grace divine, ever to remain so. I am a pilgrim in a strange country, and all my treasure is above.

I am travelling as fast as the wings of time will bear me forward, to my celestial country; though thorns, and snares, and gins, sometimes beset my path; yet my feet are shod, my sandals on, and I trample on them. Though the arrows of the archer are flying, I have a shield that turns aside the fiery darts. I have a shadow from the heat, and a refuge from the storm. I live upon the food of angels, and drink largely of the fountain of the water of life. His ways are ways of pleasantness, and all his paths are perfect peace. How great is the love wherewith he hath loved me! O how large his grace to the most unworthy! "Bless the Lord, O my soul, and all that is within me bless his holy name." I have heard from cousin J—— R——, and his soul prospers: blessed be God! I hope, dear sir, you ever do, and ever will remember, at the throne of grace, your most unworthy, but truly affectionate child in a precious Jesus,

H. A Roe.

LETTER XXI.

To Mr. Robert Roe.

Macclesfield, Jan. 14, 1780.

My dear Cousin,—I am willing to answer any question, or write in any manner that will give your soul satisfaction—break any snare of the enemy, or, in any way whatsoever, glorify God; but I am often led to think you do not want information in your judgment respecting these things; and therefore that your aim is to see how far I am, or am not, consistent with myself in my different letters. Were many people to peruse what I write to you, they would think it very presuming in me to argue points of doctrine, or experience with you, who are intended to be a teacher in Israel; yet, you so draw me in, that I dare not refuse. I rejoice to hear that your soul is more happy in God than when you wrote before. O live near to him, and press forward, and all is yours! I would again repeat, trample upon all that is past, and come this moment to Jesus by faith alone, for present, instantaneous, perfect love.

"Ready are you to receive:
Ready is your God to give."

But I must hasten to consider your objections. You ask, if I, "previous to justification, forsake all sin, and have power to keep myself from evil, by the grace I receive from the convincing Spirit of God—what need of his free justifying or sanctifying grace? On the other hand, if I offend (say you) in one point, not being faithful to the grace of conviction, am I never afterward to be accepted, even by the Gospel charter? How agrees this (you go on to ask) with trampling, as you often bid me, on my worthiness and unworthiness, and coming by faith alone?" I would here put a few questions to you, and I beseech you answer them to the Lord. Can your forsaking all sin now, (though it be pleasing to God, and what he requires and commands,) cancel your *old sins*, or obtain forgiveness for what is past? Have you no need, then, of the free justifying grace of God, to be received by faith alone? On the other hand, if you resist the convincing Spirit of God, and continue in sin, contrary to his strivings and drawings, will he continue his operations, and, in spite of you, work that faith in you which alone justifies the ungodly? Yet consistent with these things, you may, through the power of temptation, and your evil, unregenerate nature, have been overcome and given way, not being faithful to the grace of light and conviction; and yet, you may still come, hating the sin you have committed, and burdened with your past unfaithfulness, trampling on your present worthiness or unworthiness, come just as you are—a poor prodigal, a condemned malefactor, to Jesus, and receive freely, by faith alone, the mercy and the pardon you no ways deserve.

Again, you are now a believer, but feel the remains of a carnal nature. It is your happy privilege, through the Spirit, to mortify the deeds of the body, or the motions of the body of sin, that still works in your members. This is pleasing unto God, and what he requires, as fruits of that faith, whereby he hath promised you shall be able to quench every fiery dart of the devil. But, supposing you do this without once being unfaithful to the grace of justification, (and also! very few, if any, can truly plead they have been so,) will this cleanse your heart from the root of inbred sin? Ah, no! And have you no need then of the free sanctifying grace of God, to be received by faith alone? If, on the other hand, you are willingly, wilfully, or habitually unfaithful to grace given, are led captive, and overcome by your inbred sin, or outward temptations: if you *resist* the teachings of the Spirit of God, who would point you to the all-cleansing blood, and do not earnestly seek to go on to perfection, neither desire holiness, will he come forcibly, and take possession of your heart, and *dwell* there, whether you will or no? Yet, consistent with what I have urged, though you may be deeply conscious you have not been *strictly faithful* to justifying grace; nay, through surprise, or temptation, you have been vanquished, and foiled, and overcome by inward corruption, yet, coming self-condemned and humble in the dust to Jesus, will he refuse freely to forgive, yea, (and if you earnestly desire it, and come by faith alone to receive it,) to cleanse you from all unrighteousness?

You ask, How am I to learn the difference between sin and temptation? I own there is some difficulty here: I mean, in discerning between the motions of inbred sin, while it yet remains, and the temptations of Satan. Nothing but the Spirit of God, by his inward teaching, can make it clear to you. But this we know, whether our temptations are from our evil hearts when unrenewed, or from the enemy, if our will stand firm for God, and oppose all that would rise, or is offered contrary to his will, he is so far from accounting us guilty of sin, that he approves, and will reward the victory. But O! rest not without inward purity, and when your heart is cleansed from all sin, you will see more fully the nature of temptation.

Pray let us know if you are likely soon to get ordained; and if you are, whether you will accept the curacy now offered you. I hope you had a profitable time with Mr. Wesley. I had a precious season when he was here; and I think I never saw him so full of the Spirit of his Master, —so full of God. May the Lord fill your earthen vessel with all his fulness, and keep you till redemption's day, prays your affectionate cousin and friend,

H. A. Roe.

LETTER XXII.

To Miss Loxdale.

Macclesfield, May 20, 1780.

My very dear Friend,—How agreeable was the reception of your affectionate letter; but I am very sorry to find your health is so indifferent. My dear friend, let me advise you to take all the care you can of your body, for it is not *your own*, but the Lord's. And I am fully convinced we have no right to trifle with the precious talent of health, which is given us to improve to the glory of our God.

I every day experience fresh calls and fresh motives to praise and love our adorable Lord. Nor is my heart less moved at the gracious tenderness of his dealings with my dear sister. O my love, can you ever *now* distrust him for any thing? Surely such love hath destroyed unbelief forever: —surely you can *now* put no limits to his power and faithfulness—his grace his willingness to save. O praise him, and trust him forever.

"Look for his perfect love,
Look for his dear people's rest;
Hope to sit down with him above,
And share the marriage feast."

Yes, there I trust we shall meet and rejoice together!—there we shall sing, without weariness of body or soul, the wonders of his grace, and tell to all the listening heavenly throng, how rich redeeming love hath saved and ransomed, kept and preserved, delivered and strengthened, and at last brought us save where the wicked cease from troubling,—where the weary are at rest.

I rejoice that you are still pressing on to the attainment of that holiness which God calls you to. Only come by simple faith, and you shall soon experience that sweet rest,

"From self and sin set free."

I look upon this blessing as consisting, not so much in overwhelming joy, as humbling love: though joy, as an effect, will surely follow after. With me it was thus: I sunk into my own nothingness, and was humbled in the dust. Emptied of self and self-dependence, I submitted to be saved by grace. My depth of weakness was laid open to my view, but I cast myself on Jesus as my strength: emptied of all, I plunged by a simple act of faith, into his fulness of love, and found him all my salvation, and all my desire. When Satan suggested, Thou wilt soon lose what thou hast attained, I told him, Let my Lord see to that: "He that keepeth Israel, neither slumbereth nor sleepeth." Jesus is mine, with all his strength and fulness; and his grace is sufficient. I think, my dear friend, if you expect thus to be laid at the Saviour's feet, in humblest love and self-abasement, temptation that the blessing is something greater than you will be able to bear, will vanish, or at least, lose all its force; and, being thus humbled, thus united to Jesus, hang momentarily depending on him, and fear not but he will be your keeper. Faith is the bond of union, and in your union with him lies all your strength. He will water you every moment: yea, he will dwell in you as a well of water springing up into everlasting life. He is himself all you want: he is holiness—

he is heaven;—and he is yours! My soul longs for you.

> "O may you gain perfection's height,
> And into nothing fall!
> Be less than nothing in your sight,
> And Christ be all in all."

You will, you surely will! Nay, I have no doubt but you will soon prove this; for the Lord enlarges my heart in your behalf; and I trust your next will convey the happy tidings.

The Lord is peculiarly gracious to your unworthy friend, and condescends to bless my small labours for him. In visiting the sick, I found a great increase of love to God, and the souls for whom Jesus died. At some places, the neighbours coming in, the power of the Lord has been very present; and some of them, who before were asleep in sin, are crying out, "What must we do to be saved?" and so many fresh ones are sending to me daily, and begging I will call upon them, that it seems as if my employment would soon be too great for my bodily strength; but if he calls me to the work, he will give strength for it. My one desire is to spend and be spent for him. Our present maid has a deep concern upon her mind, and, I trust, will not rest short of pardon. She who has left us retains her peace, and walks uprightly. I cannot tell you the grateful feelings of my heart on this account. I thank you for your kind intention in the affair you mention—hope my God will reward every token of your undeserved love to your very unworthy, but sincere friend in him we love,

H. A. Roe.

LETTER XXIII.

To Miss Loxdale.

Macclesfield, Nov. 2, 1780.

My dear Friend,—I rejoice to find by the contents of your last, that you are pressing on to the attainment of that fulness which God calls you to enjoy; and I trust you will soon experience that blessed rest—from self and sin set free. The suggestion, that this blessing will be more than you can bear, is apparently from an enemy:—Ah, no! but it will enable *you* to bear all things. If you expect to be overwhelmed with exceeding great joy when you receive this, I think you are not expecting it in the way it is generally given. I look upon joy as an effect, or a fruit, and not the blessing itself. With me it was thus: I was humbled and self-emptied, and Jesus became my All in all! I felt myself all weakness, (yea, as I *never* did before,) and *he* was all my strength:—*I* all ignorance, *he* my wisdom :—*I* all nothingness, *he* all fulness: —*I* all helplessness, *he* omnipotence. I flew from myself, and escaped to Jesus: he received me graciously, freely, without money, without price, without worthiness, or faithfulness, and became all my salvation, and all my desire: humbled in lowest abasement at his boundless condescension, and filled with love, I felt that God was All and in all to me.

If the enemy were to suggest, though you were to feel this, you could not retain it, remember, you receive the blessing that it may keep you. You have only to hang momentarily dependent on Jesus, and he will be your keeper. Faith is the bond of union, and in your union with him lies your strength. He will water you every moment: yea, he will be in you as a well of water springing up into everlasting life. Jesus himself is all you want: —he is holiness—he is heaven—he is yours. O bring your polluted heart then, just as it is; and he will take full possession! O come by simple faith.

"Faith, mighty faith, the promise sees,
And looks to that alone:
Laughs at impossibilities,
And cries, 'It shall be done.'"

My state of health is better than it has been for some years; but, glory be to God, not half so well as my better part! O no!—so plentiful, so rich, is my Redeemer's love, that thought cannot fathom it: it seems but now beginning an eternity of bliss! O how sweet the service of such a Master, such a God!—how reasonable, how delightful all his paths! what solid, present peace!—what antepasts of heavenly joys, when we walk in communion with him! If we have any sorrow, any abiding doubts or fears, surely it is because we know not, as fully as we may know, the nature of a God of love. When we suffer him to reveal to us what he is, the lovely discovery transforms us into his image, and dispels every thought but love. Beholding him, we are changed into the same image, from glory to glory, even by the Spirit of the Lord.

My thirsty soul earnestly longs to know him more; but his love is unfathomable — yet every day brings me fresh discoveries — and I believe, what we are capable of receiving, he will reveal to all who love him. Open then your heart:—permit him, and he will give you such ravishing views of his beauty, as you never had before:--such views as will dissolve your heart in humble love, and fill your eyes with joyful tears. You will see and own,

> His every act pure blessing is,
> His path unsullied light."

May what I now feel be communicated to your

spirit, and God be your eternal portion, prays your affectionate sister and friend,

H. A. Roe.

LETTER XXIV.

To the Rev. J. Wesley.

January 6, 1782.

My very dear and honoured Sir,—I have still good news to tell you. Glory be to God, he is working graciously among us. Cousin Robert has been the instrument of four persons believing and receiving sanctification since I wrote last. One of them is a class leader, and in all who now profess this salvation, the change is very evident: they walk and follow after God as dear children, who truly love him with all their hearts. On the watch-night, a young woman, who experienced this salvation some years ago, but had lost it, received it again, as Mr. L. was saying, "Come by faith alone, if you have no worthiness, no fitness, believe only, and love shall make all things new. Delay not a moment: come now, and God will now destroy your inbred sin," &c.

Mr. L.'s word is made a blessing to very many. Several backsliders are restored, many convinced of sin, some converted, and a number longing to love God with an undivided heart, O! how I love thus to see the prosperity of Zion! I feel, indeed, a sweet assurance, through grace, that if all around me were careless and lukewarm, my soul would cleave to its only centre, with all its powers and affections; but how much more does it animate and enliven my spirit—how increase my joy—yea, how does it strengthen my hands, to see my dear brethren rejoicing and glorifying in the same precious salvation! and living as it becomes the redeemed of the Lord! There are persons, besides those I have mentioned, who can say, they feel nothing contrary to love, and are kept in perfect peace, but dare not yet profess that they are cleansed from all sin. I now meet two bands, and blessed be God we do not meet in vain. My soul dwells truly in a present heaven: the eternal Trinity is my God and my All. Every power and faculty is swallowed up in him.

> "I nothing want beneath, above,
> Happy in his perfect love."

I was surprised to hear that you had been at Chester and Wrexham; but, I trust, if you did not come to preach a funeral sermon for a friend, you came to shake Satan's kingdom.

We had a precious love feast. Some people tell me I always have precious times, and therefore judge others have so too; but I believe most that were present are agreed in this, that we have had no love feast like the last for many years. The select band is very lively. I have just been there, since I began my letter, and find another soul has received the witness of sanctification under Mr. L. this morning. I know you will join me to praise a God of love. Glory be to his holy name.

> "Our days of praise shall ne'er be past,
> While life, and thought, and being last,
> Or immortality endures."

In a day or two after I wrote to you, the pain in my face and head was suddenly removed in answer to prayer, and I have hardly felt it since. Till then I had no liberty to pray for its removal; but hearing that my bands never met during my confinement, and that several neglected to meet in the select band, whom I persuaded to go before, I said, "Lord, if thy unworthiest servant can be a blessing to their precious souls, remove this affliction, it is enough; and I will praise thee;" and the prayer was heard. In ten thousand instances I thus prove him a God that heareth and answereth prayer. I am filled with his goodness: I know not where to begin that praise that never shall end. I remain, dear and ever honoured sir, your unworthiest child in bonds of divine love,

H. A. Roe.

LETTER XXV.

To the Rev. J. Wesley.

April, 7, 1782.

Rev. and dear Sir,—Glory be to him, to whom all glory is ever due. I find him an ocean of love, without bottom or shore. He fills my happy soul with humble joy unknown. I dwell in his sacred presence: he dwells in my worthless heart, and all wrapt up in him I am.

Your last sermon on the Monday morning was made a peculiar blessing to very many precious souls, who say, they are sure *God* directed you to speak just as you did. Some others, indeed, say you preached a new doctrine, which they never heard before, except from cousin Robert Roe, respecting a *present* salvation; for they cannot believe a person can be justified or sanctified, unless they have undergone a *long* preparation, &c. Nay, they have even affirmed that he or myself *desired* you to preach that sermon, and to mention the person who was convicted, justified, and sanctified in twelve hours.

Why should we wonder at these things? The remains of the carnal mind in myself would once have strongly opposed the simplicity of faith. But O! how precious do I now prove the experience of those words, "I am crucified with Christ, nevertheless I live: yet not I, but Christ liveth in me; and the life that I now live in the flesh, I live by faith in the Son of God, who loved me, and gave himself for me." How mistaken are those who say, to speak much of living by faith, or of coming to be justified or sanctified by faith alone, is setting aside good works! For, can there be a Gospel faith which does not work by love? And does not love work all holy obedience? Excuse me, dear sir, I have been led to say more on this subject than I intended, my soul being peculiarly blessed since I began to write. Indeed, I often find it so when I write to you. He makes you in various ways an instrument of much good to my soul. How unworthy am I of his innumerable mercies! Praise the Lord, O my soul, and all that is within me praise his holy name.

A dear young woman, who received sanctification about three months ago, (who has been a follower of God for six years, and found his pardoning love at fourteen years old,) is now to all appearance on the borders of eternity; and no pen can describe the holy triumph of her soul. It is a blessing to be near her. On Tuesday last, as I was repeating and enforcing some of the passages in your last sermon, and a few parallel promises, another young woman, who had been seeking the blessing two years by works, was by faith brought into full liberty, and still retains the clear witness that she is cleansed from all sin. And while Mr. S—— offered a present salvation, a young woman was justified. J—— S—— writes word he has reason to praise God for his journey to Macclesfield, and is determined to preach an instantaneous present salvation from all sin. I trust your going to Chester will strengthen his hands. I cannot tell you how much I am filled with a spirit of prayer for you, and a sweet assurance that God is about to use you as a more peculiar instrument of good than he has ever done. I look for an abundant outpouring of the Spirit. Whenever I hear of souls being blessed, these words are applied, "Ye shall see greater things than these." May the fulness of the Triune God ever fill your happy soul! and may you still help me to love him more, prays your most unworthy, but ever affectionate,

H. A. Roe.

LETTER XXVI.

To the Rev. J. Wesley.

June 15, 1782.

Rev. and dear Sir,—I have been very ill, and my body brought very low since I saw you;

but those sweet words continually applied, caused me to rejoice with joy unspeakable and full of glory, viz., "According to my earnest expectation and my hope, that in nothing I shall be ashamed, but with all boldness, as always, so now also Christ shall be magnified in my body, whether it be by *life* or by *death;* for to me to live is Christ, and to die is gain." Oh, my dear sir, I never dwelt so much in God as I have done of late. My whole soul has been swallowed up in communion with the eternal Trinity, and peculiarly within this last fortnight, with the Holy Spirit. I have been led to pray in faith for a universal and pentecostal outpouring of His divine fulness; and it surely will descend.

Being lately on a visit to Nantwich, the dear people there, who knew me formerly, flocked around me with eagerness, and I held a prayer meeting with twelve or fourteen of them, for which I believe we shall praise God through eternity. A poor backslider was restored, and all present were filled with humble love and joy. I left five or six earnestly crying for a clean heart, and determined to meet among themselves, for all the classes were broken up or torn by divisions. When I came to Congleton on my return home, I found a young man who lately withstood cousin Robert Roe to his face, respecting sanctification by faith, now rejoicing in it, and declaring it boldly to all around. I spoke with several who felt the need of holiness, and two of them are able to testify "the blood of Jesus cleanseth them from all sin."

In this place, those who enjoy Christian perfection have had much opposition from some of their brethren. Four or five met constantly together to revile cousin Robert and all who profess it. But one of them now has been truly humbled before God, and received it himself in the very way he so much reviled, even by simple faith. And another of them says in his class, and publicly to all, that, if he had continued to revile them, he believes he should have been damned for it; but he is now determined never to rest till he receives it himself. Since you were with us, six or seven have been justified, and four or five sanctified. Cousin Robert preached at Keethlesum, about eight miles off, where one was justified and another sanctified. At Burslem he found many thirsting for holiness, some enjoying it, and others stirred up to seek it.

The children who professed sanctification when you were here, stand steadfast and unreprovable, though they have much opposition from those who do not believe the doctrine. Indeed, I believe it is a means of good to them, constraining them to walk and cleave so much the nearer to God, that he may give them wisdom and strength. For my own part, I find every trial or affliction has this blessed tendency; and as when a man is tossed in the sea, every boisterous wave sinks him lower, so when lost in the ocean of love, every severe trial, temptation, or afflictive dispensation serves to plunge me deeper into God. Still pray for me, dear, sir, and believe me ever your affectionate, though unworthy child,

H. A. Roe.

LETTER XXVII.

To the Rev. J. Wesley.

July 7, 1782.

My dear and honoured Sir,—Since my last I have been very ill, and thought I was on the borders of my heavenly country. O! with what joy did I feel this feeble body fail! How did my soul exult in the glorious prospect of eternity! My *every* faculty expanded, and all my large desires *eagerly* gasping for immortality; for the full and immediate fruition of my God. When most afflicted with pain and violent heart sickness, those words, *my God*, filled me with unutterable delight. I felt all the force of those other words,

> "Jesus comes with my distress,
> And agony is heaven."

O for a thousand tongues to praise him! O for a thousand lives to spend wholly for him! Yes, ardently as I long to see him as he is, I could be willing, if so poor a worm could bring glory to his blessed name, to live a thousand years. Indeed, my dear sir, I love him with a love that cannot be expressed, and yet I long to love him more—

> "Plunged in the Godhead's deepest sea,
> And lost in his immensity."

I see more and more lately into the extent of that promise, "What things soever ye desire when ye pray, believe that ye receive them, and ye shall have them." I have proved it in a thousand instances, and never knew it to fail in one. "If ye ask any thing in my name," says Jesus, "I *will* do it." What an open field, then, lies before us! Blessed be God, the work still goes forward, though all who profess holiness are strongly opposed, and their names cast out as evil. But we are enabled by grace to bear all things, and endure all things in a spirit of love. Cousin Robert, on entering his new house, had a meeting there, and it was a time much to be remembered. One received sanctification, and many were greatly established.

I have thoughts, if the Lord open a way, of going into Yorkshire. I leave myself in the Lord's hands, as I desire to spend and be spent for him alone. May He fill you with all his fulness; and in a particular manner, when you meet in conference, may the unction from above fill yours and every heart! May all go forth with strength renewed, and a plenitude of the Spirit be poured out on all flesh! I am now and ever, dear sir, your unworthy, but affectionate child,

H. A. Roe.

LETTER XXVIII.

To the Rev. Mr. Fletcher.

Dublin, Dec. 14, 1784.

Rev. and dear Sir,—I believe it will not be unacceptable to you to be informed how a God of love is blessing his dear people in this city. You have a peculiar right to expect this, because you were made, through mercy, the instrument of kindling a gracious flame in many hearts, and of preparing others to receive the message of salvation—a *present* salvation, even from *all* sin. Had not you and your dear partner been here before us, it is probable we should not have been received as we now are. But the sound of your Master's feet was behind you, and a gracious savour was left upon the minds of the people in general, so that when we came, we found them eager to embrace the *whole* Gospel. I had the clearest assurance, before we left England, that our appointment for Dublin was of the Lord, and every day brings me fresh proofs of it. It was also a kind Providence which brought us here on the very day that precious woman, Mrs. King (now Mrs. Johnson) was married, and, in consequence of which, went to reside at Lisburn. Had we arrived before the society suffered so great a loss, my poor services might not have been so acceptable; and had it been later, the minds of the people might have been grieved to excess. But the novelty of strangers first engaged their attention, and the word of the Lord then soon became a sin-killing and soul-saving word: so that now every one's cares and fears terminate in a determination to secure their own salvation.

Another great blessing is, Mr. Rogers and Mr. Blair (his fellow-labourer) are united as the heart of one man: Mrs. Blair, also, is a sister indeed to me in spirit and real affection, so that we are a family of love; and one small house serves us all.

And not the preachers only, but the stewards, leaders, and people, *all unite*, and have only one strife—how they may best promote each other's happiness and the cause of God. And glory, glory, glory be ever ascribed to Father, Son, and Holy Ghost, it *is* promoted! Sinners are snatched by grace as brands from the burning, and the kingdom of God and his Christ is set up in many believing hearts.

"Lo, the promise of a shower
 Drops already from above;
But the Lord shall shortly pour
 All the Spirit of his love."

In six weeks from the time of our first arrival, many were awakened, and nine received a clear sense of pardon: these returned public thanks, which greatly encouraged the seekers, and raised the expectation of all. As it was manifestly a time of refreshing from the presence of the Lord, it was thought expedient at our love feast, October 10, to give notes of admission, on that occasion, to many who were not as yet members of society, but appear desirous of salvation, so that near seven hundred souls were present; and a feast of love it was, such as I believe many will praise God for to all eternity! After several, who spoke with great freedom and simplicity, a poor penitent besought us with tears to pray for her. The kindlings of love which had been felt before now became a flame in every believing soul, and when fallen on our knees, the power of God descended of a truth: every corner of the house was filled with cries of "God be merciful to me a sinner," or "Praise the Lord, O my soul, who hath forgiven all mine iniquities!" Not one remained unaffected; and we have since found that seven were justified at that time, among whom was one that got a note of admittance in the morning, and several who came only with a faint desire were deeply convinced of sin. The next night another was justified under the word, and a second under the prayer, and a backslider healed; and soon after, while Mr. R—— explained and enforced, "Blessed are the poor in spirit, for theirs is the kingdom of heaven," dear sister R——, whom I am persuaded you well remember—for you took great pains to encourage and help her forward—even this poor, nervous, afflicted woman, who has been a seeker twenty-one years, laid hold of the promise by faith, and received the "knowledge of salvation by the remission of her sins;" and notwithstanding she is often greatly depressed by her bodily disorder, she is still enabled to claim her interest in redeeming blood. A poor vile young man, who had indulged himself in all kinds of sin with greediness, and, according to his own expression, "believed no God more supreme than himself," strayed into the chapel just as Mr. Rogers gave out the text, "Believe on the Lord Jesus Christ, and thou shalt be saved:" he was that hour cut to the heart, and is now earnestly seeking salvation, and has received much comfort. Under the same sermon one was justified, and another backslider healed.

Since this, a man and his wife came to preaching together, who had been seekers seven years, and their states nearly alike: they did not sit near each other, but were both set at liberty under the same sentence and in the same instant. They both ran to catch hold of Mr. R—— as he came from the pulpit, and there met each other, and rejoiced together with exceeding great joy. The man said he knew his wife was blest before they thus met, as well as he knew that himself was. Another person, who had been a backslider ten years, first into Antinomïan principles, and then into gross, open sin, fell lately into deep despair, and many times attempted to put an end to his life, but was often prevented by an almost miraculous providence. Friday, Nov. 12, was the last time, when he had placed a loaded pistol to his breast, and intended to discharge it the next moment; but these words came with power, "Why will ye die?" He instantly fell on his knees, and dropped the pistol. He came afterward to the preachers, who endeavoured to encourage him; and on the Tuesday following he was at our prayer meeting, where an agonizing spirit of prayer was given: he obtained *then* a comfortable hope of mercy, and at night, under Mr. Blair's preaching, was set at libetty. This he told me the next morning, with streaming eyes, and gratitude unspeakable.

Nov. 18, we had another love feast at Gravel-walk: it was a more wonderful season than even the former. We know of nine that we have reason to believe were justified; and many lukewarm professors were greatly stirred up. Two of these found peace in the blood of Jesus the week after, another on Sunday night last, who was a Papist, and another last night. A Jew is also convinced and converted; and from being, according to his sect, a Pharisee, is now zealous in his love to Jesus, though at the hazard of his life, for his own mother and other relations have attempted to murder him at different times.

One of sister Johnson's classes, and another, since now raised, are committed to my care. In the first of these are now thirty-eight members, in the latter thirty-six; and within the last quarter, ten of these have received a sense of pardon, and four others are enabled to love God with all their hearts. I have likewise undertook a class of young girls, from about nine to fourteen years of age. In a few weeks many of them began to feel awakenings, and a few were deeply convinced of sin. A month ago, one of these, ten years of age, received a clear sense of pardon : she told her companion of the same age, who prayed and wept, and would not be comforted, till she obtained the same blessing, which was in a few days. When the rest heard this, they were greatly stirred up, and the following Sabbath two more were as clearly justified, one of eleven, the other thirteen years of age. There is a great and visible change in all these, and they speak clearly and experimentally. Seven more are under conviction, and I doubt not will soon be brought into liberty. In all, we have certain accounts, since we came, of forty-six justified, eight sanctified, and one hundred added to the society.

As to myself, I never was so truly happy in *every* sense : happy in increasing union and communion with Father, Son, and Spirit, and sunk into depths of humble love. I feel my unworthiness and nothingness indescribable; yet, stupendous grace! all the communicable fulness of a Triune God is mine. I feel the equal love of the undivided Deity. As I worship the Father, so I worship the Son and the Holy Ghost—my God—

my all in all. I am happy too, in one who is truly a help to me both for soul and body, for time and eternity, and who greatly encourages me in all my labours: happy in my situation, among a lively, affectionate people, who make it their study how to manifest their love; nor have we one jarring string among us. O may we ever be kept humble at the Saviour's feet, and all our blessings (as through grace they do) prove only a scale to heavenly love. Please to remember us, in the most affectionate manner, to dear Mrs. Fletcher. We entreat an interest in both your prayers. When I last asked this favour at Leeds, I believe you granted it, and that your petitions were answered. Once more, then, pray for us, and believe me, dear sir, in Gospel love, your willing servant,

H. A. Rogers.

LETTER XXIX.

To Mr. Matthias Joyce.

Dublin, May 1, 1785.

Dear Brother,—My soul greatly rejoices in your joy. I do join with you in that song which shall never end, "Unto him that hath loved us, and washed us from our sins in his own blood, be glory forever and ever." O how precious is that life of simple faith you describe and possess! Go on, favoured servant of the Lord, and he will show you greater things than these. I do not mean there is any thing greater or higher than love; but in this ocean, what heights, what lengths, what depths! what immeasurable degrees, even in that communion with a Triune God, which it is our privilege to prove. I know you feel something of what I mean, even of equal love of Father, Son, and Holy Ghost. This we cannot *properly* feel till freed from inbred sin. Where sin remains, there cannot be that close union with the Father I now speak of; but sin destroyed, and we know the meaning of those words, "The Father himself loveth you;" and again, "I and my Father will come, and make our abode with you." Yea, the whole Deity flows in upon us. Consider that blessed scripture, "Know ye not that your body is the temple of the Holy Ghost, which is in you, which ye have of God, and ye are not your own? For ye are bought with a price." By whom? By Jesus: therefore glorify God the Father—even the Triune God—Father, Son, and Spirit, with your bodies and your spirits, which are his.

"Drawn, and redeem'd and seal'd,
We'll praise the One and Three,
With Father, Son, and Spirit fill'd
To all eternity."

I hope the Lord will carry on a gracious work in Drogheda. I am glad to hear you see so good a beginning. I never heard of so universal a revival, as I am told by many is now spreading through England, Ireland, and America; and yet I think it is but the beginning of what the Lord will shortly do. Let us not be weak in faith, and we shall see showers of blessings. The promise shall surely be accomplished; and, perhaps, hastened speedily by the universal cry of God's dear children: "The earth shall be filled with knowledge of the glory of God, as the waters cover the sea."

I doubt not but you have had a precious season with Mr. Wesley. I think I never saw him more truly filled with his blessed Master's Spirit. We have heard of two souls convinced of sin, and eight justified under him, while in Dublin; and, blessed be God, two more, since he left us, can praise a reconciled God, and one is set at perfect liberty, besides three more of the children, who have received remission of sins. I find, blessed be God, my own soul is as a watered garden; and I have access to a spring, whose waters fail not, from which I ever drink fresh supplies. O what wells of salvation!—what an unfathomable ocean of love!

A trifling affliction of body has, I think, sunk me deeper into God. Such heartfelt, solid peace, such inward nearness to, and fellowship with him, I have proved the last fortnight, as is better felt than described. It has been much of

> "That sacred awe which dares not move,
> And all the silent heaven of love."

O for an enlarged heart! O for ten thousand tongues to praise my God! As it is said, "In that day ye shall know that I am in the Father, you in me, and I in you:" so it is—the blessed day is come: I do know it: I do feel it. I know what it is to dwell in the Father, through the Son, and by the uniting power of the Holy Ghost, and ever worship an undivided Deity. These words have often been spoken to my heart, and I feel them now applied: "All that I have is thine:" yes, my Lord, and I possess a drop out of the ocean. If I had much more at present, it would lay me dead at thy feet; but all is mine in happy reversion, and what my weakness *can* bear, thou wilt impart. O make thyself room, and more of heaven bestow! Thou wilt, thou dost enlarge my heart. I grasp the God I seek, the God I love, the God I shall enjoy to all eternity! O what a word is that! A Triune God my own to all eternity! Yes, yes, he is. Wonder, O heavens! Be astonished, O earth! Be humble, O my soul; and help me to praise him, all ye hosts above! O that all the world knew the riches of Divine love! O that all believers would give him all their heart!

My brother, let you and me covenant afresh with God, to spread the savour of his grace with all our most enlarged powers, especially his full salvation, that rest from all sin, that rest of perfect love, received by simple faith, and by faith *alone.* I think I never read any thing wherein that blessing is more clearly described, than Mr. Wesley's sermon in the March and April Magazines for this year, which I believe will do much good; for, how many have been discouraged by not knowing and considering that one point, "Sin is a wilful transgression of a known law." If this were the constant rule by which we judged of what we feel, how many vain reasonings would be answered—how many subtle suggestions of the enemy? A mistake through ignorance, or through an imperfect memory, together with various hateful injections from an enemy: a dulness of spirit, occasioned by the body; or a flutter of spirit, occasioned by surprise, &c., none of these, I say, or all of them put together, would then appear a sufficient reason why a soul should cast away its confidence respecting what the Lord has wrought. Seeing these are consistent with pure love, they are not wilful transgressions of a known law.

May the Lord bless you in your soul and labours, still more abundantly, prays, dear brother, your friend and sister in Jesus,

H. A. Rogers.

LETTER XXX.

To the Rev. J. Wesley.

November, 21, 1782.

My dear and honoured Sir,—I have been much indisposed since I wrote last, but I think it is not wholly my old disorders. I believe since my cousin's death my nerves have been much affected, because any thing sudden will occasion tremours, which I can no otherwise account for, at the same time that my soul is in perfect peace and solidly happy, as also many times there is a dulness and stupidity, when at the same moment I feel a direct witness that it proceeds not from any abatement of the ardours of love divine.

Glory be to God, I feel this as a well of water ever springing up afresh, and I know the work of his grace takes still deeper root than ever in my worthless heart; and though at times the enemy suggests, if this nervous disorder takes hold of me, as on my late dear cousin, I shall not rejoice evermore, as I have done hitherto, yet I am enabled to answer him in the power of faith, "My strength shall be equal to my day." If he afflicts, I have His word of promise, "My grace is sufficient for thee." Nor can I have one painful fear: I know in whom I trust.

I was yesterday employed in visiting members of the classes with Mr. R.—a business which has been much neglected here of late, and which, I trust, will be made a blessing to many. I find it profitable. Mr. R. has suffered much through the prejudices of some; but he is as gold purified in the fire: it has been an unspeakable blessing. It has cut off his intimacy with those, who would, perhaps, have proved snares and hinderances to his soul and his labours; and united him more closely to the little flock, who are rich in faith, and heirs of the kingdom. I believe he has acted faithfully to God, to souls, and to you.

The select band is now the most precious meeting in which I ever assembled. There are forty-eight members, all truly and happily walking in

20

the narrow path: thirty-five, I have no doubt, enjoy perfect love. About six have enjoyed it before, and are now seeking it afresh, and the rest, who never enjoyed it, are thirsting for it more than gold or silver. We are all, too, united in one spirit. All in this little company are helpers of each other's joy.

I love Mrs. R. much: she is, indeed, one of the excellent ones of the earth. I feel much for you respecting the affair at Birstal: may the Lord strengthen your hands, and in doing so, defend his own cause. Your warfare shall surely yet be glorious, though it be through briers, or thorns, or scorpions. The Lord still reigneth, and will defend his dear servants. Surely he is purging his Zion, and will remove the chaff, and leave himself a pure and a peaceable remnant, whose motto shall be, "Holiness to the Lord."

The openness of my disposition has sometimes brought me into inconveniences; but with you I believe it will not, and therefore I speak freely. I am very unapt to suspect any person of guile, but experience tells me, all are not to be trusted. I feel I need the continual unction of the Holy One to teach me. O pray that this may be ever given to your ever affectionate, unworthy child in a precious Jesus,

H. A. Rogers.

LETTER XXXI.

To the Rev. J. Wesley.

CORK, Jan. 24, 1788.

MY DEAR AND HONOURED SIR,—Never had one, so every way undeserving, so much reason to praise a God of love. Day after day—nay, every hour I breathe, he loadeth me with his multiplied mercies; yea, they are more in number than the hairs of my head. If I did not love him with all my consecrated powers, and momentarily offer up my *little all;* if I were not resolved to embrace every opportunity to spend and be spent in service so divine, I should of all mortals be the most inexcusable; for O! his love to me is boundless—I prove it an ocean without a bottom or a shore. The sweet communion I have with Father, Son, and Spirit, is unspeakable! and whatsoever I ask of God in faith, it is done. In God I live: in him I move: by him I act and speak, and it is in him alone I enjoy all my mercies.

Since I wrote last we have fresh cause for praise. The Lord is doing wonders among us here. It seems very likely, at present, we shall see as great a work here as at Dublin. At the visitation of the classes this Christmas, we found the society increased from three hundred and ninety-seven members (the number it contained last conference) to five hundred and four; and the number of classes are increased from twenty-four to thirty; and fifty-six souls have found peace with God since September last. The Christmas festival was a most blessed season. On Christmas morning, at four o'clock, the preaching house, was well filled, and God was truly present to bless—many were awakened, and four justified at the watch-night on New-Year's Eve. Several also found pardon at the love feast, and many witnessed a good confession; but the time of renewing our covenant exceeded all: fourteen souls were that day born of God: some at their classes, and the rest at that sweet solemn season of the covenant. The house was truly shaken (I mean every soul therein) by the power of God. I believe none present, preachers or people, will ever forget it. I trust I never shall. It was none other than the antechamber of glory to my soul—the house of God—the gate of heaven. O how was I filled with his presence! how did I bask in the beams of his love! how was I made to feel his immeasurable fulness all my own, through covenant blood divine! Several were perfected in love, and several backsliders restored. Since this, between thirty and forty have joined the society; several of whom date their deep awakenings from the covenant night. Mr. Rogers saw it expedient on that occasion to give notes of admittance to some who were halting between two opinions; and most of them were then, and are now, determined to be the Lord's.

My class being now divided, I met twenty on a Tuesday, and eighteen on a Friday. My heart is knit to these precious souls; and, blessed be God, we never meet in vain. The Lord is pleased to bless me in all my weak labours, and he knows I ascribe to him all the good done, and all the glory. I do lie at his feet, and am astonished at his condescending love to such a worm. Last Sunday evening, thanksgiving notes were sent by four, for a sense of pardon received last week and we hear of two more, who received the same blessing that day. Several of our dear friends, who know and love the Lord, have entered into a solemn covenant with him, and with each other, never to rest till they experience perfect love. One of these has since received the blessing, and seems in all things a new creature indeed.

We have got another new place for preaching, in a very convenient and populous part of this city. Mr. R. preached there the first time, a fortnight ago, and told the congregation he would meet in a class as many as were determined to forsake their sins, and seek the kingdom of God with all their hearts. Fourteen offered themselves, and were admitted on trial; and since then, five more, so that there is a new class meets there, of nineteen members. Great good is likely to be done, as most of the hearers that attend are strangers, who, perhaps, would never have heard elsewhere. We have now five preaching houses, at different parts and proper distances; and I believe we shall see a glorious harvest of precious souls. In all, since we came, seventy-seven are enabled to rejoice in a reconciled God, and many more seem just ready to step into the pool of redeeming mercy.

We hear good news respecting the work of God in Dublin, and in other parts of the kingdom. O may the Lord ride on in the glorious and triumphant chariot of Gospel grace and salvation, till all be subdued! My dear Mr. Rogers begs me to send his duty and love to you, and joins me in daily intercessions at a throne of grace, that you may be filled with the fulness of every new covenant blessing. I am, my dear sir, your ever obliged and truly affectionate, though unworthy friend and servant,

H. A. ROGERS.

LETTER XXXII.

To one who had set out fair for the kingdom of heaven, but at this time was grown languid and faint in spiritual things, and likely to return to the spirit and customs of the world.

CORK, Jan. 16, 1789.

MY DEAR FRIEND,—I have long desired, in the bowels of love, to see your soul advance in spiritual life; and having considered your state in secret, and with solemn prayer before God, I think duty calls me to try if, by freely and fairly expostulating with you, I may, through grace, be an instrument of stirring you up to seek the Lord afresh, and in that manner which alone will avail to your salvation; even so as experimentally to feel him your God, reconciled in Christ Jesus. Short of this you cannot be happy —you are not *safe*. An unpardonable sinner is under all the curses of a broken law, especially that sentence, "Cursed is every one who continueth not in all things written in the book of the law, to do them :" which stands in full force against that soul who has never taken refuge in the one and only propitiation for sin, even Jesus Christ the righteous; for no man can come unto the Father but by him ; neither is there salvation in any other. He himself assures us, "If ye die in your sins, where I am ye cannot come," and "Except a man be born again, he cannot see the kingdom of God." Bear with one who loves you, then, while I ask a few serious questions, as in the presence of God, before whom we must shortly both appear, and in whose sight all things are naked and open.

Are you now as earnest in seeking the pardon of all your sins as you were when, two years ago, you came with deep penitential sorrow and floods of tears to join the society of God's people? Oh that you could answer me in the affirmative. You well remember the language of your soul *then* was, "The remembrance of my sins is grievous to me, the burden of them is intolerable:—a wounded spirit who can bear?" You saw yourself a barren fig tree, a cumberer of the ground—a brand ready for the burning; and that infinite justice must have sentenced you to the pit from whence there is no return, if unmerited mercy in your Divine Advocate had not prayed, "Let it still alone." Your cry was, with the publican, "God be merciful to me a sinner," and with sinking Peter, "Lord save, or I perish." For a time you acted agreeably to such convictions—promising was the prospect, and fair the bud of grace: the arms of love were ready to receive you, and angels even began to rejoice over a repenting sinner. But ah! where are *now* those fervent desires—those ardent breathings after God—those restless longings, which nothing but the knowledge of his love could satisfy? Where is that restless spirit of prayer, that love to every ordinance and means of grace! How seldom was your seat in God's house then empty? Where is fled that deep seriousness which then ever sat on your countenance, and accompanied all your conversation?—that deadness to worldly company, worldly concerns, and the good will of worldly persons? In short, that whole deportment, which loudly spoke to all, that the language of your soul was,

"None but Christ to me be given,
None but Christ in earth or heaven."

My dear friend, I could weep over you while I see the sad reverse! Alas! it is not with you now as it was *then:* you seem to have lost that blessed power, that weeping penitence, that happy victory over all the charms a delusive world can boast! Say, is it not the case? Have you not sunk back into careless ease and indifference, with respect to heavenly things—a false peace, and your spirit become light and trifling? You can now converse on worldly subjects, even as others, and join in their empty laughter; yea, and prefer such company to the lovers of Jesus. O why is this awful change? Is God no longer a just and holy God to punish sin? Is he no longer a God of truth who hath said, "The soul that sinneth, it shall die?"—"Except ye be converted, and become as little children, ye shall in no case enter into the kingdom of heaven?" Is Christ and salvation, pardon here and glory hereafter, no longer desirable? If otherwise, why, then, are you neglecting and trifling with your most important concerns? Why are you returned to that which cannot satisfy? I tremble for you! O cry mightily to God, and rest not till you are again filled with that hungering and thirsting that cannot be satisfied but in an experimental knowledge of Jesus crucified, and his nature written on your heart.

As the first step to a recovery, let me beseech you *now* lift up your soul to him who discerneth in secret, and ask him, Lord, why is thy striving Spirit departed, or just departing from me? Yea, ask your own soul, Wherein did you *resist* and *grieve* that Spirit? He convinced you, he that would follow Christ so as to be saved by him, must forsake and give up *all*. But were you faithful and obedient to these teachings? Did you not, after a little, begin to keep something back, and say, is it not a *little one?* Was there no creature delight, no beloved companion you had forsaken for Christ's sake, which you have again yielded to, and taken pleasure in?—pleasing yourself with the hope that this Agag might be spared: whereas the Spirit of Truth hath said, "The companion of fools shall be destroyed:" and you are expressly commanded, "Come ye out from among them, and be ye separate, saith the Lord:" on this condition only, saith he, "I will receive you, and will be a Father unto you, and ye shall be my sons and my daughters, saith the Lord Almighty."

While you obeyed the voice of God, you could not go to balls, plays, or cards; for his Spirit taught you, "She that liveth in pleasure is dead while she liveth." But, have you not been prevailed upon?—or, if not, have you not, in what is called *little things*, conformed to the world?—such as fashionable adorning of the body, even in *immodest* as well as *costly* array? whereas, the command is plain and positive, and easy to be understood, "That women adorn themselves in modest apparel, with shamefacedness and sobriety—not with broidered hair, or gold, or costly array;" and again, "Be not conformed to this world, but be ye transformed by the renewing of your mind;" that is, if ye would "prove the acceptable will of God." Now, consider a moment, after (contrary to checks of conscience) indulging yourself in any of these things, could you pray as before? nay, were even your desires after God and spiritual things as lively and vigorous? Ah no! the Spirit of God was grieved, and he moved not upon your spirit: he left you to yourself, and you neglected duty more and more, till now, I fear, you can at times plead with the world you had forsaken, against singularity, against shutting yourself up from carnal company, and subjecting yourself to the sneers and disdain of those who see no beauty in Christ and salvation. Alas! how changed! how trifling did you once account the scoffs and frowns of such: yea, not worth a thought, when you first felt your state as a lost sinner: then you would cry,

> "Let earth and all its trifles go:
> Give me, O Lord, thyself to know,
> Give me thy precious love."

And are you happier now? Are you in a safer state—more fit for heaven? It is true you may have less fears of hell; but this is no good sign, for you have more *cause* to fear. You were then a *repenting* sinner; and had you persevered to seek, you would, before now, have been a child of God, and an heir of glory. But you are now a *trifling* sinner, and, O think a moment! what is it you are trifling with?—with God that made you—with Jesus, who shed his blood for you—with the Holy Ghost, who awakened, and hath been long striving with you: you are trifling with eternal happiness and eternal pain, and with your own immortal soul. This is an important subject, and demands your immediate attention : in a little time it will be too late to reflect or repent. O, then, as you value eternal life, stop ! O go not a step further from your God ; but return, with weeping and supplication to the feet of him you have pierced —him who yet prays for you, or you had been in hell :—to him who is yet willing to wash you in his own blood, and by the power of that Spirit you have grieved, save you from *all*, even your most besetting sin. But delay not, or he may swear, "You shall *never* enter into his rest." Speedily cut off the right hand—pluck out the right eye—take up your cross, and give up all. You cannot serve God and mammon : you cannot be a friend of the world and not be the enemy of God : you cannot indulge the spirit of the world, without losing your own soul. And be not deceived : if you follow the fashions and vain customs thereof, *you have* the spirit of it and love it more than God. "If as the world you live, you as the world will die." God forbid this should be the case ! O fly for refuge to the hope set before you ! and let me have joy over you in time, and in the day of eternity.

I have, however, warned you ; and, perhaps, it may be your last warning, your last call, if you should now neglect. God will not always strive !

He may, before you are aware, lay the axe at the root of the tree, and cut it down. O that you may henceforward bring forth the fruits he requires—first, the fruits of repentance, then the genuine fruits of faith. Then shall I meet you with joy, among the sheep at the right hand of yonder dazzling throne!—when the Ancient of days shall sit, and the books shall be opened—when the righteous shall shine as the sun in the kingdom of their Father, and be as pillars in his house above, to go out no more! Amen, Lord Jesus, prays yours in real affection,

H. A. ROGERS.

LETTER XXXIII.

To Mrs. Condy.

CORK, Oct. 11, 1789.

MY DEAR FRIEND AND SISTER,—I believe you are well able to answer your own questions. However, as you desire it, I will freely tell you my thoughts on what *we* call Christian perfection. We do not mean hereby, the perfection of God, of angels, of disembodied spirits, or of Adam while innocent. But we mean that perfection of which *our* natures are capable through the grace of our Lord Jesus Christ, the second Adam. We are under the law to Christ, viz., the law of love —the law of liberty; or in other words, the covenant of grace. Whosoever loveth the Lord his God with all his heart, and mind, and soul, and strength, and his neighbour as himself, fulfilleth this law. The lowest degree of this salvation is to have all contrarieties to this love cast out of the soul. We may be said thus to love him with a *pure heart,* when proud *self,* and great *I,* are slain, and we feel only humility: when anger, fretfulness, and impatience, are no more; but we ever feel a meek and quiet spirit: when *I will,* and *I will not,* is all brought into subjection to the will of our heavenly Father; and our will is, that *he* should reign over us: when he really does regulate and govern our passions, affections, and desires—inordinate desires, and inordinate creature love being no more; and, lastly, unbelief (and consequently all tormenting fear, and painful anxiety) is wholly cast out. But, after all this, it remain that we go forward, that we grow in grace, till we be not only emptied of sin, but filled with all the fulness of God.

The moment any soul is justified, it is free from the power or dominion of outward and of inward sin; and may hold fast that blessed freedom to the end. But supposing a person does this, such a one will feel a mixture of evil propensities, tempers, affections, and desires, which defilement is so rooted in our nature, that none but *Jehovah Jesus* can cast out "the strong man armed, and spoil all his armour wherein he trusted." It is true, we may mortify, resist and keep *under* those evils; but Jesus alone can pluck up and destroy every plant and root which his Father planted not. We may gradually grow in grace and holiness, and hereby increase in victoriously subjecting the enemy within; but Jesus alone can *slay* the man of sin.

All salvation, too, is by faith alone as the instrument. If, then, we must be saved by faith, it is in a moment, and the *present* moment, if not our own fault; for, what wait we for, who are the children and heirs of God? and therefore heirs of the promises, which are all to us "yea and amen in Christ Jesus." If we wait for more worthiness—to suffer more, to do more, to be more *fit*, then we are seeking to be sanctified by these things, viz. by works. But if we believe we can only obtain the blessing by grace, through faith, and this salvation is the free gift of God, then let us be consistent with ourselves: let us expect it by faith—expect it in a moment, and expect it *now*—which are one and the same thing, and are inseparable. To be dying, and to be dead, indeed, unto sin, are two things. Be not *you*, my sister, content with the former: "A man may be dying for some time," says Mr. Wesley, "yet, properly speaking, he does not die till the moment the soul is separated from his body, and in that instant he begins to live the life of eternity: in like manner, a man may be dying unto sin for some time; yet he is not 'dead indeed unto sin' till sin be separated from the soul, and in that instant he begins to live the life of *pure love*." O, be you "dead indeed unto sin," and alive unto God, through Jesus Christ your Lord!"

It is the blood of Jesus alone cleanseth from all sin:—not penal sufferings, not mortifications of any kind, not any thing *we have*, not grace already received, not any thing *we are*, or *can be;* nor death, nor purgatory; no, not the purgatory of all our doings and sufferings, and strivings put together; no, no—Christ is the procuring, meritorious cause of all our salvation. He alone forgiveth sins, and he alone cleanseth from all unrighteousness. Faith is the only condition, and it shares in the Omnipotence it dares to trust. "*All things are now ready*," is the Gospel message; and Jesus saveth all them to the uttermost that come unto God by him. "I will, be thou clean," is his language to every seeking leprous soul!—to you, if not already cleansed.

Joy in the Holy Ghost is a blessed fruit of this salvation; but divine joy is not always rapturous: we may be sorrowful, yet always rejoicing, and there is suffering love, as well as exulting love. A person saved as above, may experience a degree of heaviness or dullness for a season, through bodily infirmities, close trials, or sundry temptations; but such a one cannot walk in darkness. Likewise, many mistakes are consistent with this state—I mean errors in judgment, and failures in memory; yet the will stands firm for God, and the intention is always single. Involuntary sins, (as some call them,) or sins of ignorance, (except the ignorance be wilful,) are not breaches of the law of love—for these things we have an Advocate with the Father, Jesus Christ the righteous, who is our propitiation, and washes our holiest duties in his own blood:—to whom we will ever give honour and glory. I am, my dear sister, yours in the bonds of pure love,

H. A. ROGERS.

LETTER XXXIV.

To one lately emerged out of Arian darkness.

CORK, Nov. 5, 1789.

MY DEAR MISS D.,—I received the favour of yours, and rejoice that you know in whom you have believed, and that your face is now Zionward. Go on, my dear sister: it is a blessed path: the goodly land is before—the land of sacred liberty, and glorious rest from all sin. Oh that you may soon prove, by happy experience, "perfect love casteth out all [slavish] fear!" and that the deepest humiliation before God, on account of our ignorance, helplessness, and unworthiness, is not only consistent *with*, but inseparable *from*, rejoicing evermore; for the ground of that rejoicing is, that he who hath loved, and washed me from my sins in his *own blood*, hath all the honour and glory, and is all in all forever, while I sink a poor woman at his feet—overwhelmed at his free unmerited grace—grace that plucketh me from the gulf beneath—reconciled a poor guilty rebel to her God—changed the leopard's spots, and made the Ethiop white. Thus, the more deep our sense of unworthiness, the more precious is Jesus, our interceding Advocate with the Father, who, in his exalted human nature, ever liveth to intercede for us, until that day when he shall deliver up the kingdom (viz. his mediatorial office) to God, even the Father, and the glorious Godhead of Father, Son, and Holy Ghost, shall be all in all forever. O, the preciousness of such a High Priest, such a Saviour, such a Counsellor, such a King! O for more heartfelt union with him—more of the power of his transforming love! Blessed promise, "He that hungereth and thirsteth after righteousness, shall be filled."

You have heard, I doubt not, of precious Mr. Fletcher's death, and how he proclaimed with his latest breath—GOD IS LOVE! O that we may be filled as he was with his heavenly Master's Spirit. *There* was a witness of the power of grace! a living and a dying witness that Jesus can save to the uttermost. Let me exhort, my dear friend, to come just as you are to the open fountain of his precious blood; and how soon may you feel the merit of Him you were once taught to despise, made of God unto you not only *wisdom* and *righteousness*, but also *sanctification* and *redemption*.

You see how freely I write, as if I had known you seven years. I hope you will follow my example in this, and let me know the particulars of your spiritual state, that I may rejoice yet more in your joy. My love and my dear partner's attend you. "May He that liveth, and was dead, who is the First and the Last—the bright and the morning Star," be the portion of your happy soul, prays your invariable friend,

H. A. ROGERS.

LETTER XXXV.

To Mr. Holy, of Sheffield.

CORK, March, 12. 1790.

DEAR SIR,—I have so long been silent, that I am almost ashamed to write at all. I can only say, I am more fully engaged than you can easily imagine; and more so every day. As to farther apologies, I really have not time to make them, and must rely on your good nature to excuse me. It gave me real pleasure to hear of the prosperity of your soul. I cannot doubt, from the description you gave, but the Lord hath put you in possession of what you so long desired, and you can *now* love him with all your heart; or, in other words, from moment to moment, with all your present powers. What, with all your strivings, you could not do before, viz., keep your mind from sinful wanderings, and the rising of evil tempers, fix your eye on things above—fix your affections there—this you now find is done by the power of God through faith. It is not *you* that now live, but Christ liveth in you; and your tempers, will, affections, passions, and desires, move in the will of God, sweetly attracted and governed by divine love. You feel you are helpless; but Jesus is almighty, and faith makes all his omnipotence your own. You are tempted; but sin, though offered with a pleasing bait, can find no entrance; for lo! the Lord your keeper stands omnipotently near, and till our *will* gives way we have not sinned. What some call *involuntary* sins, or sins of ignorance, we know would be breaches of that perfect law, adapted and suitable to the perfect body and perfect soul of Adam while innocent: his perfect knowledge gave him at one glance to see how he ought to act in all things; and if he acted contrary to this perfect knowledge, he sinned. But we (even when sanctified) are not perfect in knowledge, and therefore an all-wise and gracious God hath put us under a law or covenant adapted to our capacity, and which our renewed natures *are* capable of, even the law of love—love to God and every soul of man. To keep *this* law is Christian perfection. Love is the fulfilling of the law: involuntary sins, therefore, or sins of ignorance, are not sins in the Gospel sense; but to him that believeth any thing to be sin, though otherwise unessential, to him it is sin. This you know; and while you keep the law of liberty—the law of love, you feel your many weaknesses and short comings are all atoned for by the prevailing, ever-pleading blood of Jesus; and in this sense it is we every moment need the merit of his death.

I have had a touch of the fever and sore throat, lately so very prevalent in this city; but how tenderly hath the Lord sweetened all my pain, by the divine consolations of his love and constant presence: I think affliction was never so sweet before: he continually spoke to my heart, "All that I have is thine," so that every moment I was swallowed up in love and praise. My dear partner joins me in Christian love, and believe me, dear sir, to be your sincere friend and sister in Jesus,

H. A. Rogers.

LETTER XXXVI.

To a Friend.

London, Dec. 5, 1792.

My dear Sister,—As our blessed Lord has again restored me to a little strength, I feel renewed desires to devote it all to him. Wishing to be of some little use to the afflicted among his dear saints, in the course of my visits yesterday morning, I called upon Mrs. Jacques, (a poor woman, only three doors from our Spitalfields chapel,) and I was thankful I did so. She gave me a pleasing, affecting account of her husband, who died a month ago. Hoping and praying it may prove as great a blessing to your soul as it has been to mine, I here relate the particulars.

They had been married five years. For two years after their marriage they lived reputably; when it pleased the Lord to afflict Mr. Jacques with a palsy, so that he was unable to work; and about eighteen months ago he had a second stroke, which took away the use of one side entirely; and he was then confined to his bed. A blood-vessel was strained, or broke, which affected his throat, and formed a lump there as big as the head of a child. This affliction reduced him to deep poverty; but they were assisted by kind friends, who also visited and prayed constantly with them. While in health, Mr. Jacques had frequently heard the Methodists, and was enlightened respecting the way of salvation; and during his sickness, he earnestly sought the Lord; but his evidence was never clear, till a little before his death. His wife knew the Lord in her youth, but was a backslider in heart from his love; yet she earnestly desired salvation for her dying husband; and would often say, "My dear, how is it with your soul? Have you confidence in God?" &c. He would answer, "I am not happy: I have no assurance." She asked, "Do you think he has power to save you?" He said, "O yes, but I want to know he *does* save me!" Several friends prayed with him, and for him; yet the cloud remained until the Monday evening before he died. As one of our friends went into his room that night, he cried out, "Lord, save thy poor, helpless servant this night! O visit me with salvation under the prayer of this thy servant: pardon my sins, and heal my guilty soul!" The Lord heard; and before his friend rose up from prayer, so delivered him, that he cried aloud, "Now I am happy! Now I *know* Jesus has forgiven me *all*, and I shall be with him forever! I am happy! I am happy!" Thus he went on for some time. To his wife he said, "Trust the Lord, and be resigned, and seek his forgiveness with all your heart. Are you resigned?" She said, "I cannot give you up." "Not resigned!" said he, with great concern, "you *must* be resigned, for I *shall* be taken from you: I shall die this night, therefore resign me quickly!" After lying composed a little, he bid them pray. A person present did so; but he bid them pray again! They asked, "Are you not happy?" He said, "O yes, I am; but you have need yet to pray—the time is very short!" They prayed again; but he turned to his wife, and said, "Do you pray." She said, "Lord, help me to pray." And she found power earnestly to entreat the Lord to finish his work, and if any thing remained to be done, speedily to make an end of sin. This satisfied him; and he said, "That is *right*:—thank thee: the Lord is here, and I shall soon be happy forever!"—further adding, "I have much to say to thee, and the time is very short. Are you resigned?" She said, "I hope I am." "Well," said he, "that is right: then I shall soon go! Trust God, and he will take care of thee." After lying a little, with his eyes closed, he cried, "Sing—sing—I am just going!" They could not sing for tears: he seemed displeased, and cried, "Will none of you sing?" They could not answer him, and he said to his wife, "What! will not *you* sing? You ought not to weep, but to *sing*, when you see me going to God?" And then he gave out, and sung with a loud voice,

"Salvation, O the joyful sound!
What pleasure to our ears!" &c.

After which he lay composed a little, then started up, and said, "*There* is the Lord Jesus! Betsey *there* is the Lord Jesus!" And to another he said, "See! *there* he is!—The Lord Jesus!—I am going!"—and immediately dropped, as it were, asleep into his arms; for he spoke no more.

My soul was comforted by the above relation. O what is all below compared with a death like this! What are trials, which are but for a moment, when the joy which is set before us is so exceeding abundant! The poor widow now desires to meet class with me, and I bid her come. May she be joined to the Lord in bonds never to be broken. I am, my dear friend, yours in our common Lord, H. A. ROGERS.

LETTERS FROM THE REV. JOHN WESLEY TO MRS. ROGERS.

LETTER I.

WHITEHAVEN, May 3, 1776.

WITH pleasure I sit down to write to my dear Miss Roe, who has been much upon my mind since I left Macclesfield. Once I saw my dear friend, Miss Beresford: when I came again, she was in Abraham's bosom. Once I have seen her living picture, drawn by the same hand, and breathing the same spirit, and I am afraid I shall hardly see you again, until we meet in the garden of God. But if you should gradually decay, if you be sensible of the hour approaching when your spirit is to return to God; I should be glad to have notice of it, wherever I am, that if possible I might see you once more before you

> Clap your glad wing and soar away,
> And mingle with the blaze of day.

Perhaps in such a circumstance, I might be of some little comfort to your dear mamma, who would stand in much need of comfort; and it may be, our blessed Master would enable me to teach you at once, and learn of you, to die! In the mean time, see that you neglect no probable means of restoring your health; and send me, from time to time, a particular account of the state wherein you are. Do you find your own will quite given up to God, so that you have no repugnance to his will in any thing? Do you find no strivings of pride? no remains of vanity? no desire of praise, or fear of dispraise? Do you enjoy an uninterrupted sense of the loving presence of God? How far does the corruptible and decaying body press down the soul? Your disorder naturally sinks the spirits, and occasions heaviness and dejection. Can you, notwithstanding this, "rejoice evermore, and in every thing give thanks?" Certainly before the root of sin is taken away, believers may live above the power of it. Yet what a difference between the first love, and the pure love! You can explain this to Mr. Roe by your own experience. Let him follow on, and how soon may he attain it!

I am glad you wrote to Miss Yates, and hope you will write to Miss ——. As to health, they are both nearly as you are; only Miss —— is a little strengthened by a late journey. I never conversed with her so much before. I can give you her character in one line. She is "all praise, all meekness, and all love." If it will not hurt you, I desire you will write often to, my dear Hetty, Yours, affectionately.

LETTER II.

NEWCASTLE-UPON-TYNE, June 2, 1776.

MY DEAR HETTY:—It is not uncommon for a person to be thoroughly convinced of his duty to call sinners to repentance, several years before he has an opportunity of doing it. This has been the case with several of our preachers. Probably this may be the case with Mr. Roe: God may show him now what he is to do hereafter. It seems his present duty is to wait the openings of Divine providence.

If I durst, I should earnestly desire that you might continue with us a little longer. I could almost say, it is hard that I should just see you once and no more. But it is a comfort, that to die is not to be lost. Our union will be more full and perfect hereafter.

> Surely our disembodied souls shall join,
> Surely my friendly shade shall mix with thine:
> To earth-born pain superior, light shall rise
> Through the wide waves of unopposing skies:
> Together swift ascend heaven's high abode,
> Converse with angels, and rejoice with God.

Tell me, my dear Hetty, do you experience something similar to what Mr. De Renty expresses in those strong words: "I bear about with me an experimental verity, and a plenitude of the presence of the ever blessed Trinity?" Do you commune with God in the night season? Does he bid you even in sleep go on? And does he "make your very dreams devout?"

That he may fill you with all his fulness is the constant wish of, my dear Hetty,

Yours, affectionately.

LETTER III.

BRISTOL, September 16, 1776.

MY DEAR HETTY:—As I did not receive yours, of August 28, before my return from Cornwall, I was beginning to grow a little apprehensive lest your love was declining; but you have sweetly dispelled all my apprehensions of that sort, and I take knowledge that you are still the same. The happy change wrought in Miss P. R. and Miss B., may encourage you to snatch every opportunity of speaking a word for a good Master. Sometimes you see present fruit; but if not, your labour is not lost, the seed may spring up after many days. I hope, though your cousins are tried, they will not be discouraged; then all these things will "work together for good." Probably, if they stand firm, religion will, in a while, leaven the whole family. But they will have need of much patience, as well as much resolution. I am not sorry that you have met with a little blame in the affair, and I hope it was not undeserved. Happy are they that suffer for well doing! I was almost afraid that all men would speak well of you. Do you feel no intermission of your happiness in God? Do you never find any lowness of spirits? Does time never hang heavy upon your hands? How is your health? You see how inquisitive I am, because every thing relating to you nearly concerns me. I once thought I could not be well acquainted with any one till many years had elapsed; and yet I am as well acquainted with you as if I had known you from your infancy. You now are my comfort and joy! And I hope to be far longer than this little span of life, my dear Hetty, Yours, in tender affection.

LETTER IV.

BRISTOL, October 6, 1776.

MY DEAR HETTY:—To-morrow I set out for London, in and near which, if it pleases God to continue my life, I shall remain till spring. The trials which a gracious Providence sends may be precious means of growing in grace, and particularly of increasing in faith, patience, and resignation; and are they not all chosen for us by infinite wisdom and goodness? So that we may well subscribe to those beautiful lines,—

> "With patience mind thy course of duty run;
> God nothing does, or suffers to be done,
> But thou wouldst do thyself, if thou couldst see
> The end of all events as well as he."

Every thing that we can do for a parent, we ought to do: that is, every thing we can do without killing ourselves. But this we have no right to do. Our lives are not at our own disposal. Remember that, my dear Hetty, and do not carry a good principle too far. Do you still find,

> Labour is rest, and pain is sweet,
> When thou, my God, art here?

I know pain or grief does not interrupt your happiness; but does it not lessen it? You often feel sorrow for your friends: does that sorrow rather quicken than depress your soul? Does it sink you deeper into God? I cannot express the satisfaction which I receive from your open and artless manner of writing; especially when you speak of the union of spirit which you feel with, my dear Hetty,

Your ever affectionate.

LETTER V.

LONDON, February 11, 1777.

MY DEAR HETTY:—The papers of one who lately went to God are fallen into my hands. I will transcribe a few particulars. His experience is uncommon; and you may simply tell me how far your experience does or does not agree with it. But beware of hurting yourself upon the occasion: beware of unprofitable reasonings. God may have wrought the same work in you, though not in the same manner. "Just after my uniting with the Methodists, the Father was revealed to me the first time; soon after the whole Trinity. I beheld the distinct persons of the Godhead, and worshipped one undivided Jehovah, and each person separately. After this I had equal intercourse with the Son, and afterward with the Spirit, the same as with the Father and the Son. After some years, my communion was with the Son only, though at times with the Father, and not wholly without the Spirit. Of late I have found the same access to the Triune God. When I approach Jesus, the Father and the Spirit commune with me.*

"Whatever I receive now, centres in taking leave of earth, and hastening to another place. I am as one that is no more. I stand and look on what God has done—his calls, helps, mercies, forbearances, deliverances from sorrows, rescues out of evils; and I adore and devote myself to him with new ardour. If it be asked how, or in what manner, I beheld the Triune God, it is

[* In a letter to Miss Loxdale, Mr. Wesley says, "I avoid, I am afraid of, whatever is peculiar, either in the experience or the language of any one. I desire nothing, I will accept of nothing, but the common faith and common salvation; and I want you, my dear sister, to be only just such a common Christian as Jenny Cooper was." This sufficiently shows what were Mr. Wesley's own views as to such "peculiar" and "uncommon" expressions as some of the above.]

above all description. He that has seen this light of God, can no more describe it than he that has not. In two of those divine interviews, the Father spoke, while I was in an agony of prayer for perfect conformity to himself: twice more when I was in the depth of sorrow, and each time in Scripture words. It may be asked, 'Was the appearance glorious?' It was all divine, it was glory. I had no conception of it. It was God. The first time, the glory of Him I saw reached even to me. I was overwhelmed with it—body and soul were penetrated through with the rays of the Deity."

Tell me, my dear maid, if you have ever experienced any thing like these things: but do not puzzle yourself about them; only speak in simplicity. You cannot speak of these things to many; but you may say any thing without reserve to, my dear Hetty,

Yours, in tender affection.

LETTER VI.

LONDON, February 11, 1779.

MY DEAR HETTY:—It is a great mercy that, on the one hand, you have previous warning of the trials that are at hand; and, on the other, are not careful about them, but only prepared tc encounter them. We know indeed that these, as well as all things, are ordered by unerring wisdom; and are given us exactly at the right time, and in due number, weight, and measure. And they continue no longer than is best; for chance has no share in the government of the world. The Lord reigns and disposes all things, strongly and sweetly, for the good of them that love him. I rejoice to hear that you have now less hindrance in the way, and can oftener converse with his people. Be sure to improve every one of those precious opportunities of doing and receiving good.

I am often grieved to observe that, although on His part "the gifts and callings of God are without repentance;" although he never repents of any thing he has given us, but is willing to give it always; yet so very few retain the same ardour of affection which they received either when they were justified, or when they were (more fully) sanctified. Certainly none need to lose any part of their light or their love. It may increase more and more. Of this you are a witness for God; and so is our dear Miss ——. You have not lost any thing of what you have received: your love has never grown cold since the moment God visited you with great salvation. And I hope also you will ever retain the same affection for,

Yours, most tenderly.

LETTER VII.

LIVERPOOL, April 10, 1781.

MY DEAR HETTY:—Many of our brethren and sisters in London, during that great outpouring of the Spirit, spoke of several new blessings which they had attained. But after all, they could find nothing higher than pure love; on which the full assurance of hope generally attends. This the inspired writings always represent as the highest point; only there are innumerable degrees of it.

The plerophory, or full assurance of faith, is such a clear conviction of being now in the favour of God as excludes all doubt and fear concerning it. The full assurance of hope is such a clear confidence in the person who possesses it, that he shall enjoy the glory of God, as excludes all doubt and fear concerning this. And this confidence is totally different from an opinion that "no saint shall fall from grace." It has, indeed, no relation to it. Bold, presumptuous men often substitute this base counterfeit in the room of that precious confidence. But it is observable, the opinion remains just as strong while men are sinning and serving the devil, as while they are serving God. Holiness or unholiness does not affect it in the least degree. Whereas, the giving way to any thing unholy, either in heart or life, immediately clouds the full assurance of hope; which cannot subsist any longer than the heart cleaves steadfastly to God.

I am persuaded the storm which met us in the teeth, and drove us back to England, was not a casual, but a providential thing: therefore I lay aside the thought of seeing Ireland at present.

I am, my dear Hetty,
Always yours, in tender affection.

LETTER VIII.

London, December 9, 1781.

My Dear Hetty:—We may easily account for those notices which we frequently receive, either sleeping or waking, upon the Scriptural supposition that "He giveth His angels charge over us, to keep us in all our ways." How easy is it for them, who have at all times so ready an access to our souls, to impart to us whatever may be a means of increasing our holiness or our happiness! So that we may well say, with Bishop Ken,—

"O may thy angels, while we sleep,
Around our beds their vigils keep,
Their love angelical instill,
Stop every avenue of ill!"

Without needing to use any other arguments, you have a clear proof, in your own experience, that our blessed Lord is both able and willing to give us always what he gives once; and there is no necessity of ever losing what we receive in the moment of justification or sanctification. But it is his will that all the light and love which we then receive, should increase more and more unto the perfect day.

If you are employed to assist children that are brought to the birth, that groan either for the first or the pure love, happy are you! But this is not all your work. No, my Hetty, you are likewise to watch over the new-born babes. Although they have love, they have not yet either much light or much strength, so that they never had more need of your assistance, that they may neither be turned out of the way, nor hindered in running the race that is set before them.

I should not have been willing that Miss Bosanquet should have been joined to any other person than Mr. Fletcher; but I trust she may be as useful with him as she was before.

I fear our dear —— will not stay long with us. I have no answer to my last letter, and Mrs. Downes writes that she is far from well. Yet God is able to raise her up. As to Peggy Roe, I have little hope of her life: but she seemed, when I saw her, to be quite simple of heart, desiring nothing more but God. My dear Hetty, adieu! Remember in all your prayers,

Yours, most affectionately.

LETTER IX.

LONDON, January 7, 1782.

MY DEAR HETTY:—In the success of Mr. Leech's preaching, we have one proof of a thousand, that the blessing of God always attends the publishing of full salvation as attainable now, by simple faith. You should always have in readiness that little tract, "The Plain Account of Christian Perfection." There is nothing that would so effectually stop the mouths of those who call this "a new doctrine." All who thus object are really (though they suspect nothing less) seeking sanctification by works. If it be by works, then certainly these will need time, in order to the doing of these works. But if it is by faith, it is plain, a moment is as a thousand years. Then God says, (in the spiritual, as in the outward world,) Let there be light, and there is light.

I am in great hopes, as J. S. got his own soul much quickened in Macclesfield, he will now be a blessing to many at Chester. A few witnesses of pure love remain there still; but several are gone to Abraham's bosom. Encourage those in M. who enjoy it, to speak explicitly what they do experience; and to go on, till they know all that "love of God that passeth knowledge."

Give all the help you can, my dear Hetty, to them, and to Yours, most affectionately.

LETTER X.

DARLINGTON, June 25, 1782.

MY DEAR HETTY:—It is certain there has been, for these forty years, such an outpouring of the Spirit, and such an increase of vital religion, as has not been in England for many centuries; and it does not appear that the work of God at all decays. In many places there is a considerable increase of it; so that we have reason to hope that the time is at hand when the kingdom of God shall come with power, and all the people of this poor heathen land shall know him, from the least to the greatest.

I am glad you had so good an opportunity of talking with Mr. S——. Surely, if prayer was made for him, so useful an instrument as he was would not be suffered to lose all his usefulness. I wish you could make such little excursions oftener, as you always find your labour is not in vain.

This afternoon I was agreeably surprised by a letter from our dear Miss ——. It seems as if God in answer to many prayers, has lent her to us a little longer. "He bringeth down to the grave, and bringeth up again. Wise are all his ways!"

Take particular care, my dear Hetty, of the children: they are glorious monuments of Divine grace, and I think you have a particular affection for them, and a gift to profit them. I always am, my dear friend,

Yours, most affectionately.

LETTER XI.

BRISTOL, October 1, 1782.

MY DEAR HETTY:—I received yours two days after date, and read it yesterday to Miss Stockdale, and poor Peggy Roe, who is still strangely detained in life. But she is permitted to stay in the body a little longer, that she may be more ready for the Bridegroom.

You did exceedingly well to send me so circumstantial an account of Robert Roe's last illness and happy death. It may incite many to run the race that is set before them with more courage and patience.

The removal of so useful an instrument as your late cousin, in the midst, or rather in the dawn, of his usefulness, (especially while the harvest is so great, and the faithful labourers so few,) is an instance of the Divine economy which leaves our reason behind: our little narrow minds cannot comprehend it. We can only wonder and adore. How is your health? I sometimes fear, lest you also (as those I tenderly love generally have been) should be snatched away. But let us live to-day. I always am Affectionately yours.

LETTER XII.

BRISTOL, March 15, 1783.

MY DEAR HETTY:—I shall not be able to visit Macclesfield quite so soon as usual this year; for the preaching houses at Hinckley and Nottingham are to be opened, which I take in my way. I expect to be at Nottingham on the 1st of April; but how long I shall stay there, I cannot yet determine. Thence I shall probably come, by Derby, to Macclesfield.

I intended to have written a good deal more, but I am hardly able. For a few days, I have had just such a fever as I had a few years ago in Ireland. But all is well. I am in no pain, but the wheel of life seems scarcely able to move; yet I made shift to preach this morning to a crowded audience, and hope to say something to them this afternoon. I love that word, "And Ishmael died in the presence of all his brethren." Still pray for, my dear Hetty,

Yours, most affectionately.

LETTER XIII.

LONDON, October 12, 1787.

MY DEAR HETTY:—I do not doubt but your calling at Dublin would be an acceptable time, especially as R. H. was there.

After we left you at Manchester, we pushed on, and, in all haste, set out for the Isle of Jersey. But a storm drove us into Yarmouth, in the Isle of Wight. There Dr. Coke and I preached in the market-place by turns, two evenings and two mornings. A second storm drove us to the Isle of Purbeck, just where the Indiaman was lost. There I had an opportunity of preaching to a little society, which I had not seen for thirteen years. We hoped to reach Guernsey the next evening, but could get no farther than the Isle of Alderney. I preached on the beach in the morning, and the next afternoon came safe to Guernsey. Here is an open door: high and low, rich and poor, receive the word gladly; so that I could not regret being detained by contrary winds several days longer than we intended. The same thing befel us in the Isle of Jersey, where also there was an open door; even the governor, and the chief of the people, being quite civil and friendly.

Jane Bisson I saw every day. She is nineteen years old, about the size of Miss ——, and has a peculiar mixture of seriousness, sprightliness, and sweetness, both in her looks and behaviour. Wherever we were, she was the servant of all. I think she exceeds Madam Guion in deep communion with God.

I hope you will see a revival in Cork also. See that you take particular care of the tender lambs, not forgetting poor P. L. Peace be with all your spirits! I am, with kind love to James Rogers, my dear Hetty, Yours, most affectionately.

LETTER XIV.

May 28, 1788.

My Dear Hetty:—My not hearing from you for so long a time would have given me concern, but I knew it was not from want of affection. I am glad to hear you prosper in your soul: rest in nothing you have attained; but press on till you are filled with all the fullness of God. In this day of God's power, I hope many of the back-sliders in Cork will be brought back: there are great numbers of them in and about the city, and many are of the genteeler sort. It seems you have a particular mission to these: perhaps they will hear none but you. I hope you have already found out Mrs. Forbes, (Captain Forbes's wife,) and that now she is more than almost persuaded to be a Christian. The pearl on my eye is but just discernible, and dulls the sight a little, but not much: as it grows no worse, I do not much regard it.

Mr. Smyth's society, I verily believe, will do us no harm: and every one may speak of me as he will. I am just flying away as a shadow. It more than makes me amends, that James and you still love and pray for, my dear Hetty,

Your most affectionate.

LETTER XV.

FEBRUARY 9, 1789.

MY DEAR HETTY:—I am glad to hear that you do not grow weary or faint in your mind; that you are rather increasing in the way of holiness. Go on in the name of the Lord, and in the power of his might, doing the will of God from the heart.

It was a providence indeed, the flood did not begin in the night, rather than in the day. So it is that judgment is usually mixed with mercy, that sinners may be awakened and not destroyed. I liked well to lodge at brother Laffan's when I was in Cork last: but certainly I shall like much better to lodge with brother Rogers and you. I shall be more at home with you, than I could be any where else in Cork. I still find (blessed be God) a gradual increase of strength, and my sight is rather better than worse. If my life and health be continued, I shall endeavour to reach Dublin about the end of March; and Cork, before the end of June. Peace be with your spirits! I am, my dear Hetty, Yours, most affectionately.

FUNERAL SERMON FOR MRS. ROGERS BY THE REV. THOS. COKE, LL.D.

"It is appointed unto men once to die." Heb. ix. 27.

If the remains of our departed sister, in memory of whom the present discourse is delivered, were now before your eyes, with all the pomp and splendour of modern funerals, it is not improbable there are some whose minds would be affected with a solemn but superstitious awe which the preacher has neither the power nor inclination to raise. He is conscious that those who had the privilege of being acquainted with our respected sister, need nothing more than the recollection of that amiable woman, under the blessing of God, to infuse into them that spirit of true solemnity which alone becomes the Christian on these occasions. But yet, that which rises above every other consideration, is the momentous truth held out to us in my text, that great statute law of Heaven, "It is appointed unto men once to die."

For the due improvement of this weighty subject, we shall, under the blessing of the Most High,

First, Give an explanation of the text.

Secondly, Consider the grand point held forth to our view,—the certainty of death.

Thirdly, Lay down some considerations against the fear of death, for the use and comfort of believers.

Fourthly, draw some inferences from the foregoing heads of my discourse: And,

Lastly, Present you with an epitome of the experience, death, and character of our deceased friend, Mrs. Hester Ann Rogers.

I. We are to explain the text.

1st. The proposition is indefinite, therefore universal, "all must die." It is not confined to any sex or description. The whole race is included. But yet there have been, and still shall be, exceptions to the general rule. 1. Enoch, that holy man, who walked with God three hundred years, and then "was not, for God took him. By faith he was translated" into heaven. When he had, for so long a time, borne, by example and prophecy, his faithful testimony against the sins of a wicked world, just mature for destruction, his merciful Redeemer, the God of Israel, with whose smile and intimacy he had been divinely honoured for centuries, took him into his everlasting arms, and fitted him at once for consummate glory. 2. Elijah, the great and highly honoured prophet, who had power to open and shut the heavens, and to call down celestial fire, when he had finished his suffering life in the midst of a crooked, adulterous, idolatrous people, his friend and his God took him, soul and body together, in a chariot of fire, to the heaven of heavens. These are the exceptions we have had already.

And, in respect to futurity, "we shall not all sleep, but we shall be changed in a moment, in the twinkling of an eye, at the last trump; for the trumpet shall sound," and instantly all the faithful who are then alive, shall put on incorruption and immortality, and shall afterward enter into their Master's joy, without suffering the usual lot of mortality.

The above excepted, we must all pass through the valley of the shadow of death, and return to the dust from whence we came. And truly, my brethren, I know not whether I should not prefer, if the choice were given me, to tread the steps my Saviour trod before me, and to pass after him through the door of death, than to be at once translated to the realms of bliss. He has sanctified the grave by lying in it; and every path in which we follow the Lamb is strowed with blessings to the faithful. He will take care of our sacred dust: every thing which is essential to humanity will he preserve in the hollow of his hand till he completely mould it by almighty power, and give it a lustre to which the sun shall appear as darkness.

2dly. All must die once, but all shall not die the second death. There is the comfort of the believer. That divine and ineffable union which subsists between God and the Christian's soul, shall preserve the consecrated body, which here below is the temple of the Holy Ghost. As the whole humanity of Christ was united to his Godhead, even when his soul and body were separated; so the soul and body of the faithful are united to Christ, even when they are separated by death; for we are the "bone of his bone, and the flesh of his flesh." When death shall untie those secret and sweet bands, those vital knots which fasten soul and body together, then shall the sanctified and immortal spirit burst through its tenement of clay, and take possession of its everlasting home. On such "the second death hath no power." To them death is only a sleep, a happy passage out of the prison of the body into a state of perfect freedom—out of an earthly house, where the better part groans, "into a building of God, a house not made with hands, eternal in the heavens." But,

3dly. We must all undergo the first death.

This is the irrevocable decree of Heaven: not from the necessity of nature, but as the punishment of sin. Man was made immortal: sin alone brought death into the world, and all our wo. "By sin," says St. Paul, "death entered into the world." And shall we nourish and indulge our great enemy? Shall we harbour, yea, shall we serve the murderer of Christ? Shall we not exert ourselves to the utmost against the greatest foe of God and man? Shall a little temporary joy or profit induce us to sacrifice everlasting happiness, and to embrace everlasting burnings?—May the awful decree, "It is appointed unto man once to die," have such an influence on our minds, and be so accompanied by the operations of grace upon our hearts, that we may always be enabled to say with holy triumph, "O death, where is thy sting? O grave, where is thy victory? Thanks be to God, who giveth us the victory through our Lord Jesus Christ."

II. But we now proceed to consider the second point,—the unavoidableness and certainty of death.

It needs no proof. Every thing else on this side of the grave, is attended with probability or possibility only:—this alone with certainty. If it be inquired, will such a child be rich or poor, be learned or ignorant, be honourable or contemptible? the answer is, perhaps it may, perhaps not. But if it be inquired shall he die? the answer contains no perhaps: it is simply, he certainly shall.

I shall therefore only consider the present head in a way of application. For it is the heart alone which wants to be awakened on the present subject. Such is the sottishness of men in general, that they will not duly consider the transitoriness of all sublunary things, the mortality of our bodies, and the infinitely momentous concerns of eternity. Let us, therefore, examine into the grand reasons of this stupidity of man. We shall find it, perhaps, to proceed from the following particulars:—

1st. Immense multitudes are so immerged in the pleasures, honours, or riches of this world, that every thought of the certainty or approach of death is drowned therein. As soon as an idea on the important subject springs up in the mind, it sinks and is lost in the innumerable ideas which continually crowd in concerning the things of time and sense: it is devoured by the worldly thoughts which are incessantly buzzing in the souls of carnal men. One is eagerly pursuing things of time, and so abhorrent of reflection, that, with a variety of invented delights, he imps the wings of time to make them fly the faster; and is never contented but when the senses are gratified.—Another is eat up by ambition : he forgets he is mortal; and power, and titles, and worldly honours are the only food of his soul. A third, like the fool in the parable, trusts in his riches. He says to his soul, "Soul, thou hast goods laid up for many years: eat, drink, and be merry:" whereas he might as well lay a plaster to his clothes to heal the wounds of his body, as imagine it can bring happiness into his soul through any thing which the honours, riches, or pleasures of this world can possibly afford him. If he will believe the Spirit of God, the sum total of them all is, "Vanity of vanities, all is vanity and vexation of spirit." If vanity can satisfy you, if vexation of spirit can give you content, if you can gather grapes of thorns, or figs of thistles, then go and doat upon the creatures.

2dly. Men in general are continually viewing death as at a distance; and thereby entirely lose sight of the awful certainty and unavoidableness of it. When they are young, the heat of blood, the incessant flow of the animal spirits, a vicious education, and the constant company of the dissipated and unawakened, drive away every thought of death, as if the solemn moment were at the utmost distance from them. Those who are grown up to manhood, and are strong and healthy, think it quite sufficient to provide for death when sickness gives the summons. Those who are sickly and diseased, buoy up themselves in their false confidence by their hopes of recovery; and even the aged (strange as it seems!) regard their few remaining days as if they were years. Such is the state of the unregenerate; such the dreadful consequence of a heart hardened to divine things by original and actual sin! What if God were to summon you away, sinners, in an hour or a moment! how dreadful would be the alarm! And should we not be every moment prepared, by living in the favour God, and in the light of his countenance; for who can assure himself for a moment to come? For aught you know, the film, the bubble, which holds your lives, is now breaking! O, did we but seriously consider by what small pins this frame of man is tacked together, it would appear to us a miracle that we live for a single hour.

3dly. The apprehensions, the terrors arising in the minds of the unregenerate from reflection upon death, keep them from any due considerations on the certainty and unavoidableness of it. The agonies of death, the senseless corpse, the gnawing worm, the stench of rottenness, and all the other attendants of that grim king of terrors, form far too miserable a subject for the jovial world or the dissipated throng to reflect upon for a moment. But, though the consideration of these things is very unwelcome, yea, very dismal to the minds of sinners, yet there is far worse behind; and that is the sin which deserves death, and the hell which follows it. To be forever shut up in utter darkness, to be the sport of devils, as far as devils can sport themselves with any thing, to be banished forever from the source of happiness, to have the soul eternally tormented by the worm which dieth not, and the immortalized body by a fire suited to its ever dying, but never annihilated substance,—these subjects afford ideas which, if thoroughly attended to, and applied by the grace of God, would soon stir up the soul to enter into that state of favour with the Lord which would make dissolution a privilege, and death a kind messenger without a sting, to open the gate to everlasting joys.

III. But this leads me to the third head of my discourse, namely, to lay down some considerations against the fear of death, for the use and comfort of believers.

1st. If the soul be immortal, if it were created and redeemed for the eternal enjoyment of God, and consequently enter after death on an infinitely better life than this, the believer may certainly be well contented, yea, glad to die. The glorious view, which faith opens to the spiritual eye, far overbalances all the frightful objects with which death is surrounded. The scenes of pure perennial bliss, where saints eternally bask themselves in the bright beams of the countenance of their God, and bathe themselves in the rivers of pleasures which flow at his right hand forevermore, are sufficient, though only viewed in prospect, to elevate the soul above every terrifying thought which can possibly assail it. An old heathen philosopher, Tullius Cicero in his dream of Scipio, beautifully observes, "If I were now disengaged from my cumbrous body, and on the wing for Elysium, [the place where the ancient Romans supposed the virtuous would dwell after death,] and some superior being should meet me in my flight, and make me an offer of returning and reanimating my body, I should without hesitation reject his offer: so much rather would I go to Elysium, to reside with Socrates and Plato, and all the ancient worthies, and spend my time in conversing with them." But could a heathen thus triumph in the thought of enjoying his poor miserable paradise, and prefer it even to life, how much more may a Christian triumph in the exulting thought, that he shall spend an eternity with the wisest, the holiest, the happiest beings that ever came out of the creative hand of God: yea, that he shall spend an eternity with Jesus, the Mediator of the new covenant, the joy of his heart, and the delight of his eyes: where he shall fix his ever-waking eyes on the infinite beauty of his adorable Lord; yea, if it were possible, would think eternity itself too short for the beholding and admiring such transcendent excellences, and for the solemnizing those heavenly espousals between Christ and his most beloved spouse, when all the powers of heaven shall triumph for joy, and a concert of seraphim forever sing the wedding song.

2dly. The whole life of a Christian is founded on a hope which cannot be accomplished but by dying. How exceedingly mistaken must he be, who fears that which alone can gratify his highest wishes, and is the great end of all his pursuits. What does the Christian chiefly hope for? Is it not the full enjoyment of his God in the realms of bliss? Is it not the restoration of his whole nature to the full image of God, in which it was at first created; and the recovery of that paradise, which he has lost by the fall—a paradise, the glories of which shall be inconceivably heightened by the union of the divine and human natures in the person of the second Adam, the Son of God? Is it not to live forever with his adorable and most beloved Saviour, to be with him where He is and to behold the glory which the Father has given him? Is it not to sit with Christ on hi throne, according to his most gracious promise even as Christ sits with his Father on the throne? Is it not to join the redeemed and the innumerable hosts of angels, in singing continually alleluiahs, salvation, and glory and honour, and power, to God and the Lamb? In short, is it not to see God face to face, to enjoy the beatific vision, to experience an inconceivably closer union and communion with God, than we possibly can during the present scene of things; to be forever blest in the close embraces of the sovereign Good? But can we be possessors of these mighty joys without passing through the valley of death? And shall a Christian be afraid of that which alone can enable him to realize the glorious hope, which is the very support of his life? Should it not rather be the language of his soul, "I desire to be dissolved, and to be with Christ, which is far better."

3dly. Death is no more than a quiet sleep. Thus it is frequently represented in the oracles of God. "Behold thou shalt sleep with thy fathers.* Many that sleep in the dust shall awake.† Our friend Lazareth sleepeth.‡ Stephen fell asleep.§ I would not have you be ignorant, brethren, con-

* Deut. xxxi. 16, and 2 Sam. vii. 12. † Dan. xii. 2.
‡ John xi. 11. § Acts vii. 60.

cerning them which are asleep, that ye sorrow not even as others, which have no hope. For if we believe that Jesus died and rose again, even so them also which sleep in Jesus, will God bring with him For we which are alive and remain unto the coming of the Lord, shall not prevent them which are asleep.* Some are fallen asleep. They are fallen asleep in Christ.† The fathers fell asleep."‡ The inspired writers seem to delight in the metaphor when applied to the death of the faithful; and what can be more expressive? The weary labourer lays himself down to sleep till the morning, and the Christian takes his sleep in the grave till the morning of the resurrection, only with this essential difference: the common sleep of nature deprives us of the natural light, but the sleep of death brings the believer to the vision of the true, and otherwise inaccessible light. Why, then, should the Christian be afraid of death? Surely, he may take the serpent into his bosom; for he has not only lost his sting, but is reconciled to the believer, and become one of his party. Therefore says Saint Paul, "Whether life or death, all is yours:" and again, "To me, to live is Christ, and to die is gain." And well may the Christian

* 1 Thess. iv. 13, 14, 15.
† 1Cor. xv. 6, 18
‡ 2 Pet. iii. 4.

rejoice in death, and welcome the pleasing messenger; for it is the hand of death which draws the curtain, and lets him in to see God face to face in heaven, that palace of inestimable pleasure and delight, where the strongest beams of glory shall beat fully upon our faces, and we shall be made strong enough to bear them. Neither does death do any real injury to our bodies, since they shall be new moulded at the resurrection: when "this mortal shall put on immortality, and this corruptible put on incorruption:" when these dull lumps shall become as impalpable as the angelic nature, subtle as a ray of light, bright as the sun, nimble as lightning.—Who is there that is truly armed with this helmet of salvation, this hope of heaven, who would for a moment desire to have the law of death reversed? Surely a holy soul may frequently be breathing forth desires (though with due resignation) after the kind office of death, to deliver it into so great and incomprehensible a glory.

IV. I now proceed, in the fourth place, to draw some inferences from what has been advanced.

1st. If death be so certain and unavoidable, and it be "appointed unto men once to die," what exquisite folly is it to suffer our affections to cleave to any thing here below! How painful must the parting be when we are drawn from our dearest idols, from our chief joy!—How different is the concluding scene of the pious and the unregenerate! Angels are waiting to receive the former, and to accompany them to their beloved Bridegroom, their adorable Lord: whilst devils are ready to seize upon the latter, and to bring them to their place of torment. Some of the voluptuous heathens were accustomed to bring in the resemblance of an anatomy to their feasts, in order to remind their guests of their favourite motto, "Let us eat and drink, for to-morrow we die:" let us indulge ourselves in every pleasure of sense, since annihilation daily approaches, and we shall then sink into an eternal sleep. How much better is the advice of the apostle: "But this I say, brethren, the time is short: it remaineth, that both they that have wives be as though they had none; and they that weep, as though they wept not; and they that rejoice, as though they rejoiced not; and they that buy, as though they possessed not; and they that use this world, as not abusing it: for the fashion of this world passeth away."* Why should any thing this world can allure us with, be of any price in a wise man's esteem? Both they and we perish in the using: they are

* 1 Cor. vii. 29, 30, 31.

dying comforts, and we must die who enjoy them And, therefore,

2dly. As we must all shortly die, let us labour to be always in readiness and preparation for the awful hour. On this head of my discourse I shall only lay down a few short directions, and then proceed to the more immediate subject of our meeting.

1. Wean your hearts from the love of the world. Death must and will pluck you from it. Why, then, should you toil, and waste your lives on so precarious, so transitory an object? Every thing below is fading; but your precious souls are immortal. Be not, therefore, unequally yoked: join not your ever-living souls to dying comforts: this would be a tyranny worse than that which was exercised by those of old, who tied living bodies to dead carcasses. When you take your eternal farewell of all sublunary enjoyments, what lingering looks will you cast on those dear nothings, those miserable follies, which you clasped round your heart, unless Almighty grace has wrenched your affections from them: whilst the soul which is crucified to the world, and the world to it,—which sits loose to every thing below, spreads its wings and takes its glad flight to realms where bliss and love immortal reign. Soon will the films fall off from the eyes of worldlings. When they

stand before the awful bar of God, with what astonishment will they behold the men whom they once despised, shining as the stars of the firmament at the right hand of the Judge! "They shall be troubled with terrible fear, and shall be amazed at the strangeness of the salvation of the righteous, so far beyond all which they looked for; and repenting and groaning for anguish of spirit, they shall say within themselves, These were they whom we had sometimes in derision, and a proverb of reproach. We fools accounted their lives madness; and their end to be without honour. Now are they numbered among the children of God, and their lot is among the saints!" And then will the final separation take place: those who were here dead to the world, and walked with God, shall ascend up to the marriage supper of the Lamb, and be ever with their Lord, while the others sink down into the place prepared for the devil and his angels.

2. Would you be prepared for death, then delay not your conversion (if you be unregenerate) for another day. Get an interest in Christ as soon as possible. By earnest prayer and active faith, press into the liberty of the children of God. Remember him who has said, "Many shall seek to enter in, and shall not be able." It is not an empty wish or languishing endeavour which will

serve the turn. He that is but almost a Christian shall but almost be saved. You must "strive to enter in at the strait gate." To those who thus knock, it shall certainly be opened. God delights to bless the earnestly seeking soul.

3. Live every day as if it were your last, and the next were allotted for eternity. It may be so; and when we consider the importance of eternal things, of the everlasting happiness of the blessed, and the everlasting misery of the impenitent, it should lead us to leave nothing to the hazard,—for there is no end of procrastination. There will be the same tempting devil, and the same treacherous heart to-morrow as to-day, only made more treacherous by delay. Therefore, "now is the accepted time, now is the day of salvation. Now, while it is called to-day, harden not your hearts." Do you think you can be happy too soon? Or do you think that God will accept of the dregs of your life, when you have given the strength of it to vanity, folly, and the devil? Begin, therefore, to live to God every day and every hour.

4. You who are believers, be constant in the exercise of a holy life. Let your fellowship be with the Father, and his Son Jesus Christ. Labour to walk in the light, as God is in the light, and the blood of Christ Jesus his Son shall cleanse

you from all sin. Walk as heirs of heaven, led and moved by the Spirit of Christ in you. Live habitually by faith in the Son of God, who loved you, and gave himself for you. Be much in the exercise of the presence of God; and he will more and more smile upon you, and more and more reveal himself to you. You shall be strong in the Lord, and in the power of his might, and shall overcome the wicked one: yea, you shall be more than conquerors, through him that hath loved you.

5. Lastly, Take care to preserve an abiding witness of the favour of God. Watch unto prayer for this. There is nothing else will support you in the dying hour: there is nothing else will make you comfortable through life. To retain a clear sense of your interest in Jesus Christ, a constant assurance of the love of God—O this will turn the waste wilderness of the world into a little paradise: it will enable you to triumph with the poet:—

"Should [Providence] command me to the farthest verge
Of the green earth, to distant barb'rous climes,
'Tis naught to me:
Since God is ever present, ever felt,
In the void waste as in the city full;
And where he vital breathes there must be joy."

Above all, at the hour of death, what can support us but this mighty blessing; and it will support the believer. For whom will it not comfort to think that death will change his bottle into a spring? Though here our water sometimes fails us, yet, in heaven, where we are going, we shall bathe ourselves in an infinite ocean of delights, lying at the breasts of an infinite fountain of life and sweetness. Whoever has such an assurance, cannot but welcome death, embracing it not only with contentment, but delight; and while the soul is struggling and striving to unclasp itself, and to get loose from the body, it cannot but say, with holy longings and pantings, "Come, Lord Jesus, come quickly."

V. I proceed, in the fifth and last place, to present you with an epitome of the experience, death, and character of our deceased friend, Mrs. Hester Ann Rogers.

She was born at Macclesfield, in Cheshire, on the 31st of January, 1756—of which place her father was minister for many years. She was trained up in the observance of all outward duties, and in the fear of those sins, which, in these modern times, are too often deemed accomplishments. She was followed by divine impressions from her childhood, and was early drawn out to secret prayer. From four years old, she never remembered going to bed without saying her prayers, except once. When she wanted any thing, or was in pain or grief, she fled to God in secret; and it would be incredible to some, how often she received manifest answers to prayer in that early period of her life.

In the ninth year of her age, her pious father dying, her mother was prevailed on to let her learn to dance, in order to raise her spirits and improve her carriage.—This was a fatal stab to her divine impressions: it paved the way to lightness, trifling, love of pleasure, and various evils. As she soon made a proficiency, she delighted much in this ensnaring folly. Yet in all this she was not left without keen convictions, gentle drawings, and many short-lived good resolutions.

When she arrived at the age of fourteen, the Lord visited her with affliction: during this illness she had an alarming dream, which, together with the danger attending her disorder, made a deep impression on her mind for some time. But alas! her health and strength were no sooner restored, than (being solicited by her companions in gay life) she again returned to her former follies, such as balls, plays, dress, assemblies, &c., the love of which continued to grow upon her more and more, for upwards of two years, and nearly engrossed the whole of her time.

After this she was deeply wrought upon by a

sermon which the Rev. Mr. Simpson, of Macclesfield, preached on, "What shall it profit a man, if he gain the whole world and lose his own soul;" and soon after felt further convictions under another which he preached upon the new birth, from John iii, 3. She now saw and felt as she had never done before, that she must experience that divine change or perish.

In April, 1774, on the Sunday before Easter, Mr. Simpson preached from John vi. 44, "No man can come unto me, except the Father, which hath sent me, draw him." Under this sermon she felt herself indeed a lost, perishing sinner, a rebel against repeated convictions, and a condemned criminal by the law of God, who deserved to be sentenced to eternal pain! She felt she had broken her baptismal vow, her sacramental vows, and had no title to any mercy or any hope! She wept aloud, so that all around her were amazed; nor was she any longer ashamed to own the cause. She went home, ran up stairs, and fell on her knees, and made a solemn vow to renounce and forsake all her sinful pleasures and trifling companions.

She could not eat or sleep, or take any comfort. The curses throughout the whole Bible seemed pointed all at her, and she could not claim a single promise. Thus she continued till Good

Friday. After many conflicts she ventured once more to approach the Lord's table. As the minister was reading that sentence in the communion service, "If any man sin, we have an Advocate," &c., a ray of divine light was darted into her soul, and she was enabled to believe there was mercy for her: she felt a degree of love to God spring up in her heart, and in a measure could rejoice in him. But alas! this was only for a short season! She had never yet heard the Methodists, nor had she lost all her prejudices against them; but a neighbour who had lately found peace with God, advised her strongly to hear them: she resolved to go privately and went accordingly at five o'clock one morning. The text was, "Comfort ye, comfort ye my people, saith your God." She thought every word the preacher said was for her: he spoke to her heart, as if he had known all the secret workings there. She was much comforted, her prejudices were now fully removed, and she received a full and clear conviction, "these are the people of God."

She met with a little pamphlet, entitled, "The great duty of believing on the Son of God." She was much encouraged on reading this; and would gladly have spent the night in prayer; but her mother (with whom she slept) would not suffer it. She therefore went to bed, but could not sleep;

and at four in the morning rose again, that she might wrestle with the Lord. She prayed, but it seemed in vain! the heavens appeared as brass; and hope seemed almost sunk into despair! When suddenly the Lord spake that promise to her heart: "Believe on the Lord Jesus Christ and thou shalt be saved." She revived, and cried, "Lord, I know this is thy word, and I can depend upon it." Again it came, "Only believe." "Lord Jesus," said she, "I will, I do believe: I now venture my whole salvation upon thee as God! I put my guilty soul into thy hands: thy blood is sufficient! I cast my soul upon thee for time and eternity." Then did he appear to her salvation: in that moment her bands were loosed: her soul was set at liberty; and the love of God so shed abroad in her heart, that she rejoiced with joy unspeakable; and for eight months she experienced no interruption to her bliss.

But now the Lord began to reveal in her heart, that sin was not all destroyed; for though she had constant victory over it, yet she felt the remains of anger, pride, self-will, and unbelief often rising, which occasioned a degree of heaviness and sorrow. At first she was much amazed to feel such things.

About this time the Lord was pleased to make the preaching of Mr. Duncan Wright a great blessing to her. He clearly explained the nature of salvation from inbred sin; and showed it to be as freely promised in Scripture, and as fully purchased by the blood of Jesus, as pardon. Henceforth she could not rest, but cried to the Lord night and day, to cast out the strong man, and all his armour of unbelief and sin.

On the morning of February, 22, 1776, when at prayer, her intercourse was open with her Beloved, and various promises were presented to her view. She thought, shall I now ask small blessings only of my God? Lord, make this the moment of my full salvation! Baptize me now with the Holy Ghost, and the fire of pure love. Now, cleanse the thoughts of my heart, let me perfectly love thee."

Thus she continued agonizing till the Lord applied that promise, "I will circumcise thy heart, and thou shalt love the Lord thy God with all thy heart." She said, "Lord, thou art faithful, and this is thy word: I cast my whole soul upon thy promise. Now, Lord, I do believe, this moment thou dost save. Yea, Lord, my soul is delivered of her burden. I am emptied of all, I am at thy feet, a helpless, worthless worm; but I take hold of thee as my fulness! Every thing that I want, thou art. Thou art wisdom, strength, love, holiness: yea, and thou art mine! Love sinks me into nothing: it overflows my soul. O my Jesus, thou art all in all. In thee I behold and feel all the fulness of the Godhead mine! I am now one with God:—the intercourse is open:—sin, inbred sin, no longer hinders the close communion, and God is all my own!"

She now walked in the unclouded light of his countenance; and yet she did not feel so much rapturous joy as she had been led to expect; but was rather, as it were, overwhelmed with that

"Sacred awe, which dares not move,
And all the silent heaven of love."

She resolved at first not to declare openly what the Lord had wrought; but it was seen in her countenance: and when asked respecting it, she durst not deny the wonders of his love! and she soon found that repeating his goodness confirmed her own faith more and more.

From this time we may clearly preceive the increase of her joy in God and her deep communion with him, from her private diary, where she writes as follows:

"On Trinity Sunday, June, 1776, I met in the select society at six in the morning, and it was a blessed season to my soul.

"Mr. Wright dwelt a little on the equal love of each person in the adorable Trinity, in a manner which I found truly profitable: afterward he preached from Ephes. ii. 18, "Through him we both have access by one Spirit unto the Father." He showed the distinct relative offices of Father, Son, and Spirit, in man's salvation, and that the love of the Father was ever equal; as also that of the Son, and that of the Holy Ghost: that all the designs of the Son were the designs of the Father also, and of the Holy Ghost. He also spoke much of the near union and communion with God, which believers might enjoy, especially those perfected in love. My soul was led into depths unspeakable, and saw such a fulness of God ready for me to plunge into, that what I now felt seemed only as a drop compared with the ocean! As I came into the chapel yard, I felt peculiar union with the adorable Jesus, in all his offices of redeeming love; and that verse of a hymn was so powerfully sweet as I had never felt it before:—

'The opening heavens around me shine,
With beams of sacred bliss;
While Jesus shows his mercy mine,
And whispers I am his.'

"I was deeply penetrated with his presence, and stood as if unable to move, and was insensible to all around me. While thus lost in communion with my Saviour, he spoke those words to my heart,—'All that I have is thine! I am

Jesus, in whom dwells all the fulness of the Godhead bodily—I am thine!—My Spirit is thine!—My Father is thine!—They love thee, as I love thee—the whole Deity is thine!—All God is and all he has, is thine!—He even now overshadows thee!—He now covers thee with a cloud of his presence.' All this was so realized to my soul, in a manner I cannot explain, that I sunk down motionless, being unable to sustain the weight of his glorious presence and fulness of love. At the altar this was renewed to me, but not in so large a measure. I believe, indeed, if this had continued as I felt it before, but for one hour, mortality must have been dissolved, and the soul dislodged from its tenement of clay.

"Friday, 21.—I prove, through boundless mercy and free grace, an increasing intercourse and communion with my God every day. I live and move in him alone!—Wherever I go, whatever I do, I feel the presence of the great Three One.—'Yea, he dwelleth with me, and shall be in me.' This is his promise to my soul. I feel I am under his loving eye, and the continual guidance of his Spirit. I do, indeed, dwell in God, and God in me! O love unsearchable to such a worm?—

'I loathe myself when God I see,
And into nothing fall!'

"Sunday, 23.—In meeting with the select society again, I had unspeakable communion with the blessed Trinity! I had the same at the preaching also. Mr. Percival's text was, 'O God, thou art my God.' A sense of the Divine presence almost overcame my body. All the day I have been filled with a solemn weight of love, and swallowed up in God the eternal Father, Saviour, Comforter. At church, while that anthem was sung, 'I know that my Redeemer liveth,' &c., I was so overwhelmed with the power of God, and had such a foretaste of his glory, I thought I should have died! O the depths of his indulgent, condescending love! He knows my trials, and the need I have of such consolations to strengthen and support my weakness. I live by faith—this is my soul's strong anchor, which lays hold on omnipotence, and receives a momentary supply for every want. My God is always near—he is my one object, the centre and end of all my desires. He is my all in all."

After a wonderful chain of divine leadings and remarkable providences, on August 19, 1784, she was married to Mr. Rogers, in whom the Lord gave her a helpmate for glory; just such a partner as she needed to strengthen her. He made them of one heart and one soul; and for above ten years crowned their union with his constant smile.

Soon after their marriage they went to Dublin, where Mr. Rogers was appointed to labour. In that city they were gladly received, and the Lord gave them the hearts of the people. They saw a blessed revival of the work of God; and in three years the number in the society was increased more than double. From thence they removed to Cork, where also the Lord graciously revived his work. His word greatly prospered and prevailed; and many in that city still remember with gratitude the happy seasons which they enjoyed together. And it appears from what our dear friend wrote of herself when there, that she never before was more happy in her own soul, nor enjoyed deeper communion with her God than during her stay in that city. After spending three years in Cork, they removed to London; and for two years resided in Mr. Wesley's house at the new chapel; where they also had the happiness of seeing the work of God prosper: many souls were brought into Christian liberty; and in two years not less than five hundred were added to the society, in the city and suburbs. Here, indeed, it might be said, "The walls of Jerusalem were built in troublesome times." The awful event of Mr. Wesley's death, which happened during the residence of Mr. and Mrs. Rogers at the City Road, rendered their situation exceedingly critical and trying, as many of you well know.

In August, 1792, the Conference stationed Mr. Rogers here, (at Spitalfields,) in order to put this chapel and the adjoining dwelling house into a state of good repair, in which labour of love he was truly indefatigable: you now reap the benefit, and are thankful that you can here retire, and worship God in peace. Notwithstanding the work necessary to be done upon the premises was great, yet, before the end of October, Mrs. Rogers and the children were comfortably placed in their new habitation; and a few days afterward she wrote in her diary as follows:

"I feel grateful to my God that I am placed here, though but for a season; where I can enjoy more of retirement, and less of busy life. My God is with me, and I trust he will draw and unite more fully to himself his helpless creature! I have power with him in prayer, and I know he will answer my enlarged requests, for myself, my other self, and our offspring. I long for a yet larger measure of the mind of Christ; more of every grace, and a deeper communion with my God. All temptations respecting conflicts with Satan in death are vanished. I know my Joshua will be with me in Jordan, and see me safe through! Sometimes I have thought I shall have to pass that river before it be long; but that I leave to him. I feel no desires of life, but when I see my dear husband oppressed with trials, and my living seems as if it would be a help and comfort to him; or, when a silent wish arises, to see my children grown, and partakers of regenerating grace; but I am kept from anxiety."

During her state of pregnancy, she had much bodily affliction, and was reduced very low. The state of her soul will best appear from her own words; as also the narrow escape from death which she then had, at the time of her delivery.

"January 1, 1793.—I had not much sleep, yet I arose refreshed, and resolved to live for God alone. I feel him mine; and that I am offered to him without reserve. I know various bodily oppressions, natural to my present state, hinder my rejoicing as much in him as at other times; but my trust is fixed on his almighty love! and I feel I cannot trust in vain. He is my strong helper; and my painful feelings do work for my good, for they lead me to cast my helplessness upon his fulness, and to seek my all from him alone. Yes, and I trust to prove the utmost of these sweet lines:—

'I shall suffer and fulfil
All my Father's gracious will:
Be in all alike resign'd
Jesus' is a patient mind.'

"On April the 20th, I suffered much in labour pains, and at night saw it needful to send for the doctor. He came, and hoped I should soon be delivered; but at midnight my pains left me. I was tolerably easy all the next day; and enabled in patience to wait the Lord's leisure. I slept better that night than I had done for some weeks, and was greatly refreshed. In the morning lingering labour came on again; and the pain was so excruciating and constant, (though unavailable,) that I thought I must have expired! Having continued in this state about six hours, my labour came on with uncommon violence and rapidity, so that in a few minutes I was mercifully delivered of a lovely girl. But O! it was nature's agony indeed! For a little time gratitude unspeakable overflowed my heart, and body and soul experienced a heaven.—But this was soon passed, and I was thrown back upon the verge of eternity. Mr. Jones laboured to save me till the sweat ran down his temples for three hours; and for twelve hours I was between life and death! I felt, however, no fears of dying; and all within was peace. When capable of thought, I could view a blessed eternity with delight. I recovered very slowly, and at times suffered much; but the Lord continued to comfort my soul; and though few thought I should be restored, yet I believed I should. My dear husband suffered much on my account, and I believe his tenderness greatly contributed to my recovery.

"The Leeds Conference drawing near, my dear partner left me on July 21, and in the night after, my Hester was seized with a malignant fever. The weather was uncommonly hot; and what my fatigue and weakness were, my God only knows! But he held me up that I did not sink; and my soul was happy in his love. In this time of affliction I had peculiar intercourse with God in prayer, both with the family and in secret; and I received manifest answers. On the seventh day the fever came to a crisis—my child was quite delirious, and very ill indeed; but I felt fully resigned to the will of God respecting her life or death? About nine in the evening, her piercing cries through agonizing pain in her head, were very pitiable; and I entreated the Lord, in the prayer of faith, to give her ease. He heard—he answered! The pain was instantaneously removed, and she fell into a slumber; but it soon appeared to be the sleep of death! Her feet, legs and hands were cold, her nails blue, and she was motionless till a little past four in the morning. Just then, a blister which I had put on her back began to rise, and signs of life appeared: by degrees warmth returned to her arms, hands, and feet, then motion, and lastly speech. After this, a mighty change appeared: her fever was gone, and the next day she sat up some hours, and continued to recover in a most wonderful manner. What cannot the Lord do? Upon the whole, when I look back, I can only wonder and adore! repeating with the poet,

I stand and admire thy outstretch'd arm,
Having walk'd through the fire, and suffered no harm.

"Out of weakness surely I have been made strong, both as it respects body and soul.—What a feeble frame! Yet, how am I strengthened of the Lord, to bear fatigue, loss of rest, and painful sensations! How helpless and unworthy; yet comforted in my God—strengthened to do his will, to offer up my child, and with entire resignation to say, 'It is the Lord, let him do what seemeth him good!' How sweet also my prospects into a glorious eternity! and when weakest, no gloomy fears of entering those abodes;—but the blessed testimony, that where Jesus is, ('My Lord and my God!') there shall his servant be, and shall see his face—'his Godhead without a veil, wrapped up in Father, Son, and Spirit, forevermore.'"

Upon leaving London, she writes as follows:—

"Sunday, Sept. 1.—I heard Mr. Rogers at the new chapel in the morning, and had a blessed season. He also preached at Spitalfields in the evening, from, 'Finally, brethren, farewell.' The singers at both places took leave by hymns adapted for the purpose, very sweet and affecting. A mixture of love and friendly grief, together with deep gratitude to God, filled my soul. Lord, remember this dear people with tenfold blessings! on the two following days the simple-hearted affection, shown by very many of God's dear children, affected me much. I saw my dear and only brother on Tuesday evening. I felt much at parting. I think we shall not meet again on earth. After this, I called upon our valuable friends, Tooth, Whitfield, Jones, and several others; and then hastened to meet my dear husband at our kind friend's Mr. Senols, where we supped. O thou God of Love, preserve these until we meet them all again, where pain and parting are no more! On Wednesday we dined at Mr. Ball's, and then hastened in a coach, with our children, to Mr. T. Shakspeares', in Smithfield. It was Bartholomew's fair; and such a scene, or rather manifold scenes of folly, my eyes never beheld, as were exhibited where once dying martyrs for Jesus offered up their latest breath! With difficulty, but, thank God, with safety, we got through. I found my body very weak, and expected to faint; but I had not been long in the coach before I was better. Through much mercy we arrived next day at Birmingham, where our friends received us kindly. On the ensuing Sabbath Mr. Rogers preached from 'I determined not to know any thing among you, save Jesus Christ, and him crucified.' The word was with power, and my soul was greatly comforted."

It was thought a change of air and situation would be useful to our dear friend, and have been a means, under God, of strengthening her delicate constitution; but an obstinate windy complaint, with which she was attacked near three years before her dissolution, baffled all human skill, and repelled the force of every medicine, and never left her till the day of her death. During the last three or four months of her life, out of various other things, the following are extracted:—

"Since I came to Birmingham the Lord has been very present with me: I have indeed been fed with the hidden manna of his love! I have been peculiarly drawn out in prayer for the conversion of souls; and notwithstanding the enemy has laboured by various means to hinder this, yet the Lord hath given me to rejoice also herein. I feel my soul animated to praise my great Source of bliss: may all I have, and all I am, be his devoted sacrifice forever, I feel it good to live by faith: it brings deep peace and present power. I never can watch so well as when I thus momentarily believe. I have of late felt very poorly in body; and have had a degree of dulness hanging on my spirit; but I fly to the Lord—I wrestle with him for its removal: and I ever find he is a present God when I call upon him. And O, how he opens his heaven of love afresh in my soul, by giving me unspeakable views of what my Jesus suffered in the body for me! and the love and sympathy he still feels to every suffering member. I have felt of late a deepening of the graces of faith, resignation, and entire dependence on my God. And O, how good is the Lord, that he should thus prepare me for what he knew would touch me in the tenderest part!

"After a very restless night, my dear Patty broke out very full of the small pox; and for a fortnight I had much exercise for faith and patience. But this was very little to what I felt on the return of my dearest husband from Barr, where (on May 19, 1793) he had a kind of apoplectic fit. He fell down as sudden as if he had been shot—and still continues very unwell. Yet in secret prayer, the Lord assured me he should not die, but live! O, what should I do at a time like this, if I had not a constant intercourse with my God? But blessed be his dear name, I have access to him. He is indeed my refuge and strength, a very present help in trouble; and fills my soul with strong consolation.

"July 15, 1794.—For some time I have felt a desire, if the Lord saw good, to accompany my dear husband to the Bristol Conference. It would be a gratification to see the dear children; but much more do I desire to go on account of my dear partner's health, who has not yet recovered his late awful attack. I was in suspense, however, until this day, whether I could go or not; but now I see an opening in providence; and although there is a hazard with respect to myself in taking such a journey in my present state, yet the Lord assures me he will preserve my going out and my coming in; and greatly comforts my soul. On Tuesday, 22, we set off at four in the morning, with Mr. Pawson, and as many more of the preachers as the coach could contain. We had a comfortable journey. I felt the Lord truly with me, and my body was in a wonderful manner strengthened; so that I was astonished to feel no more fatigued when, about ten o'clock, we arrived at our kind friend's, Mr. Hartland. We had also a refreshing sleep, and arose, both of us, in better health than when we left home. May I deeply feel my many mercies as so many various pledges of my Father's love! We found our three sweet boys, thank God, all in health, and overjoyed at seeing us. Joseph is making swift progress in the printing business, and likely to make an excellent workman. Benjamin is approved by his master, beloved by his school-fellows, and, above all, I trust he truly fears God. My James is very childish, (he is but eight years old,) yet I think I see in him the dawnings of a noble spirit, which, if governed by grace, will one day give us comfort in him also, and make him a blessing to thousands.

"After different scenes of manifold consolations during the time of conference, on August 10, we arose before three o'clock in the morning, and set off at four, on our journey home. Our friends were very affectionate, and our dear children also got up to see us set off, and we left them all well, though sorrowful to part. I claimed my Lord's promise to preserve me in coming in, as in going out; and I proved him faithful. He did wonderfully strengthen my poor body, and sustain my soul with his heartfelt presence. We arrived safe in our habitation by nine in the evening, and found the three children we had left, all well. And though I felt inexpressibly weary, yet, to be brought safe in so critical a situation, (not two months from the time of my expected confinement,) filled my soul with unspeakable gratitude."

During the few remaining weeks of her life,

she continued to breathe the following sweet language of a saint truly ripe for God:—

"Monday, Sept. 1.—I had a good day: my intercourse with heaven is truly open, and my soul stayed upon my God. Tuesday, 2, was a blessed day of nearness to God. His word was precious food; and I found my heart enlarged in praise and love. Wednesday, 3, was also a day of inward comfort, though of bodily weakness. I had a precious time in meeting my class. And although the poor sinners were baiting a bull by the window, I believe all, as well as myself, so felt the Divine presence, as not to be disturbed by the rabble. Thursday, 4, I had much cramp and little sleep in the night, which in some degree has weakened the animal frame; but I feel peace in my God. Friday, 5.—I believe in answer to prayer, I had refreshing sleep, and was better in body this day, and my soul comforted in my God." Thus she goes on from day to day, expressing the same unshaken confidence and comfort in her God, even until she could write and speak no more!—The last words she was able to write in her journal are these:—"My body is very poorly, and has been so most of the week. O! what a clog to the spirit! Yet I am kept in a praying, depending, resigned frame, determined to trust my God with my all."

On the 10th of October, 1794, the expected time of her travail being come, she was in great pain most of the day, and about eight o'clock in the evening she was delivered of a fine boy. She was not a little disturbed by her inveterate windy disorder during her labour, but after her delivery she seemed much relieved. She lay composed for more than half an hour, with heaven in her countenance, praising God for his great mercy, and expressing her gratitude to all around her. She took Mr. Rogers by the hand, and said, "My dear, the Lord has been very kind to us: O, he is good, indeed he is good! But I'll tell you more by and by." She thanked the doctor, and told him she would remember his kindness and attention another day, and expressed her entire satisfaction in all he had done. But, alas! in a few minutes after this, her terrible complaint returned with redoubled violence, and instantly threw her whole frame into a state of agitation not to be described. A medicine just then arrived from the doctor, which she took; but all in vain. After a severe struggle for about fifteen minutes, bathed all over with a clammy, cold sweat, she laid her head on her husband's bosom, and said, "I am going." Mr. Rogers, recovering a little from the dreadful feelings he had experienced, found a desire to propose a question or two to his dear wife, relative to the state of her soul, not for his own satisfaction, for (as he observed to me) he could as soon call in question the truth of revelation, and of all religious experience from the beginning, as doubt of her eternal happiness; but he did this that God might be glorified, as in her life, so by her death. In the presence of many of her friends who were standing by he said to her, "My dearest creature, is Jesus precious?" She replied, "Yes, O yes, yes." He added, "My dearest love, I know Jesus Christ has long been your all in all, can you now tell us he is so?" She replied, "I can—he is—yes—but I am not able to speak." He again said, "O, my dearest, it is enough." She then attempted to lift up her face to his, and kissed him with her quivering lips and latest breath. About ten o'clock (two hours after her delivery) she gently fell asleep in Jesus, in the thirty-ninth year of her age, leaving her inanimate clay in her dearest husband's arms, and seven children to lament their unspeakable loss.

Thus lived, and thus died one of the best of women. Almost every thing that is good may be said of her, if she be viewed as a daughter, a wife, a mother, a friend, a private Christian, or as a public person; particularly as a leader of classes and bands, in the Methodist society. Almighty grace, to which alone be ascribed all the glory, got to itself indeed a victory in this amiable woman.

Her filial duty is hardly to be exceeded. Whilst she indulged herself in those pleasures which the world calls innocent, but which the children of God in all ages have known to be inconsistent with vital religion, she enjoyed the smiles of her mother, and of a flattering world. But no sooner did she become a confessor of Christ, but the clouds of persecution lowered, and afterward fell down upon her with great severity. Her mother not only confined her for a considerable time, but at last gave her the alternative of leaving her house, or of becoming her proper servant. She preferred the latter; and, though brought up in the most delicate manner, and of a very respectable family, she submitted to the degradation, and for several months went through all the most menial offices with a patience and meekness not to be shaken. Her mother finding her incorrigibly pious and steady to her God, (enthusiastic as her mother would have termed it,) for the sake of her own honour, raised her again from the ashes to the state of a child. But all this time Miss Roe discovered nothing but the height of filial affection; and continued so to do in every instance till her mother's death.

Her conjugal affection was equally great and

steady; and indeed (as may be observed from what has been already said) Mr. Rogers stood in need of such a helpmeet for him. When he was stationed in London as the assistant preacher, his steady attachment to the Methodist discipline raised up many powerful and bitter enemies against him. His sufferings were inexpressible, and his constitution very much impaired thereby; though at the same time it must be observed, that a unanimous vote of thanks was granted him by the Methodist Conference, for his exertions and his immovable patience and fortitude in defence of Methodism. Mrs. Rogers was, to my knowledge, during those three years of severe trial, his support indeed. More true conjugal love could not, I think, be manifested by a wife to her husband, than was by her, both at that time, and, I verily believe, upon all occasions. It seems probable, that she had received some secret intimations of her death, before she was taken in labour, which appears to be proved by a copy of verses which were found among some of her choice papers a little after her death. Those glowing effusions, which may be expected to flow from the heart of a most affectionate wife, are so evidently displayed in these lines, that I transcribe the whole:

"My hour is come, and angels round me wait,
To take me to their glorious happy state:

Where, free from sickness, death, and every pain,
I shall with God in endless pleasures reign.

"Transporting thought! Thou dearest man, adieu!
I feel no sorrow but in leaving you:
O thou, my comfort, thought, and only care,
In these last words thy kindness I'll declare.

"In truth, in constancy, in faithful love,
Few could you equal, none superior prove:
Compell'd by frequent sickness to complain,
You strove to lessen and t' assuage my pain.

"A tender care you never fail'd to show,
A constant sharer in my present wo.

"More I would say, my gratitude to own,
But breath forsakes me, and my pulse is gone:
Adieu, dear man! ———— O spare
This flood of grief, and of thy health take care.

"My blessing to my babes: thou wilt be kind
To the dear infants whom I leave behind:
Train them to virtue, piety and truth,
And form their manners early in their youth.

"Farewell to all who now on me attend,
The faithful servant, and the weeping friend:
The time is short till we shall meet again,
With Christ, to share the glories of his reign."

Her maternal care and affection shone equally bright. Though she devoted much of her time to religious duties in public and private, yet nothing seemed to be left undone which could make her children comfortable and happy. She even prevented all their wants; and was equally, nay, if it were possible, more, attentive to Mr. Rogers's children by his former wife than to her own. To the whole of them she delighted to give "precept upon precept, precept upon precept, line upon line, line upon line, here a little and there a little!" watering the whole of her labours upon them with many tears, and daily fervent prayers.

As a friend, she was faithful, and immovable in her attachments: nothing but her friends forsaking God, could induce her to abate her love for them. She was formed for society, and possessed the most delicate feelings which could arise from the social principle. And when some of her dearest intimates treated her with neglect, on account of some disputes in the connection which they had nothing to do with, she could still weep, and love, and pray for them, not as unworthy of her friendship, or of the favour of God, but as led away from her by misinformation and error of understanding, and perhaps also by some deviations from the perfect love of God.

But her *forte*, her greatest excellence, consisted in the enjoyment of her God. A very considerable part of her life evidenced, that salvation from sin, and salvation from sufferings, are very different things. Her firm patience under deep afflictions has been rarely, if ever, exceeded. Her conduct in the hour of nature's sorrow, in every instance, astonished all who were near her; and her sufferings on those occasions were very exquisite. Her animal spirits were astonishingly good at all times. She hardly ever in her life was in what is generally termed low spirits. She was ever cheerful, never light; and always ready to lift up the hands of her husband, and her friends, and to encourage their hearts. She enjoyed for many years that glorious blessing, which St. John in the fourth chapter of his first epistle speaks of, as his own experience and that of many of whom he was writing—that "perfect love of God, which casteth out all fear that hath torment." In short, she walked with God, she lived in the blaze of gospel day, and Christ was her all in all.

And as a public person she was useful in a high degree. She never, indeed, assumed the authority of teaching in the church; but she visited the fatherless and widows in their affliction, and delighted to pour out her soul in prayer for them. Very many dying persons entered into the liberty of God's children, under her prayers and exhortations; for she possessed a peculiar gift in bringing a present salvation home to the soul. The profit received in Macclesfield from her holy conversation, for years before she married, induced pious and mourning souls to visit her; and a very considerable part of her time was daily spent in answering cases of conscience, spreading forth the loveliness and excellences of Christ to penitents, and in building up believers in their most holy faith. She then was a leader of classes and bands, and a mother in Israel to the young believers intrusted to her care. After her marriage she still became more extensively useful. Mr. Rogers, on his entering into a circuit, would only give a few to her care, desiring her to complete the class out of the world; and soon, by her conversation and prayers, and attention to every soul within her reach, would the number spring up to thirty or forty; and then her almost cruel husband, in this respect, for the glory of God, would transplant all the believers to other classes, and keep her thus continually working at the mine. In the city of Dublin only, Mr. Rogers himself confesses, some hundreds of those whom he received into society, were brought to Christ, or were awakened, by her gentle, but incessant labours of love. In Cork also, and in London, a similar success attended her pious exertions. Thus did the Lord mould this blessed woman into his image, as the potter does his clay, and use her for his glory, as the ready writer does his pen, until she had served him in her generation, and he said unto her, It is enough, come up higher. GO, AND DO THOU LIKEWISE.

APPENDIX TO THE FUNERAL SERMON FOR MRS. ROGERS.

BY HER HUSBAND.

As this tremendous stroke of Divine Providence has wounded me in the tenderest nerve, I hope any irregularity of thought, or impropriety of expression, however censurable on other occasions, will be pardoned by the candid reader in the present instance —especially as he will perceive, in the preceding sermon, that mine is more than a common loss.

The valuable pamphlet lately published by my dear companion, which contains a clear account of her experience from her childhood, supersedes many remarkable occurrences which should otherwise have followed in this supplement; and, as that little performance either is or may be, in the possession of any friend who desires it, I am unwilling to say the same things, which are ranged there in a better manner than I feel adequate to, under my present circumstances. If what follows is made useful to any of my friends, the return I desire is a constant interest in their sympathetic prayers, that I may be supported under my irreparable loss, and enabled to conduct myself in all things, during this most awful, trying scene, not like a stoic, but as a Christian.

In my dear companion, I have certainly lost one of the best helpmates man was ever united to. Her feeling sympathy and faithful love were, I believe, seldom equalled and never exceeded! With hers, my soul still feels, as it were, entwined, and interwoven. She was (under God) the centre and constant spring of all my domestic happiness. In her I have not only lost one of the most valuable and faithful wives; but my dear children at the same time are bereft of a most tender and affectionate parent, who always had their interest and happiness at heart.

But, what is incomparably more afflictive still to me, I have lost, in her, my best help in spiritual things. She always gave me uncommon assistance in my labours, and greatly soothed all my cares and anxieties for the church's weal or wo. She was ever my comforter in the time of sorrow. The evenness of her temper and the cheerfulness of her disposition, both in sickness and in health, were wonderful! I never saw, for one moment, any thing like gloom in her countenance; neither do I remember one trifling word ever to drop from her lips; but, on the contrary, she was always ready for spiritual conversation; and no company pained her mind equal to that where religious subjects were unpleasing or impracticable. Witness her own words soon after our arrival in Dublin :—

"Mrs. —— invited us to dinner, where we met with much gay company. Dr. —— took up the attention of the whole, with his trifling, ridiculous conversation, so that it was a very unprofitable season; and I cried to the Lord in my spirit, that we might have no more such visits as these!"—And, thank God, we had no more such while we continued in that city; but, on the contrary, our visits in general, were serious, spiritual, and profitable, so that some time afterward she remarks :

"We dined with Mr. S——, and Mr. Henry Brook was with us. He ap[illegible] to be a man of deep piety, and the conversat[illegible]as profitable. Blessed be God, all our visits since the first, have been more to his glory. My soul feels much nearness to the people, and a sweet assurance we shall be blessed among them, and made a blessing —O, for a heart-reviving shower of grace, and pentecostal blessings! The Lord I know sent us here, and surely it is for the good of souls.—My God let this be promoted, and thou shalt have the endless praise!"

Such was our union of soul and sentiment, that the secrets of our hearts were always open to each other. And it was no small consolation to me, that I had one upon earth so dear to God, who both knew and approved of all the motives from which I acted in public, as well as in private life. Hence it was, that from a conviction of her duty to God, she was ever ready to resist the unkindness of my opponents, and warn me against the craftiness of pretended friends; and her penetration herein was astonishing; so that I do not remember I ever relied upon her judgment, or acted by her advice, but I found it good.

As to her literary abilities, they were rather out of the common way. She had a critical knowledge of the English tongue! and her application to reading from her infancy made her capable of conversing on almost any subject, whether of an historical, philosophical, or theological nature.

With respect to the labours of her pen, she was of all I ever knew among her sex, the most assiduous. Writing seemed to be her peculiar talent; and she took great delight therein, even from her childhood. And yet, she never on that account, or, indeed, on any other, once neglected any part of her domestic duty. She might be truly said to husband her time in order to improve this talent. While I was absent an hour one morning breakfasting with a friend,—(and although she was prevented by sickness from accompanying me,) upon my return she with her usual smile, presented me with the following acrostic upon our marriage union:—

"J esus, the source supreme of our delight,
A nd soul of all our joys, of all our might,
M ade us of twain inseparably one,
N ever to love as he hath loved his own:
S o may we love—as Jesus loves his bride,
A nd nothing shall his love from her divide:
N othing made twain the souls whom God hath joined;
D eath only leaves mortality behind.

H eaven shall complete our union here begun,
E ndless as vast eternal circles run.
S ay, shall not then thy spirit join with mine,
T o praise the wonders of the plan divine?
E ach vie with other, which shall swiftest move,
R eady to strike afresh our harps above,
A nd bless the Saviour, through whose love we love!
N o hand but thine, dear Jesus, mark'd the road,
N o wisdom, love, or power, but that of God.
R esolved to bless—He to each other gave,
O h, that through life—His utmost power to save,
G race upon grace, our happy souls may prove,
E nwrapp'd, implunged, and swallow'd up in love:
R eady to clap the wing—His call obey,
S oar up together—Love in endless day!"

My dear partner never considered herself a poet, and rarely attempted any thing of the kind; nevertheless, these lines will show she was not entirely without this talent also.

Some of her letters with a few other productions in prose, have appeared in print; but these are very small compared with the numerous manuscripts she has left. Besides the vast quantity of letters which she wrote to her pious correspondents, she kept a diary of her life, from the time of her conversion to God, (which was in the seventeenth year of her age,) till within a few days of her death. So that I am favoured with, I believe, not less than three thousand quarto pages, all written by her own hand; and every page clearly discovers that, for the space of more than twenty years, she enjoyed constant fellowship and communion with a Triune God; and that she never forsook her first love, nor lost a sense of the Divine favour, from the day of her conversion to the hour of her death! None but those who live in the same spirit can properly conceive the degree of intimacy which subsisted between her and her God. That the reader may be excited to press after the same enjoyment, I will here give him a small specimen of the almost uninterrupted language of her heart and pen.

"I was so happy in the night, that I had very little sleep, and I awoke with these words, 'The temple of an indwelling God!' My soul sunk into depths of nothingness, and enjoys closer union with him this day than ever before. Every moment I feel such a weight of love, as almost overpowers the faculties of nature! I know I could bear no more and live; but I often feel ready to cry, O, give me more and let me die!—I long to be freed from the earth! But help me, Lord, to wait resigned, willing to suffer or do for thee. I need not lay this body down to feel thy presence! Thou dwellest in my heart, and shalt forever dwell! Thou art my present heaven, my soul's eternal all.

"I went to bed last night so full of the love of God, I could not sleep for several hours; but continued in secret intercourse with my Saviour. At preaching this morning I was so overcome with the love and presence and exceeding glory of my *Triune God*, that I sunk down unable to support it! I was long before I could stand or speak! All this day I have been lost in depth of love unutterable. At the love-feast I was again overwhelmed with his immediate presence! All around me is God!

'Within his circling arms I lie,
Beset on every side!'"

Some time after this she writes,

"As I came from meeting, I was so overpowered by the presence of God, that, had not a friend supported me, I could not have walked home! I was lost in the depths of love, and admitted, as it were, into the immediate presence of my Lord's glory! Yet I cannot explain it, for I saw no manner of similitude; and was humbled into the dust before him! It is often impressed on my mind, the Lord is preparing me for some close trial. My whole soul cries out, Thy will be done! Only let thy grace be sufficient for me.

> 'Unsustain'd by thee, I fall;
> Send the help for which I call:
> Weaker than a bruised reed,
> Help I every moment need!'

"Yes,—but,

> 'I all thy power shall prove:—
> Thy nature and thy name is love.'

"Blessed be God, I feel this day an increase of holy nearness to him, and fellowship with him. At the prayer-meeting my body was quite overcome for half an hour together, so did my Lord unfold his fulness of love to my ravished soul. I seemed as in the presence of his glory, confounded and overwhelmed with a sense of his purity and his justice, his grace and love, and was constrained to lie at his feet, in speechless adoration, and humblest praise; while my body was covered with a cold sweat, and all around thought I was dying! Well mightest thou say, O most adorable *Jehovah*, 'No man can see my face and live!' For, when thou displayest only one faint ray, one glimpse of thy glorious presence, this frail tabernacle is ready to crumble into dust before thee!—But, O, I shall one day be capable of beholding thee, face to face! These eyes shall see thy glory! and gaze for ever in ecstatic bliss! Now, this corruptible clay cannot support itself under the weight of thy love; but then it shall have put on incorruption, and be able to enjoy the full and eternal fruition of thy glory.

"Mr. P. preached from, 'The grace of the Lord Jesus Christ, and the love of God, and the communion of the Holy Ghost, be with you all.' Before he had spoken ten minutes, I was filled with the Triune God, and sunk motionless under an exceeding great weight of love! My outward senses were locked up; but my spirit seemed surrounded with glory inexpressible! I beheld Jesus, and was, as it were, overshadowed, and weighed down by the presence and exceeding glory of the whole Deity: I knew not where I was, or whether in the body! But all was unutterable bliss and glory. After I came to myself, I continued full of the divine presence, and a weight of love, such as enfeebled my whole frame. For many days and nights I could eat little, and had seldom more than an hour's sleep in twenty-four.

"Afterward, I passed through scenes of close trial, (for which the Lord had thus been graciously preparing me,) and, for a season, had not those peculiar manifestations; but his grace was sufficient, and he brought me through waves, and clouds, and storms unhurt! To him be glory for ever and ever."

As the quotations in the preceding sermon are chiefly taken from my companion's later manuscripts, I have transcribed these from what she wrote at an earlier period, which, when compared together, show, that as she begun so she finished her happy course! And although (as she observes) her ecstatic joy was sometimes checked by various trials, yet the same ground for rejoicing continued: viz. faith, and a pure conscience. And, besides the testimony of her own papers, I am witness that many times I have seen her as happy in God as she could well be, and exist below, so that I have been even afraid it would prove too much for the earthen vessel to bear!

She had a singular taste for reading, from her youth. In her unawakened state, her delight was in the perusal of entertaining novels and romances; and when a well-written history fell in her way, she thought little of reading three or four hundred octavo pages in a day, till she got through it; which she did with this advantage, that she generally made the substance of it her own. But since her acquaintance with vital religion, Rollin's Ancient History was her chief favourite, as she said she found most of God in it; and because it clearly illustrated the prophecies, and confirmed the truth of revelation.

But, of late years, (though she still read different authors at convenient opportunities,) the *Bible* was her chief study, and in it she took uncommon delight. Our usual rule was, to read one chapter every morning as a part of family worship; but for some time before the Lord took my dearest partner, we agreed to read three: one out of the Old Testament in the morning, one out of the Gospel at noon, and one at night out of the Acts or some of the Epistles. And, besides these, when unable to attend upon the public ministry of the word, she would call the servant to read by her, when even sickness and pain forbade her doing it herself. And, at intervals, when her strength would allow it, she often made remarks, and drew practical inferences as they went on.

In our course of reading to the family one morning, about three weeks before the time of her delivery, when we came to these words, in Gen. xxxv. 17–20, I perceived a silent tear stealing down her cheek. The passage referred to reads thus: "And it came to pass when she was in hard labour, that the midwife said unto her, Fear not: thou shalt have this son also. And it came to pass as her soul was departing (for she died) that she called his name Ben-oni; but his father called him Benjamin. And Rachel died, and was buried in the way to Ephrath, which is Bethlehem. And Jacob set a pillar upon her grave: that is the pillar of Rachel's grave to this day." Some time after this, in my absence, she desired the maid to read to her again the same chapter, which considerably affected her. Yet I could not then learn that she had the least presentiment of her death, any more than what is common to women in similar circumstances. But indeed it was a subject which neither of us could bear to enter into the spirit of. And, therefore, if at any time it was impressed upon our minds, we endeavoured to put it away.

When alone, she often read the Bible kneeling: on which occasion, we frequently find her breaking forth in language of this sort: "Reading the word of God in private this day was an unspeakable blessing. O, how precious are the promises! What a depth in these words: 'For all the promises of God in him are yea, and in him, amen, unto the glory of God.' Yes, my soul, they are so to thee! The Father delights to fulfil and the Spirit to seal them on my heart. O, that dear invaluable truth!

'Ready art thou to receive:
Readier is thy God to give.'

"The Lord poured his love abundantly into my soul while worshipping before him; and I was enabled to renew my covenant, to be wholly and forever his! O, how precious are his ways to my soul, suited to my weakness, worthy of a God! I am nothing! He is all. I momentarily live upon his smiles, and dwell under the shadow of his wings: I desire nothing but to please him, to grow in inward conformity to his will, and sink deeper into humble love—to let the light of what his grace hath bestowed shine on all around, and to live and die proclaiming, *God is love.*"

I think myself bound, in justice to her amiable character, here to remark, that notwithstanding the tenderness of her affection for me, and the great sensibility of her feelings at my leaving her, (which I had often done when she was sick, and in pain,) yet she never, to my knowledge, once attempted to prevent me from going on my Lord's errand. No: she knew the importance of the message too well to do that. As to her own usefulness in the church of God, it will best appear when the light of eternity discovers it: in Macclesfield, Dublin, Cork, and London, her name will be precious to her numerous and kind friends, (and especially to the children of her faith and prayers,) while memory lasts; and, I believe, numbers of these will bless God in an eternal world, that they ever saw her face. Perhaps some may be found even in Birmingham, where she closed her useful, happy life, to whom the name of Mrs. Rogers will long be precious!

And yet, notwithstanding her extraordinary zeal for God and the salvation of souls, her good sense, joined with that Christian modesty ever becoming her sex, taught her as to the manner how to proceed in saving souls from death. The sphere in which she moved was, to visit the sick; to teach her own sex in private; and to pray, whenever providentially called upon, whether in public or private. And to her might be applied that scripture: "Whosoever hath, (or uses what he hath,) to him shall be given, and he shall have more abundantly." The divine unction attending her prayer, added to the manner in which she pleaded with God for instantaneous blessings, was very extraordinary, and generally felt by all present. A conviction from God, that she ought to use this talent, constrained her even to hold meetings in her neighbours' houses for the purpose of praying with the distressed in soul, and with as many more as chose to attend.

During our stay in Dublin, she met weekly three women's classes, consisting of about thirty members each, in all ninety, to whom she was called to speak individually, besides the many occasional conversations she had with others about the state of their souls. At Cork she met two large classes, mostly new members, to whom she had been useful, and was indeed the chief instrument in bringing them into the society, as was also the case with very many of those she met in Dublin.

In London, although called to the charge of Mr. Wesley's family in addition to her own, she at once filled the place of housekeeper at the City Road, (in which station she acquitted herself with honour for two years,) and at the same time, had the charge of two large classes. Her third and last year in London was not less profitable to her friends, many of them followed her to Spitalfields, where several new members were added to her classes; and I believe most of those who attended that means of grace with her, both in that and other places, found it good for their souls. While speaking to, and praying with them, many, very many, have been enabled to witness a clear sense of God's forgiving love; and others at the same time have obtained salvation from inbred sin—a doctrine this, of which she had the clearest views, and to its validity, her own conduct bore a constant testimony.

> "Through all her words the soul within,
> The honest, artless soul was seen,
> Ingenuous, pure, and free:
> Candour and love were sweetly join'd
> With easy nobleness of mind,
> And true simplicity."

And although she clearly perceived the need of a gradual work, daily exhorting believers to grow in grace, yet she saw it her duty to bid those who felt the burden of indwelling sin look for the total destruction of it in one moment—ever pressing them to believe for the blessing—to believe now—insisting, "If thou canst believe, all things are possible to him that believeth." And the Lord set his seal to the truths she enforced. Many through her means were instantaneously delivered from the remains of a carnal mind, so as to "rejoice evermore, pray without ceasing, and in every thing give thanks."

As great a matter as the attaining this blessing may appear, it is a yet greater thing to hold it fast. And as the following circumstance had a most blessed effect on the mind of my dear companion when she was comparatively a babe in this grace, greatly tending to establish her therein, I will, for the sake of others, transcribe the following account just as she wrote it at the time. And but few events did I ever hear her mention with greater pleasure than it.

"Leeds, Aug. 24, 1781.—That dear man of God, Mr. Fletcher, came with Miss Bosanquet, (now Mrs. Fletcher,) to dine at Mr. Smith's in Park-Row, and also to meet the select society. After dinner I took an opportunity to beg he would explain an expression he once used to Miss Loxdale in a letter, viz. 'That on all who are renewed in love, God bestows the gift of prophecy.' He called for the Bible: then read, and sweetly explained the second chapter of the Acts, observing: To prophesy in the sense he meant, was to magnify God with the new heart of love and the new tongue of praise, as they did, who on the day of pentecost were filled with the Holy Ghost! And he insisted that believers are now called to make the same confession: seeing, we may all prove the same baptismal fire, showing, that the day of pentecost was only the opening of the dispensation of the Holy Ghost, the great promise of the Father! and that the latter-day glory, which he believed was near at hand, should far exceed the first effusion of the Spirit. And, therefore, seeing they then bore witness to the grace of our Lord, so should we; and, like them, spread the flame of love. Then, after singing a hymn, he cried—O, to be filled with the Holy Ghost: I want to be filled. O my friends, let us wrestle for a more abundant outpouring of the Spirit. To me he said, Come, my sisters, will you covenant with me this day, to pray for the fulness of the Spirit? Will you be a witness for Jesus?—I answered, with flowing tears, 'In the strength of Jesus, I will.' He cried, Glory, glory, glory be to God: Lord, strengthen thy handmaid to keep this covenant, even unto death. He then said, My dear brethren and sisters, God is here: I feel him in this place; but I would hide my face in the dust, because I have been ashamed to declare what he hath done for me. For many years I have grieved his Spirit; but I am deeply humbled; and he has again restored my soul. Last Wednesday evening he spoke to me by these words, 'Reckon yourselves therefore to be dead indeed unto sin, but alive unto God through Jesus Christ our Lord.' I obeyed the voice of God: I now obey it, and I tell you all, to the praise of his love, 'I am free from sin!' Yes, I rejoice to declare it, and to bear witness to the glory of his grace, that I am dead unto sin, and alive unto God through Jesus Christ, who is my Lord and King. I received this blessing four or five times before; but I lost it by not observing the order of God, who has told us, 'With the heart man believeth unto righteousness, and with the mouth confession is made unto salvation.' But the enemy offered his bait under various colours to keep me from a public declaration of what my Lord had wrought.

"When I first received this grace, Satan bid me wait a while, till I saw more of the fruits: I resolved to do so, but I soon began to doubt of the witness, which, before, I had felt in my heart;

and was in a little time sensible I had lost both. A second time, after receiving this salvation, (with shame I confess it,) I was kept from being a witness for my Lord, by the suggestion, 'Thou art a public character: the eyes of all are upon thee; and if, as before, by any means thou lose the blessing, it will be a dishonour to the doctrine of heart holiness,' &c. I held my peace, and again forfeited the gift of God! At another time I was prevailed upon to hide it by reasoning, How few, even of the children of God, will receive this testimony, many of them supposing every transgression of the Adamic law is sin; and, therefore, if I profess myself to be free from sin, all these will give my profession the lie: because I am not free, in their sense: I am not free from ignorance, mistakes, and various infirmities: I will, therefore, enjoy what God has wrought in me, but I will not say, I am perfect in love. Alas! I soon found again, 'He that hideth his Lord's talent, and improveth it not, from that unprofitable servant shall be taken away even that he hath.'

"Now, my brethren, you see my folly! I have confessed it in your presence, and now I resolve, before you all, to confess my Master: I will confess him to all the world; and I declare unto you, in the presence of God, the *holy Trinity*, I am now 'dead indeed unto sin.' I do not say, 'I am crucified with Christ;' because some of our well-meaning brethren say, By this can only be meant a gradual dying; but I profess unto you, I am dead unto sin, and alive unto God! And remember all this is 'through Jesus Christ our Lord.' He is my *Prophet, Priest,* and *King:* my indwelling holiness: *my all in all* I wait for the fulfilment of that prayer, 'That they all may be one: as thou, Father, art in me, and I in thee, that they also may be one in us; and that they be one, even as we are one.' O, for that pure baptismal flame! O, for the fulness of the dispensation of the Holy Ghost: pray, pray—pray for this: this shall make us all of one heart and of one soul: pray for gifts, for the gift of utterance; and confess your royal Master. A man without gifts is like the king in disguise: he appears as a subject only. You are kings and priests unto God. Put on, therefore, your robes, and wear on your garments, '*Holiness to the Lord.*'

"A few days after this, I heard Mr. Fletcher preach from the same subject, which greatly encouraged and strengthened me. Inviting all who felt their need of full redemption, to believe now for this great salvation, he observed, 'As when you reckon with your creditor, or with your host; and, as when you have paid all, you reckon yourselves free, so now reckon with God. Jesus hath paid all: and he hath paid for thee—hath purchased thy pardon and holiness. Therefore, it is now God's command, "Reckon thyself dead unto sin;" and thou art alive unto God from this hour! O, begin, begin to reckon now: fear not, believe, believe, believe; and continue to believe every moment, so shalt thou continue free; for it is retained as it is received, by faith alone. And whosoever thou art that perseveringly believest, it will be as a fire in thy bosom, and constrain thee to confess with thy mouth the Lord and King Jesus; and in spreading the sacred flame of love, thou shalt still be saved to the uttermost.'

"He also dwelt largely on those words, 'Where sin abounded, grace did much more abound.' He asked, how did sin abound? Had it not overspread your whole soul? Were not all your passions, tempers, propensities, and affections, inordinate and evil? Did not pride, anger, self-will, and unbelief, all reign in you? And when the Spirit of God strove with you, did you not repel all his convictions, and put him far from you? Well, my brethren, 'Ye were *then* the servants of sin, and were free from righteousness; but now being made free from sin, ye become servants to God;' and holiness shall overspread your whole soul, so that all your tempers and passions shall be henceforth regulated and governed by Him who now sitteth upon the throne of your heart, making all things new. They shall therefore all be holy.—And as you once resisted the Holy Spirit, so now you shall have power as easily to resist all the subtle frauds or fierce attacks of Satan: yea, his suggestions to evil shall be like a ball thrown against a wall of brass. It shall rebound back again; and you shall know what that meaneth, 'The prince of this world cometh, and hath nothing in me.'

"He then, with lifted hands cried 'Who will thus be saved? Who will believe the report. You are only in an improper sense called believers who reject this! Who is a believer? One that believes a few things which his God has spoken? Nay, but one that believes all that ever proceeded even out of his mouth. Here, then, is the word of the Lord: 'As sin abounded, grace shall much more abound!' As no good thing was in you by nature, so now no evil thing shall remain. Do you believe this? or are you a half believer only? Come, Jesus is offered to thee as a perfect Saviour: take him, and he will make thee a perfect saint. O, ye half believers, will ye still plead for the murderers of your Lord? Which of these will you hide as a serpent in your bosom? Shall it be anger, pride, self-will, or accursed unbelief? O, be no longer befooled: bring these enemies to thy Lord, and let him slay them.

"Some days after this, being in Mr. Fletcher's company, he took me by my hand, and said, 'Glory be to God, for you, my sister, still bear a noble testimony for your Lord. Do you repent your confession of his salvation?' I answered, 'Blessed be God, I do not.' At going away, he again took me by the hand, saying, with eyes and heart lifted up, 'Bless her, Heavenly Power!' It seemed as if an instant answer was given, and a beam of glory let down! I was filled with deep humility and love; yea, my whole soul overflowed with unutterable sweetness."

As my beloved companion enjoyed that purity of heart mentioned by our Lord in Matt. v. 8, so did she see God in all things. She greatly delighted in secret retirement and private intercourse with him. She had strong confidence in a particular providence presiding over all that respected her; and as she believed that "the very hairs of our head are numbered, and that a sparrow cannot fall to the ground without our heavenly Father," so was she led to ask of God various things which many professors of religion seldom think of praying for. And it is remarkable how many are the instances which she has recorded as direct answers to her prayers. I will here transcribe two or three.

"June 29, 1782.—This day the Lord instantaneously removed a rapid mortification in my dear mother's leg, in answer to prayer. The doctor having given his opinion that in a few hours it would be fatal, I flew to my Almighty refuge, and felt I had power with God, through faith in that promise: 'The prayer of faith shall save the sick.' And, when in half an hour I looked again at the wound, all the bad symptoms were gone; and the same doctor, standing astonished, said, no danger now appeared. I could not forbear weeping aloud for joy and gratitude, praising the God of my life."

"Nov. 29, 1785.—A lady of genteel appearance, whom I had not seen before, requested to speak with me. I found she had come secretly to hear preaching for some months, and was under deep awakenings. Her husband is a man of fortune, but a professed infidel—believes in neither God, devil, heaven, nor hell—mocks at the Scriptures, especially the New Testament; and will neither attend any place of public worship himself, nor suffer her to do so. And what added to her affliction, his bad state of health determined him to go to live in France. She cried, 'What will become of me there? No means of grace: no friend to fly to: in a country of idolaters abroad, and infidels at home: my sinful heart and the temptations of Satan to struggle with: I shall lose all my good desires, and my poor soul will be ruined!'

"I asked, 'Is there no way to prevent this?' She answered, 'No.' I said, 'But the Lord can prevent it; and if not for his glory, he will.' 'Ha!' said she, 'I fear nothing can prevent it: the carriage is preparing, and the time is fixed.' I replied, 'Only put the whole into the Lord's hand, and you are safe. Trust in God, and make it a matter of prayer; and if the journey be not for your good, though it come to the last hour he will prevent it. Nay, if you should even set out, *he* can, by a thousand means, turn you back, and he will. Did he not suffer the three Hebrew children to be cast into the furnace? Yet the fire had no power to consume. Daniel was cast into the den; but the God you are called to trust shut the lions' jaws. St. John was put into the caldron of boiling oil; yet he received no harm. This God, who is the same yesterday, to-day, and for ever, will prevent this journey if you trust in him; or he will make it a blessing to your soul.' I then went to prayer, and at parting bid her pray much for her husband, and believe all things are possible with God.

"Some time after she called on me, and told me she had taken my advice and prayed for her husband, who, a few nights ago, had a remarkable dream, which much affected and astonished him. He thought he was giving orders to his coach-maker about his new carriage, and more especially about one of the wheels, when the man turned about and said, in a very solemn manner, 'Sir, you need not trouble yourself about that wheel, for the Lord Jesus Christ has the whole management of it.' He was filled with surprise, and awoke. I again commended her to God in prayer, and she returned home not a little comforted.

"A few days afterward, a note was sent to request public thanks to Almighty God for his power and love manifested in behalf of a person whose name is unknown. The messenger, calling on me at the same time, said, 'Thank God, this journey is prevented at last!' I asked, 'But how was this brought to pass?' She said, 'Only two days ago, all was fixed for the journey; and on this day they were to set off. But the Lord afflicted the physician who advised them to go. And Mr. ——, finding himself very poorly, called in another doctor, who assured him he could not undergo the journey, and that France is not a proper place for his constitution, and therefore all thoughts of going are at an end.'

"O how my soul was filled with wonder, love, and praise! Who that considers the above, will

not see omnipotence, love, and faithfulness, exerted in answer to prayer? Who would not wish for such a friend? Who would not love, serve, and confide in such a God? Who would not own, 'He heareth prayer, and to him should all flesh come!' And how wonderful is such a dream of the Lord Jesus Christ by a man of such principles! Surely it was all of God, and to him alone is due all the glory."

"March 5, 1790.—In private, I had peculiar liberty in praying for my dear husband, that he might experience all the depth of Jesus' love more abundantly than ever, and be the happy means of leading me also into further degrees of inward salvation—that our union might ever tend to a yet closer union with our God, and all our outward mercies lead to this. While I prayed, I felt assured my Lord was well pleased, and would send an answer to my largest desires. Next morning Mr. Rogers awoke very happy, having had a precious view of the deep things of God: he dreamed that he felt the clear witness of sanctification, and his soul seemed full of gratitude and love. In taking a ride out together, and laying open our whole hearts to each other, as we frequently did, I found my soul unspeakably happy, while we resolved to be more spiritual, more devoted to God, and more zealous in saving souls, than ever. This was made a great blessing to me; and doubly so, as I believe it an answer to my prayer."

The last instance I shall cite took place only a little before her death. "June 10, 1794.—I had a peculiar season in wrestling prayer with my God this night, on account of my dear little Mary. The great weakness of her limbs for three months past, and her seeming total inability to walk, has caused much pain to my dear husband as well as myself. It appears to me I had used every possible means in vain. But this night I had power to cry unto my God, and tell him, 'Thou art the same yesterday, to-day, and forever: thou art my God.' Thou hast said, 'Call upon me in the day of trouble, and I will hear thee.' Thou hast healed cripples, made the lame to walk, yea, raised even the dead, in answer to praying faith! Lord, hear me now: stoop to my request: let the child's feet and ankle bones receive strength, give power to walk, and let me soon know thou hast heard my prayer. And I had power to believe it should be done; and my soul was filled with the Divine presence. Thursday, the 12th.—I already see an answer to my prayer in the child. She is greatly strengthened in her limbs. How good, how faithful, how condescending is the Lord! We may—I may, like Abraham, like Moses, like Elijah, ask and obtain."

Such were the habits of intimacy which my

dear partner enjoyed with her beloved Saviour, that even when her outward senses were locked up by sleep, he would frequently speak to her heart; and in dreams and visions of the night, appeared to strengthen her in times of trial—warn her of danger, or prepare her for trouble before it came. One instance out of many I will here mention. It happened about four years after our marriage, and was attended with much comfort to her mind ever after, when she recurred to it.

"Having been exercised with an uncommon sense of various short-comings and daily infirmities for some days past, I awoke this morning, lost, overwhelmed, and swallowed up in love, joy, and praise, occasioned by the following dream. I thought I was in an elegant house, and was desired by one to go into that room, (pointing the way,) and I should see the late Mrs. Rogers. I wondered, but obeyed: I thought I entered the room, which was hung all round with clean white linen; and upon a bed I saw the beautiful corpse of my dear departed sister and friend! I looked, and loved the precious remains, when, to my great astonishment, her eyes opened! She smiled on me, and raised herself up. I exclaimed, in a rapture of joyful surprise, 'Is it possible? Has the Lord permitted you to revive, so as to speak to me?' She replied, with unutterable sweetness, 'All things, my dear, are possible with God. He has permitted it for your comfort.' 'O,' said I, 'what would I have often given, to converse one hour with you, since you were taken?' She said, 'There was no need, my dear, God has been with you.' I answered, 'Yes, he has; but O, tell me, have I acted my part aright in your place? Does God, in this, approve of me?' She smiled again, and said, 'He does; and in all things he is well pleased; and he will yet strengthen and bless you to the end! He loves you, and he will save you in every time of trouble, especially in your approaching trial. You have nothing to fear; for you will be happy in life, in death, and forever. You are dear to God; and it is to comfort you he permits me to appear and tell you this.'

"This was but a few weeks before my Hester was born. And what I felt was unutterable indeed: love unspeakable and ravishing delight filled my whole soul; I was quite overpowered: I thought in my dream she said much more; but this is all I can distinctly recollect. And it so overcame me with transport, that I awoke; but my body was bathed in sweat, and my soul, as in the dream, filled with God, with heaven, and with unspeakable bliss, so that I could not refrain awaking my dear husband to tell him; and I could sleep no more, but continued praising God until the morning. The more I considered his condescending goodness herein, the more I am lost in love, self-abasement, and speechless gratitude."

This dream was made a great blessing to us both; and it is attended with no small consolation to me, especially under my present circumstances, to conceive that the inhabitants of heaven know well the transactions of earth! And (to waive the almost innumerable and well-authenticated instances of recent date) that they do so is beyond a doubt; or, how could they be said to "rejoice over every sinner that repenteth?" And when Moses and Elijah conversed with our Lord, it was on the bitter cup he was to drink in Jerusalem: of consequence, they remembered that place, as well as those prophecies which were to be fulfilled upon that occasion. And if the pious poor retain so lively a sensation in the other world, of the favours conferred on them in this, as to wait for the arrival of their kind benefactors, in order to "receive them into everlasting habitations," Luke xvi. 11, what kind offices may we not expect from those who, for many years, were our faithful companions in the kingdom and patience of Jesus? "Are they not *all* (as well as the angels) ministering spirits, sent forth to minister for them who shall be heirs of salvation?" And what angel (except the Angel of the Covenant, who took upon him our nature, and was touched with the feeling of our infirmities) is so well qualified for this office and guardianship as they? And it is even probable a part of their heaven consists in the pleasure of attending those who are yet probationers in this world of wo, especially when they see us attentive to the will of Him that sent them.

Hard as it was to part, my dear companion would have found it harder still, but for the same persuasion which constantly rested with her, as appears from her own words, saying, "I feel myself very poorly in body, and several symptoms threaten my dissolution. But my soul is kept in perfect peace: I know, 'For me to live is Christ, and to die is gain.' It seems as if the Lord had been of late preparing me for himself. And yet, when I think of leaving the dearest of earthly comforts, it is like rending of self from self; of nature from nature; and of flesh from the bone! Nevertheless, when I reflect the separation is only for a moment, compared with eternity, and that death itself cannot disunite our spirits, it greatly helps me to say, Lord, not as I will, but as thou wilt."

It seems easy to learn from this and other touches in the preceding pages, that, be our attainments in piety what they will, they have not the least tendency to dissolve the endearing ties of natural affection: on the contrary, that religion, by refining, tends to increase, both the fervour and constancy of our love. But what are all other ties, of which the human heart is capable, compared with that holy and spiritual union, ever subsisting between those whom God, in every sense hath made one?

I am conscious, the tenderest of maternal ties possessed the heart of my dear companion; yet these, when it came to the point, were dissolved with comparative ease! as were, also, all her other friendly attachments—with one only exception, of *myself*.

"Not even in death, her friendship dies!
With grateful pity and surprise
I ask, how can it be?
Loosen'd from all she leaves behind,
Yet still—she cleaves to ME.

"On me she rests her dying head,
And catching, grasps a broken reed,
But will not let me part:
Till Jesus visits her again,
By nobler love dissolves the chain,
And frees her struggling heart."

God alone can tell you what I felt in that dread moment, when her Lord gave the signal for dismission and I was called to return the last parting kiss! For some time I could only breathe, as it were, in silent accents, "O, my God, let my latter end be like hers: come, O, come quickly, and prepare me to follow her. It is still the language of my bleeding heart,—

> "O, let me on her image dwell,
> The soul-transporting spectacle,
> On whom even angels gaze:
> A pious saint matured for God,
> And shaking off her earthly clod,
> To see his open face.
>
> "I see the generous friend sincere,
> Her voice still vibrates in my ear,
> The voice of truth and love;
> It calls me to put off my clay,
> And bids me soar with her away
> To fairer worlds above."

Well, thank God, a moment cannot always last. And

> "He who set my partner free,
> Shall quickly send for you and me!"

Only let us take care that our loins are girt, and our lights burning as bright as hers, when our Lord cometh, and all shall be well! All who knew my valuable companion, will allow that these pages contain but a small part of what might be said upon so every way amiable a character. But there is a day coming when her real value shall be made manifest.

The honour of being united to such a woman

fills my soul with unfeigned gratitude before God! And although at present I am left to feel my loss, I am supported from above in a manner that exceeds all description. The heartfelt presence of God, which, from the time he took my all of earthly treasure, I have not wanted, for one moment, more than compensates for the absence of all created good, if I can suppose her absent, who, under God, was the centre of all earthly treasure to me. And now, unto Him who had a prior right, I freely resign *this all*, because his right is infinitely superior to mine. In the act of offering a sacrifice so pleasing to my God, I feel that our union in him is of eternal duration; and that as sure as my beloved partner now sleeps in Jesus, even so surely will God bring her with him, and present her to me again: "For the Lord Jesus himself shall descend from heaven with a shout, with the voice of the archangel, and with the trump of God; and then we shall be caught up together in the clouds, to meet the Lord in the air; and so shall we ever be with the Lord." Thus comforted, and knowing the time is short, I shall here take leave of my beloved wife, leaving her to rest in his arms, where,

Supremely bless'd with perfect peace,
She loves me now without excess,
Or passionate alloy:

Serene she waits my spirit's flight,
To range with her the plains of light,
And climb the mount of joy.

Reposed in those Elysian seats,
Where JONATHAN his DAVID meets,
Our souls shall soon embrace:
The utmost power of friendship prove,
Commenced on earth, matured above,
In ecstasies of praise.

How shall we sing and triumph there,
Our dangers and escapes compare,
Our days of flesh and wo:
How comprehend the plan divine
And sweetly in his praises join,
Through whom we meet below:

Through whom in paradise we meet,
Great Author of our joy complete,
The Jesus we proclaim:
While all the saints stand listening round,
And all the realms of bliss resound
Salvation to the Lamb.

The Lamb has brought us through the fire!
The Lamb shall raise our raptures higher,
When all from earth are driven:
Our glorious Head shall cleave the skies,
And bid his church triumphant rise
From PARADISE to HEAVEN.

JAMES ROGERS.

Birmingham, March 29, 1795.

ELEGIAC POEMS.

THOUGHTS ON A FUTURE STATE,

OCCASIONED BY THE DEATH OF MRS. HESTER ANN ROGERS

BY A YOUNG LADY WHO MET IN HER CLASS.

Air-built and baseless all, are earth's delights,
And grief intrudes into their noblest heights:
To changes subject, and to ills a prey,
They bud and wither in a winter's day;
And like the unfriendly plant of sense too quick,
Bloom at a distance, but when touch'd grow sick:
What calls on man to look beyond this sphere,
Since he's immortal, and all is mortal here!
If endless life, and lasting summers wait,
To crown us when we leave this wint'ry state,
How should each change instruct us to be wise,
And tell us we are natives of the skies!
But, sure of bliss, (if aught deserves the name,)
Fair friendship's pleasures must the title claim!
Her joys are mighty, but they often fail,
For while in mortal robes, e'en *she* is frail,
Ah yes, Celestia! friendship's tears must flow,
While memory lasts, or we thy absence know:

Full oft we trace the happy moments fled,
When we to noblest joys by thee were led;
And whilst we talk'd of heaven, and learn'd the way,
Mercy divine let in a beam of day,
Till faith and hope exulting soar'd on high,
And each affection centred in the sky:
We long'd to clap th' immortal wing, and praise
In louder songs, the Source of boundless grace,
Where no dull sense, or intermediate cloud,
Can ever the Redeemer's presence shroud,
But love unbounded, and ecstatic joy,
Burst forth in endless songs without annoy.

But scenes elapsed I'll leave, while I presume,
With daring thought, to penetrate the gloom
That hides immortal things from mortal view,
And humbly thy enraptured flight pursue
To worlds of bliss, complete fruition's height,
Perfect existence, and immediate sight.

O, had we seen thee when the veil withdrew,
And thy freed spirit from its prison flew!
What floods of glory burst upon thy sight,
What songs melodious rung the ether bright,
As heavenly spirits led thee through the sky,
'Midst blazing suns, and rolling worlds on high,
While joyful friends throng'd thick the heavenly way,
And hail'd thee to the bright abodes of day:
Then joining in their songs of triumph high,
The loud hosannas echo'd through the sky.

And now what mighty joys thy powers surprise,
Stretch'd out from mortal to immortal size:
Surrounded, fill'd, absorb'd in Godhead's sea,
And wrapp'd in visions of the Deity,
Yet not o'erwhelm'd, bewilder'd, or confused,
Thy nature so with the divine infused,
So fitted to thy state, so pure and high,
That heaven's profound suit thy capacity.

Thy glow-worm knowledge here by faith begun,
In open vision bursts into a sun:
Through organs weak no longer dribbled in,
Nor labours purblind reason scrapes to win;
But senses large, congenial with the skies,
'Wake to new life, and into action rise,
By intuition now, all ear, all sight,
Perception all, and piercing as the light,
Thou need'st no medium to convey delight,
With open face thou view'st the eternal Three,
In union join'd, a glorious Trinity!
And at the view increasing raptures flow,
While proving "'tis eternal life to know."*
Thou view'st unveil'd the attributes divine,
Which in unrivall'd beauty round thee shine,
Adoring the transcending harmony,
Which joins them all in man's redemption free.

Alike by thee his government 's survey'd,
Where'er his all-creative power 's display'd,

* John xvii. 3.

Allow'd his circling providence to trace
From heaven's first order to the reptile race:
Here wonders now create sublime delight,
And holy praise breaks forth at every sight.

Nor less his grace thy searching mind employs,
Since "angels o'er a penitent rejoice:"*
Here they discover mercy's richest store,
And endless cause to wonder and adore.
Now thou well know'st the secret works of grace,
Which first attracted thee to seek his face,
From hence pursuing all the steps divine,
Which through thy life in ceaseless mercies shine:
The end discovering of each grief and pain,
Why they were sent, and what the endless gain:
Alike survey'd in every hidden snare,
Escap'd by thee through providential care:
A thousand blessings now to thee are known,
O'er which on earth a pierceless veil was thrown.
What funds of pleasure must such views supply,
And themes for praise throughout eternity!
Creation's works are open to thy sight,
From lifeless matter to the seraph bright:
What wonders in the world of spirits shine,
Expressive of their origin divine!
Here beings high and things inanimate,
Which still retain their pure primeval state,

* Luke xv. 10.

Are understood by thee, whose piercing eye
Can into being's inmost essence pry;
And if revisiting this nether sphere,
How differently each object must appear!
No longer can the surface bound thy sight,
But nature's secret springs are brought to light;
And God appears diffused throughout the whole,
The source of life,—creation's living soul.

Is such thy knowledge of thy glorious Lord?
Then sure thy love in measure must accord:
Possessing now the end thy soul pursued,
In near fruition of its perfect good:
No more (as here) frail nature sinks opprest,
When with peculiar revelation blest;
Then words were lost in love's immense abyss,
And silence best express'd th' unutter'd bliss.
(What proof that love is heaven's commencement here,
Since mortal language sinks beneath its sphere.
Praise aims in vain to set its glories forth,
And only songs celestial gave it birth:)
But now at large uncircumscribed and free,
Thy vast affections feed on Deity:
Ecstatic love in holy rapture flows,
Increasing ever as thy knowledge grows
In full enjoyment and immediate sight,
Of him whose beauties are thy sole delight,
Thy praise unwearied, must forever flow,
And pleasures no embarrassment can know:

Renew'd by having his continual smile,
No doubt intruding thy delights to spoil,
But large returns forever flow to thee,
Of mutual love and sweet complacency.
And joy (love's first offspring) lives to prove,
And celebrate the jubilee above:
Immediate draughts receiving from the throne,
While thy loved Saviour makes his joy thy own:
Thou sharest in all his glorious victories,
Exulting o'er its vanquish'd enemies,
Ascribing endless glories to his name,
And ever crying, "Worthy is the Lamb
Who wash'd our robes and conquer'd all our foes,
And now on us eternal life bestows."
And fresh discoveries of unfathom'd love
Will through eternity thy joys improve.

Are such the glories of thy perfect state?
Then thy employments must alike be great;
(For spirit is to action ever bent,
And torpid rest is not its element.)
Art thou engaged in acts to us unknown
Of solemn worship 'fore the eternal throne,
Which all thy mighty faculties employ,
And give full scope to wonder, love, and joy?
Or sent to this terrene on errands kind,
Perhaps to soothe thy partner's fainting mind,
When deep-felt grief's impetuous tempests blow,
Or secret tears from silent anguish flow?

Then to administer the cordial sweet,
And lead his views to yon celestial seat,
Where kindred souls in sweet enjoyment meet?
Or dost thou come a guardian angel bright
O'er the dear objects of thy late delight,
Averting danger, and instilling truth
In soft instructions to their tender youth?
Or dost thou visit those with kind solace
Who were thy pupils in the school of grace?
O, have I ever felt thy friendly power
Conducting me through dark temptation's hour,
And taken, when unconscious of thy aid,
The cup of comfort by thy hand convey'd?
Reviving thought! it wipes the tear of wo,
Since friendship lives more perfect than below.
Nor less 'tis likely that thy guardian hand
Supports thy friends along thy shadowy land,
When life is hov'ring on the short'ning breath,
And its warm current gently cools in death:
Then bearing the triumphant soul away,
Thou aid'st its anthems in the courts of day,
And mixing with the brilliant hosts above,
Recount'st the wonders of redeeming love:
While list'ning angels hear with sweet surprise,
And gusts of hallelujahs ring the skies.
Now fellowship is perfect and complete, [meet,
Where thought communes with thought, and notions
And swift as lightning distant souls can reach,
With clear expression far surpassing speech:

Thus fitted for sublime society,
With beings of consummate purity,
Thou hold'st high converse with angelic choirs,
Cherub, and seraph, and with human sires,
With all the glorious hosts around the throne,
Perhaps with beings yet to us unknown,
Gather'd from num'rous worlds remote from ours,
And form'd with various faculties and powers:
While all the victories of grace declare,
And countless acts of providential care:
Then joining in melodious strains of praise,
To mercy's Centre, and the Source of grace,
Each happy soul takes in large draughts of joy,
And unconceived delights thy powers employ.

Say, does some spirit (perhaps thy infant son,*
For sure by thee he's still beloved and known,)
Direct thy flight along the ethereal way,
Where suns unnumber'd burn, and comets stray,
To some new workmanship of power divine,
Where beings in Adamic glory shine,
And uncursed nature all harmonious glows,
And shining fair its Maker's glory shows.
Here wonders rise on wonders to thy view,
In objects fair, immaculate and new:
And seem with thee in concert sweet to join,
In one delightful hymn of praise divine.

---

* Who died in the year 1789, at the age of six weeks.

Are such as these thy blest employs on high?
While God is all in all, and ever nigh;
For wide-extended space is full of him,
Nor aught thy ever-waking sight can dim:
Hence, though engaged at nature's utmost bound,
Thy heaven—thy God, must still thy soul surround.

But cease, my vent'rous thought, too apt to fly
To things for thy capacity too high:
Since ear hath never heard, nor eye beheld,
Th' immortal glories of the upper world,
And all is bold chimera at the best,
In darkness form'd, and wrapt in errors, rest
Nor thought can paint, nor language give them birth,
And faint descriptions but degrade their worth
Hence I'm constrain'd the subject to dismiss,
Till made with her a fellow-heir of bliss.

May 15, 1795.

AN ELEGY ON THE

DEATH OF MRS. HESTER ANN ROGERS.

BY AGNES BULMER,

A Lady who enjoyed the Privilege of her Maternal Instructions in the way to Glory.

SAY, shall the muse, in plaintive weeping strains,
  A dear departed pious friend lament!
Or join the host on yonder glorious plains,
  To greet, with triumph, the victorious saint?

A conquering warrior, who return'd from fight,
  Has gloriously her every foe subdued,
And now reposes in the plains of light,
  And triumphs in the presence of her God.

Can we, who sojourn in the vale of life,
  (Who still each anxious, painful trial, know,)
Desire to lengthen out the mortal strife,
  Of one so fully meet from earth to go?

Can we the breathings of her spirit trace,
  Behold the ardour of her panting soul;
Her steadfast care to run th' appointed race,
  Her longing to attain the heavenly goal:

Her deep communion with the God of love,
  To feel whose presence was her soul's delight:
Her life of faith concealed with Christ above,
  Now changed into the beatific sight:

Say, can we view, and wish to stop her flight,
  Even for a moment to the world recall?
O, that her glory on our souls may light,
  On us some portion of her spirit fall!

No, surely, here we'll bid our tears farewell,
  And triumph with the saint to glory gone;
With her the praise of our Redeemer tell—
  Above, below, the triumph is but one.

Ah, no! 'tis not the dead demands our tears,
  But for ourselves, alas! our sorrows flow:
We joy in her escape from grief and fears,
  To where the tree of life and pleasures grow.

But by a double tie she claim'd our love,
  And lo, at once, we mourn a friend and guide!
Oft has she led our soul to things above,
  And sweetly pointed to the Crucified.

Deeply experienced, Satan's wiles she knew,
  And bid us of his dang'rous baits beware;
Set forth the Saviour's love forever new,
  Watching our souls with constant tender care.

Full well she knew the goodness of her Lord,
  And wish'd that all with her his love might feel:
For this his mercy she to all declared
  With humble gratitude and pious zeal.

To youth, or age, her kind advice she gave,
  Alike by youth or age beloved, revered,

To all adapted, all their souls to save,
  Some roused by threat'ning, some by comfort
    cheer'd.

Yet while she labour'd thus, with pious zeal,
  She ne'er despised the social calls of life,
But with a conscientious care fulfill'd
  The duties of a parent, child, and wife.

Thus while on earth her Master's work she wrought,
  And now her Lord has said, "Enough is done,
Thy arms lay down—the fight of faith is fought,
  The prize of everlasting glory's won."

Thrice happy saint! No more our tears shall flow,
  No more our selfish hearts thy loss shall mourn;
Be this our aim, like thee our God to know,
  That with like joy we may to heaven return.

And thou, dear partner of her joys and cares,
  What consolation can a friend impart,
(A child of your united faith and prayers,)
  To ease the sorrows of a wounded heart?

Short is the time of man's appointed space,
  Soon will this transitory life be gone:
Then shall your soul its dearer part embrace,
  And stand with her before yon glorious throne!

Even now, by faith, your soul with hers shall join,
  And learn the strains of the seraphic throng,
Till all renew'd in purity divine,
  You sing in heaven the never ceasing song!

THE END.

www.ingramcontent.com/pod-product-compliance
Lightning Source LLC
LaVergne TN
LVHW020607110826
845149LV00002B/399

* 9 7 8 1 4 1 8 1 8 8 0 7 8 *